McGRAW-HILL'S ESSENTIAL

ESL Grammar

A Handbook for Intermediate and Advanced ESL Students

MARK LESTER, PH.D.

New York   Chicago   San Francisco   Lisbon   London   Madrid   Mexico City
Milan   New Delhi   San Juan   Seoul   Singapore   Sydney   Toronto

The **McGraw·Hill** Companies

Library of Congress Cataloging-in-Publication Data

Lester, Mark.
     McGraw-Hill's essential ESL grammar : a handbook for intermediate and
advanced ESL students / Mark Lester.
          p.   cm.
     Includes index.
     ISBN-10: 0-07-149642-4 (alk. paper)
     ISBN-13: 978-0-07-149642-1
     1. English language—Textbooks for foreign speakers.   2. English language—
Grammar—Problems, exercises, etc.   I. Title.   II. Title: Essential ESL grammar.

PE1128.L4568   2008
428.2'4—dc22   2007034986

2 3 4 5 6 7 8 9 10 11 12 13 14 15 16 17 18 19 20 21 22   FGR/FGR   0 9 8

ISBN 978-0-07-149642-1
MHID   0-07-149642-4

McGraw-Hill books are available at special quantity discounts to use as premiums
and sales promotions or for use in corporate training programs. To contact a
representative, please visit the Contact Us pages at www.mhprofessional.com.

Also in this series:

McGraw-Hill's Essential American Idioms Dictionary
McGraw-Hill's Essential American Slang Dictionary
McGraw-Hill's Essential Phrasal Verbs Dictionary

This book is printed on acid-free paper.

Contents

Introduction v

PART **I** **Noun Phrases** 1

  1 Nouns 3
  2 Adjectives 21
  3 Determiners 29
  4 Post-Noun Modifiers 49
  5 Pronouns 75
  6 Gerunds and Infinitives 87
  7 Noun Clauses 103

PART **II** **Verb Phrases** 119

  8 Basic Verb Forms 121
  9 Verb Tenses and Modals 135
 10 Special Verbs 169
 11 Verb Complements I: Simple Complements 193
 12 Verb Complements II: Multiple Complements 203
 13 Predicate Adjective Complements 223
 14 Adverbs 237
 15 Using Adverbs 249

PART **III** **Sentences** 273

 16 Conjunctions 275
 17 Questions 297
 18 The Passive 319

Index 335

Introduction

This book is for nonnative speakers of English who have already attained extensive fluency in classroom English. It is designed to help you move to the next level of functioning comfortably in a fully English-speaking environment. For example, your job may take you to an English-speaking country, or your duties may require you to interact extensively with native English speakers in person, on the telephone, or on the Internet.

Even though the book includes many topics covered in other ESL books, it is not a textbook. It is an advanced-level reference work designed to give you instant access to detailed information about specific topics that you need to know and apply now. Each section of the book is a self-contained module. Unlike with a textbook, you do not need to start on page 1. Just use the table of contents or the index to locate the topic you need, and then go right to it.

The most important feature of this book is the immense amount of information about English grammar in general and about four specific areas of English grammar that are most likely to cause difficulties:

• **Areas of unusual grammatical complexity.** Nonnative speakers find certain areas of grammar especially difficult to master. The reason is simple: the grammatical mechanisms involved are indeed quite complicated. Unless you fully understand how these mechanisms work, you will never master the areas they govern. This book explains these mechanisms in much greater detail than most ESL textbooks attempt to do.

• **Areas of unusual irregularity.** Many grammatical options are controlled by particular words, often verbs. This book is full of lists that tell the reader which words control which specific grammatical structures. For example, it is impossible to predict in general whether a particular verb will permit a gerund, an infinitive, or both as an object. The only way you can tell is to look at the lists provided to see which construction is allowable. No other book (outside specialized linguistic reference works) provides such extensive listings of idiosyncratic, word-controlled grammatical structures.

• **Areas in which native speakers routinely use special forms in conversational English.** If your only use of English is as a formal, written language (as is the case for many nonnative speakers), and you don't foresee any need to ever talk to a native speaker of English under fifty years old, then this area is not a concern for you.

For everybody else, however, this may well be the most difficult of the four areas. Unless you have had extensive direct contact with native speakers of English in informal situations, you simply have not had the opportunity to acquire this type of English. It is not just a matter of contractions and rapid speech (though these will cause you plenty of problems); there are also well-established, predictable shifts in grammar that take place in casual conversation. Here's an illustration:

In formal English, the standard passive is formed with the helping verb *be*. For example:

We *were* interrupted.

In informal conversational English, most native speakers actually use the helping verb *get* instead of *be*. For example:

We *got* interrupted.

One of the key features of this book is the discussion of this kind of grammatical substitution wherever it is significant. (This occurs surprisingly often.)

• **Areas in which both native and nonnative speakers often make mistakes.** As you become more like a native speaker, you are bound to start making the same mistakes that native speakers do. For example, like native speakers, you will have problems distinguishing between restrictive and nonrestrictive adjective clauses in more complicated sentences. You will also have problems knowing when and how to use direct and indirect quotation. This book has extensive treatments of these predictable problem areas, far beyond what you would ever encounter in an ESL textbook (and most books for native speakers, for that matter).

This book is divided into three parts: Noun Phrases, Verb Phrases, and Sentences.

Part I, Noun Phrases: Noun phrases (nouns together with all their modifiers) are one of the fundamental building blocks of English. Noun phrases function as the subjects of sentences, the objects or complements of verbs, and the objects of prepositions. Part I addresses the various components that make up noun phrases. The first four chapters describe nouns and noun modifiers. The remaining three chapters discuss grammatical entities other than nouns that can also function as noun phrases. They are pronouns, gerund and infinitive phrases, and noun clauses.

Part II, Verb Phrases: Part II is devoted to verb phrases, the second of the two fundamental building blocks of English. Verb phrases are verbs together with all of the verbs' complements (structures required by particular verbs) and optional modifiers. The first three chapters deal specifically with verb forms and verb tenses. The next three chapters deal with verb complements: nouns, adjectives, adverbs, and other grammatical structures that are required by particular verbs and predicate adjectives to form complete sentences. The final two chapters deal with optional adverb modifiers of verbs.

Part III, Sentences: In this section we will examine three topics that affect entire sentences. These topics have been picked for two reasons: they are a major part of English grammar, but even more important, they pose certain difficulties for nonnative speakers. Chapter 16 explores conjunctions: ways in which words, phrases, and entire independent clauses (sentences) are joined together. Chapter 17 focuses on how questions are formed. We conclude with a study of the passive in Chapter 18.

Note: Throughout the text, **X** signifies ungrammatical, **?** signifies questionable, **X?** signifies borderline ungrammatical, and **//** signifies the sound of a letter.

PART I

Noun Phrases

Nouns

This chapter is divided into three sections. The first two sections describe in detail the two basic types of nouns: **proper nouns** and **common nouns**. Proper nouns are the names of specific individuals; common nouns are the names of categories. The third section describes how we form possessive nouns.

Proper Nouns

Here are some examples of proper nouns:

Specific persons: Dorothy, Miss Marple, Senator Smith, Uncle Fred
Specific places: Chicago, Jordan, Red Sea, Mount Olympus
Specific things: New York Times, Microsoft Corporation

Capitalization of Proper Nouns

The most obvious feature of proper nouns is that they are capitalized. However, the conventions of capitalization are anything but simple. Here are some of the more important capitalization rules for persons, places, and things:

Capitalization of Persons. Capitalize all parts of the name, including *Jr.* and *Sr.*:

Fred Smith Sr.
Martin Luther King Jr.

When civil, military, religious, and professional titles *precede* a name and are used as part of the name, they are capitalized:

General Patton
Pope Benedict XVI
President Bush

However, if the title *follows* the name or is used to talk *about* a person, then the title is considered a common noun and is not capitalized. For example, compare the following:

Proper noun: *Governor* Schwarzenegger was reelected.
Common: Arnold Schwarzenegger, the *governor* of California, was an actor.
Common: Arnold Schwarzenegger is the *governor* of California.

The names of groups of people (linguistic, religious, racial) are normally capitalized. For example:

Catholics
Chinese
Latinos

Capitalization of Places. Geographical terms (for example, *street, river, ocean*) that are part of a name are also capitalized. For example:

Atlantic Ocean	Great Barrier Reef
Deep Creek	Lake Erie
Elm Street	Mississippi River
Empire State Building	Rocky Mountains

The names of distinct regions are usually capitalized. For example:

Mid Atlantic	the South
the Midwest	Southeast Asia

Popular names of places are usually capitalized (and not enclosed in quotation marks). For example:

Badlands (South Dakota)   Eastern Shore (Chesapeake Bay)
Bay Area (California)   Fertile Crescent

Strangely enough, words derived from geographical names are generally *not* capitalized. For example:

china (dishes)   plaster of paris
french fries   venetian blinds

Capitalization of Things. The complete names of private and public organizations of all kinds are capitalized. For example:

Cheney High School   Peace Corps
Green Bay Packers (football team)   Xerox Corporation
New York Philharmonic

The names of historical, political, and economic events are generally capitalized. For example:

Boston Tea Party   New Deal
Great Depression

The names of acts, treaties, laws, and government programs are generally capitalized. For example:

Declaration of Independence   Marshall Plan
Federal Housing Act   Monroe Doctrine

The names of months and the days of the week are capitalized, but *not* the names of the seasons. For example:

fall   summer
February   Wednesday
spring   winter

Plural Forms of Proper Nouns

Plural proper nouns are uncommon, not because there is any grammatical restriction on them, but because we rarely need to use them. Here are some examples of plural proper nouns:

> We have had three hot *Julys* in a row.
> The *Smiths* went to the beach this weekend.
> There are two *New Yorks*, one for the rich and another for the rest of us.

Do not use an apostrophe for the plural of proper nouns. For example:

X We have known the *Johnson's* for a long time.

For the use of definite articles with plural proper nouns, see Chapter 3.

Common Nouns

Common nouns refer to persons, places, things, and ideas (abstractions). Here are some examples:

Persons: student, women, reporter, father, employee
Places: city, river, mountains, forest, sidewalk
Things: computer, book, water, elephant
Ideas: justice, love, friendship, honesty, respect

Common nouns are divided into two main categories: **noncount** and **count.** Noncount nouns are nouns that cannot be used in the plural. The term *noncount* refers to the fact that these nouns are literally not countable; that is, they cannot be used with number words. Most common nouns are count nouns; they can be counted and used in the plural. The distinction between noncount and count nouns is of particular importance in determining which article to use. This topic is covered in detail in Chapter 3.

Noncount Nouns

Many noncount nouns are generic names for categories of things. For example, the noncount noun *luggage* is a generic or collective term that refers to an entire category of objects that we use for carrying things while we travel, such as *backpacks, briefcases, handbags, suitcases,* and *valises.* The generic noun *luggage* is not countable, while all of the specific nouns are countable:

Noncount: X one luggage, two luggages
Count: one backpack, two backpacks
               one briefcase, two briefcases
               one handbag, two handbags
               one suitcase, two suitcases

Most noncount nouns fall into one of ten semantic categories:

Abstractions:	beauty, charity, faith, hope, knowledge, justice, luck, reliability
Academic fields:	anthropology, chemistry, economics, literature, physics
Food:	butter, cheese, chicken, pepper, rice, salt
Gerunds (-*ing* verb forms used as nouns):	hoping, running, smiling, winning
Languages:	Arabic, Chinese, English, Russian, Spanish
Liquids and gases:	beer, blood, coffee, gasoline, water, air, oxygen
Materials:	cement, glass, gold, paper, plastic, silk, wood, wool
Natural phenomena:	electricity, gravity, matter, space
Sports and games:	baseball, chess, football, poker, soccer, tennis
Weather words:	fog, pollution, rain, snow, wind

Many noncount nouns can be used as count nouns but with a predictable shift in meaning—to convey something like "different kinds of." Here are some examples:

gasoline—**noncount:** The price of *gasoline* is outrageous. (liquid)
gasoline—**count:** The station sells three *gasolines*. (different grades of gasoline)

Spanish—**noncount:** I am learning *Spanish*. (language)
Spanish—**count:** There are several *Spanishes* in America. (different kinds of Spanish)

cheese—**noncount:** I love *cheese*. (food)
cheese—**count:** The store sells a variety of *cheeses*. (different kinds of cheese)

Some noncount nouns have count noun counterparts but with different meanings. Here are some examples:

iron—**noncount:** The chain is made of *iron*. (material)
iron—**count:** The hotel will provide *irons*. (electric appliances for pressing clothes)

paper—**noncount:** Books are made of *paper*. (material)
paper—**count:** I left my *papers* on the desk. (documents)

chicken—**noncount:** *Chicken* is a heart-healthy meat. (food)
chicken—**count:** There were a dozen *chickens* in the yard. (living animals)

coffee—**noncount:** Too much *coffee* makes me nervous. (liquid)
coffee—**count:** We would like two *coffees*, please. (cups or servings of coffee)

Plural Forms of Count Nouns

The distinctive feature of count nouns is that they can be used in the plural. Most nouns form their plural with -*(e)s*, but there are also a number of irregular plural forms. Most irregular plurals are either nouns of **English**

origin that have retained older ways of forming the plural or **Latin words** that have retained their Latin plurals. In addition, there are a small number of **plural-only nouns**, and finally there is a difference between British and American English on whether **collective nouns** are singular or plural.

Regular Plurals. The regular plural is most often written as -*s*. For example:

Singular	Plural
cat	cats
dog	dogs
llama	llamas

If the regular plural is pronounced as a separate syllable, the regular plural is spelled -*es*. For example:

Singular	Plural
batch	batches
bench	benches
box	boxes
class	classes
wish	wishes

There are two special spelling rules for regular plurals:
Words ending in a consonant + *y*. When a word ends in a consonant + *y*, the plural is formed by the following rule:

CHANGE THE *Y* TO *I* AND ADD -*ES*

Singular	Plural
baby	babies
family	families
lady	ladies
story	stories

However, if the word ends in a vowel plus *y*, the preceding rule does not apply, because the letter *y* is does not represent a separate vowel. The *y* is part of the spelling of the vowel and therefore cannot be changed:

Singular	Plural
boy	boys
key	keys
subway	subways

Words ending in a consonant + **o.** There are two spellings for words that end in a consonant + *o*. In one group, the plural is formed by adding -*s* in the normal way. In a second group, the plural is formed by adding -*es*. Unfortunately, there is no way to predict the group to which any particular word belongs. You simply have to look up each word ending in a consonant + *o*. Here are some examples of each group:

-*s* Plurals		-*es* Plurals	
Singular	**Plural**	**Singular**	**Plural**
ego	egos	hero	heroes
kilo	kilos	potato	potatoes
memo	memos	tomato	tomatoes
zero	zeros	volcano	volcanoes

Irregular Plurals of English Origin. Seven words form their plural by a vowel change alone:

Singular	Plural
foot	feet (See note.)
goose	geese
louse	lice
man	men
mouse	mice
tooth	teeth
woman	women

Note: In addition to the usual plural form *feet*, the noun *foot* has a second plural form, *foot*, when we use the word to refer to length or measurement. For example:

I bought a six-*foot* ladder.

He is six *foot* three inches tall.

Some words ending in *f* form their plurals by changing the *f* to *v* and adding -*es*. Here are the most common words that follow this pattern:

Singular	Plural
half	halves
knife	knives
leaf	leaves
life	lives
loaf	loaves
self	selves (also the plural *themselves*)
thief	thieves
wolf	wolves

Some words have a plural form that is identical to their singular form. Most of these words refer to animals or fish. For example:

Singular	Plural
a cod	two cod
a deer	two deer
a fish	two fish
a sheep	two sheep
a shrimp	two shrimp
a trout	two trout

Since the singular and plural forms of these nouns are identical, the actual number of the noun can be determined only by subject-verb agreement or by the use of an indefinite article. For example:

Singular: The *deer* was standing in the middle of the road.

Plural: The *deer* were moving across the field.

Singular: I saw a *deer* in the backyard.

Plural: I saw some *deer* in the backyard.

If one of these words is used as an object with a definite article, then the number is inherently ambiguous. For example:

Look at the *deer*! (one deer or many deer?)

Two words retain the old plural ending -*en*:

Singular	Plural
child	children
ox	oxen

Irregular Plurals of Latin Origin. English uses thousands of words of Latin origin. In formal or scientific writing, the original Latin forms of the plural are often used. While the irregularity of Latin grammar is almost beyond belief, there are two patterns that are regular enough to merit our attention:

Plurals of Latin words ending in -**us.** The plurals of these words typically end in -*i*. For example:

Singular	Plural
alumnus	alumni
focus	foci
locus	loci
stimulus	stimuli
syllabus	syllabi

Plurals of Latin words ending in -**um.** The plurals of these words typically end in -*a*. For example:

Singular	Plural
addendum	addenda
curriculum	curricula
datum	data (See note.)
memorandum	memoranda
spectrum	spectra
stratum	strata

Note: *Data* is often used as a kind of collective singular except in formal scientific papers. For example:

The *data* is very clear in this matter.

Plural-Only Nouns. Some plural nouns have no corresponding singular form at all or else have a singular form that differs substantially from the meaning of the plural.

One group of plural-only nouns refers to tools or articles of clothing that have two equal parts joined together:

Tools:	bellows, binoculars, (eye)glasses, forceps, pincers, scissors, sheers, spectacles, tongs, tweezers
Clothing:	braces, briefs, flannels, jeans, pants, pajamas, shorts, slacks, suspenders, tights, tops, trousers, trunks

Here are some other plural-only nouns with idiomatic meanings:

accommodations (living arrangements)
arms (weapons)
brains (intellect)
communications (means of communication)
credentials (records or documents)
customs (duty)

funds (money)
guts (courage)
looks (appearance)
manners (behavior)
pains (trouble, effort)
wits (intelligence)

A few plural-only nouns have no plural marking: *cattle, livestock, poultry, people, police.* Here are some examples with the plural verb underlined:

The *police* <u>are</u> investigating the crime.
People <u>were</u> beginning to talk.

Collective Nouns

Collective nouns refer to groups of people either individually or collectively. Here are some examples:

audience   class
committee   government
team

Logically, we can think of a *team*, for example, as being either a unit (singular) or a group of individuals (plural). In American English, collective nouns are almost always treated as singular nouns; in British English, collective nouns are almost always treated as plural nouns. For example, compare the following sentences with the verbs underlined:

| **American:** | The *team* is on the field. |
| **British:** | The *team* are on the field. |

| **American:** | The American *government* has announced a new policy. |
| **British:** | Her Majesty's *government* have announced a new policy. |

Possessive Forms of Nouns

Modern English is a hybrid of two languages: Old English (Anglo-Saxon) and French. Reflecting this mixed heritage, Modern English has two ways of forming the possessive: the Old English way, which uses an **inflectional ending** (*'s* and *s'*), and an *of* **possessive** that is a kind of loan-translation of the French way of forming the possessive. Here is an example of each:

| **Inflectional possessive:** | *Shakespeare's* plays |
| ***Of* possessive:** | the plays *of* Shakespeare |

Inflectional Possessives

It is essentially a historical accident that the regular plural and the possessive inflections are pronounced exactly alike, with the same sibilant sounds. Up until the sixteenth century, the plural and the possessives were also spelled alike: *-s*. During the sixteenth century, however, the apostrophe began to be used for the possessive ending to distinguish it from the plural ending. For example:

Plural	Possessive
boys	boy's
girls	girl's
friends	friend's

The use of the apostrophe *after* the -*s* to signal the possessive use of a plural noun did not become widely accepted until the nineteenth century:

Plural	Plural Possessive
boys	boys'
girls	girls'
friends	friends'

While it is correct to call -*s*' the "plural possessive," it is a mistake to think of the -*'s* as the "singular possessive." The problem with this definition arises with the possessive forms of irregular nouns that become plural by changing their vowel rather than by adding a plural -*s*. For example:

Singular Noun	Possessive	Plural Noun	Possessive
man	man's	men	men's
woman	woman's	women	women's
child	child's	children	children's

As you can see, -*'s* is used with these plural possessive nouns, not -*s*'. Using the -*s*' with these nouns would mean (incorrectly, of course) that the /s/ is what makes these nouns plural. What actually makes them plural is the change in their vowels.

A much better way to think of plurals and possessive is as follows:

Plural Only	Possessive Only	Both Plural and Possessive
-s	-'s	-s'

This analysis will help ensure that you will always use the right form.

Mercifully, the spelling of the possessive forms is regular (though there are a few exceptions for proper nouns, which are discussed later in this section). Here are some examples using words that form their plurals in different ways.

WORDS ENDING IN A CONSONANT + *Y*

Singular		Plural	
Noun	**Possessive**	**Noun**	**Possessive**
baby	baby's	babies	babies'
family	family's	families	families'

WORDS ENDING IN *O*

Singular		Plural	
Noun	**Possessive**	**Noun**	**Possessive**
ego	ego's	egos	egos'
memo	memo's	memos	memos'
hero	hero's	heroes	heroes'
volcano	volcano's	volcanoes	volcanoes'

Notice that in the last two examples, the singular possessive and the plural forms are spelled differently.

WORDS ENDING IN *F*

Singular		Plural	
Noun	**Possessive**	**Noun**	**Possessive**
thief	thief's	thieves	thieves'
wolf	wolf's	wolves	wolves'

The possessives of some proper nouns ending in a sibilant sound are often spelled with just an apostrophe. For example:

In *Jesus*' name (this spelling is conventional)
Ramses' tomb
Charles *Dickens*' novels
Kansas' main city

The Meaning of the Inflectional Possessive. As its name would suggest, the possessive is most commonly used to show ownership or possession. For example:

Ralph's car
My *family's* house

However, the possessive is used in many other meanings, the two most important being relationships and measurement:

Relationships
Ralph's neighbor (Ralph does not own his neighbor.)
My *family's* doctor (The family does not own the doctor.)

Measurement
Time: an *hour's* delay; a *week's* postponement; two *years'* duration
Value: the *euro's* value; the *dollar's* decline; five *dollars'* worth

Of *Possessive*
While the inflectional possessive and the *of* possessive mean the same thing, they are not always interchangeable. For example:

Inflectional possessive:	*Sarah's* taxi
Of **possessive:**	X the taxi *of Sarah*
Inflectional possessive:	X a *soup's* bowl
Of **possessive:**	a bowl *of soup*

Let us use the term *possessive noun* to refer to both (a) nouns that can have inflectional possessive *'s* or *s'*, and (b) nouns that follow *of*. In the first of the preceding examples, the possessive noun would be *Sarah*. In the second example, the possessive noun would be *soup*.

Here is a general rule that will help you decide which form of the possessive noun to use:

If the possessive noun is **animate,** use the inflectional possessive.
If the possessive noun is **inanimate,** use the *of* possessive.

Here are some examples with **animate** possessive nouns:

Inflectional		Of Possessive
the *gentleman's* hat	X?	the hat *of the gentleman*
the *cat's* dish	X	the dish *of the cat*
our *family's* house	X	the house *of our family*

Here are some examples with **inanimate** possessive nouns:

Of Possessive		Inflectional
a map *of Australia*	X?	*Australia's* map
a glass *of water*	X	*water's* glass
the back *of the room*	X	the *room's* back

As with most broad generalizations, the rule about possessives is overly black-and-white. The first part, which says that animate nouns require the inflectional possessive, does seem to hold true. The real problem is with the second part, which says that inanimate nouns use only the *of* possessive.

We can (but do not have to) use the inflectional possessive with the following types of inanimate nouns:

Inanimate possessive nouns that are a product of human creation. For example:

Inflectional	Of Possessive
the *ecomony's* growth	the growth *of the economy*
the *performance's* success	the success *of the performance*
the *game's* rules	the rules *of the game*

Natural phenomena. For example:

Inflectional	Of Possessive
the *storm's* damage	the damage *of the storm*
the *tide's* surge	the surge *of the tide*
the *sun's* glare	the glare *of the sun*
the *earth's* climate	the climate *of the earth*

Possessive nouns that express location or time. For example:

Inflectional	*Of* **Possessive**
the *city's* population	the population *of the city*
the *river's* bank	the bank *of the river*
this *year's* profits	the profits *of this year*
today's lesson	the lesson *of today*

When the inflectional and *of* possessive forms are both grammatical, there are still stylistic differences between them.

In general, the inflectional forms are somewhat less formal, and the *of* possessive forms are more formal. For example, if you were writing a report, you would probably choose *the population of the city* rather than *the city's population* as the title of a section.

Everything else being equal, the inflectional possessive implies shared or previous knowledge, while the *of* possessive does not. For example, compare the following:

Inflectional:	We met *Jim's friend* last night.
Of **possessive:**	We met *a friend of Jim's* last night.

The inflectional sentence implies that the listener already knows who Jim's friend is. The *of* possessive sentence implies that the listener is not expected to know who Jim's friend is.

Double Possessive

We use a special form of the possessive when the possessive noun is a personal pronoun or an animate noun. This construction is sometimes called a **double possessive** or **double genitive**. The pronoun or animate noun is itself used in the possessive form.

If the possessive is a pronoun, the pronoun must be in the possessive pronoun form (as opposed to the possessive adjective form). For example, compare the following possessive nouns:

In object form:	X	He is a friend of *me*.
In possessive adjective form:	X	He is a friend of *my*.
In possessive pronoun form:		He is a friend of *mine*.

If the possessive noun is an animate noun (most commonly a proper noun), we have the option of using the possessive form or not. For example:

He is a friend of *Sam*.
He is a friend of *Sam's*.

He was a contemporary of *Mozart*.
He was a contemporary of *Mozart's*.

It is a policy of the *company*.
It is a policy of the *company's*.

Adjectives

The term *adjective* can be used to refer to any word that modifies a noun. In this book, however, we divide all noun modifiers into three groups and treat each in a separate chapter: "true" adjectives in this chapter, determiners (all pre-adjective noun modifiers) in Chapter 3, and post-noun modifiers in Chapter 4.

In this chapter we will discuss three aspects of adjectives: their comparative and superlative forms, how adjectives can be derived from the present and past participle forms of verbs, and the sequence and punctuation of multiple adjectives.

"True" adjectives are noun modifiers that have the following four characteristics:

1. They immediately precede the nouns they modify (and thus follow all other pre-noun modifiers).

2. They have **comparative** and **superlative** forms.

3. They can be used as **predicate adjectives**.

4. They are an "**open class**."

To better understand the difference between adjectives (as defined here) and other types of pre-noun modifiers, look at the following sentence with all noun modifiers in italics:

All the brave soldiers deserve medals.

1. The adjective *brave* immediately precedes the noun *soldiers*. The other two noun modifiers cannot be placed in between the adjective *brave* and the noun *soldiers*:

    X *All brave the* soldiers deserve medals.

    X *The brave all* soldiers deserve medals.

2. Only *brave* has comparative and superlative forms:

    Comparative: *braver*

    Superlative: *bravest*

3. Only *brave* can be used as a predicate adjective:

    All those soldiers are *brave*.

    X   All brave soldiers are *the*.

    X? The brave soldiers are *all*.

The last example is marginally grammatical, but only if *all* is used as an indefinite pronoun meaning "everything."

4. Finally, of all the pre-noun modifiers, only adjectives are an "open" class. That is, we can create new adjectives. For example, in computer jargon, *lossy* (rhymes with *bossy*) is an adjective that describes programs that degrade data when the program is run, as in the following sentences:

    That is a very *lossy* program. (modifying adjective)

    This program is *lossier* than that program. (comparative adjective)

    His company's program is *lossy*. (predicate adjective)

    Articles and all other pre-adjective noun modifiers are "closed" classes. That is, there have not been any new articles or other pre-adjective modifiers added to English in hundreds of years (nor are there likely to be any new ones for hundreds of years to come).

Comparative and Superlative Forms of Adjectives

One-syllable adjectives tend to use the Old English way of forming comparatives and superlatives—with -er and -est. Three-syllable adjectives always use a translated version of the French way of forming the comparative and superlative—with *more* and *most*. Here are some examples:

One Syllable	Three Syllables
brave, braver, bravest	ambitious, more ambitious, most ambitious
calm, calmer, calmest	beautiful, more beautiful, most beautiful
nice, nicer, nicest	generous, more generous, most generous
smart, smarter, smartest	impatient, more impatient, most impatient

Two-syllable adjectives pose a problem. Some two-syllable adjectives use the -er/-est pattern, while other two-syllable adjectives use the *more/most* pattern. Some, such as *polite*, can even be used in either pattern:

Jane is *politer* than Mary. Jane is the *politest* person in her class.
Jane is *more polite* than Mary. Jane is the *most polite* person in her class.

Here are some useful generalizations about which pattern to use.

-er/-est

Two-syllable adjectives that end in an unstressed vowel sound tend to use the -er/-est pattern. Two-syllable adjectives ending in *le* and *y* are especially common. For example:

le: able, feeble, gentle, noble, simple
y: dopy, early, easy, happy, funny, noisy, wealthy, pretty, tacky

Adjective	Comparative	Superlative
simple	simpler	simplest
early	earlier	earliest
happy	happier	happiest

Notice that the spelling of comparative and superlative forms of adjectives that end in *y* follow a rule similar to the rule that governs the plural form of nouns that end in *y*: change the *y* to *i* and add *-er* or *-est*.

More/Most

Two-syllable adjectives that are stressed on the second syllable tend to use the *more/most* pattern. For example:

Adjective	Comparative	Superlative
alert	more alert	most alert
bizarre	more bizarre	most bizarre
precise	more precise	most precise
secure	more secure	most secure

Irregular Comparative and Superlative Forms

A few irregular comparatives and superlatives survive from older forms of English:

Adjective	Comparative	Superlative
bad	worse	worst
good	better	best

The adjective *far* is peculiar in that it has two sets of comparative and superlative forms with slightly different meanings:

Adjective	Comparative	Superlative
far	farther	farthest
far	further	furthest

We use *farther* and *farthest* for distance in space. For example:

Please take the *farthest* seat.

We use *further* and *furthest* for all other kinds of sequences or progressions. For example:

Are there any *further* questions?

Adjectives Derived from Present and Past Participles

Many adjectives are derived from the **present-participle** and the **past-participle** forms of verbs (see Chapter 8 for detailed descriptions of participles). For example:

Present Participle	**Past Participle**
amusing	amused
charming	charmed
discouraging	discouraged
failing	failed
tempting	tempted

The process of turning a participle verb form into an adjective is common in languages around the world. What is unusual about English is that there are two different participle forms that can be turned into adjectives. Moreover, the two different participle forms often have different, even contradictory, meanings. The two participle forms are particularly difficult for nonnative speakers of English whose native language has only one form of participle. To see how different the two forms can be, compare the following sentences:

Present participle: He is a *boring* teacher.
Past participle: He is a *bored* teacher.

In the first sentence, the present participle means that the teacher bores his students. In the second sentence, the past participle means that the students bore the teacher—exactly the opposite meaning of the present participle.

Here is a way to remember which form of the participle to use. Participles used as adjectives still preserve many of their underlying verb functions. The noun being modified by the participle is either the *subject* of that underlying verb or the *object* of that underlying verb.

If the noun being modified is the underlying subject—that is, the noun is doing the action of the participle—then use the *-ing* present-participle form. For example, in the phrase *the boring teacher*, the teacher is the one doing the boring.

If the noun being modified is the underlying object—that is, the noun is the recipient of the action of the participle—then use the past-participle form. For example, in the phrase *the bored teacher*, the teacher is the recipient of the action of the verb.

Here are some more examples of both types of participles, using the same verbs as the source for the two participles:

Present Participle	**Past Participle**
an *amusing* proposal	an *amused* audience
(the proposal amuses)	(something amused the audience)
the *blistering* sun	his *blistered* skin
(the sun blisters)	(something blistered his skin)
an *interesting* idea	an *interested* listener
(the idea interests)	(something interested the listener)
an *exhausting* test	the *exhausted* workers
(the test exhausts)	(something exhausted the workers)

Sequence and Punctuation of Multiple Adjectives

English often uses two or three (rarely more) adjectives to modify the same noun. When this occurs, there is a definite left-to-right sequence of the adjectives based on their meaning. For example, we can say:

big old house

but not

X *old big* house

We can say:

old blue house

but not

X *blue old* house

From these two examples, we can deduce that these three adjectives must be used in this relative left-to-right sequence:

big old blue house

Generalizing from these examples to whole categories of adjectives, we can make the following rule about order of adjectives: size, age, and color. For example:

Size	Age	Color	Noun
big	old	blue	house
small	new	paisley	shirt
tiny	ancient	black	car
huge	brand-new	shiny	TV

We can identify as many as seven classes of adjectives based on their left-to-right sequence:

Opinion	Size	Shape	Condition	Age	Color	Origin/ Material	Noun
pretty		upright		modern		French	clock
	little		broken		red		doll
amusing				new		Spanish	director
disgusting				old	black		towel
	big		remodeled			brick	mansion
attractive		oval				pottery	bowl

When adjectives are used in their normal left-to-right sequence as shown here, they are not separated by commas. However, when we use two or more adjectives from the *same* class, then we must separate them by commas. By far the most common use of multiple adjectives is in the category of **opinion**. For example:

a *charming, handsome* actor
an *amusing, refreshing* comedy
his *cruel, demeaning* comments
the *confusing, repetitive, overblown* performance

There are two other characteristics of multiple adjectives from the same class: they can be used in any order, and we can also separate them by *and*, neither of which is possible with adjectives from different classes. Here are some examples:

an *amusing, refreshing* comedy
an *amusing* and *refreshing* comedy
a *refreshing, amusing* comedy
a *refreshing* and *amusing* comedy

his *cruel, demeaning* comments
his *cruel* and *demeaning* comments
his *demeaning, cruel* comments
his *demeaning* and *cruel* comments

Determiners

The term *determiner* refers collectively to all classes of noun modifiers that precede adjectives. In this chapter we examine four of the most important types of determiners: **articles**, **possessives**, **demonstratives**, and **quantifiers**. Here is an example of each type of determiner:

Did you ever find *the* books? (article)
Did you ever find *your* books? (possessive)
Did you ever find *those* books? (demonstrative)
Did you ever find *any* books? (quantifier)

With the exception of a few quantifiers, the four types of determiners are mutually exclusive. That is, we cannot combine multiple determiners to modify a single noun. For example:

X Did you ever find *the your* books?
X Did you ever find *those any* books?

Articles

There are two types of articles: the **definite article**, *the*, and the **indefinite articles**, *a/an* and *some*.

The Definite Article

The definite article, *the*, is normally unstressed. It is pronounced to rhyme with *duh* before words beginning with a consonant sound. It is pronounced to rhyme with *see* before words beginning with a vowel sound.

Using the Definite Article with Common Nouns. The definite article, *the*, can be used with all types of common nouns—with singular and plural **count nouns** and with **noncount nouns**. (Briefly, count nouns have singular and plural forms. Noncount nouns cannot be used with number words and have no plural forms. Noncount nouns are described in some detail in Chapter 1. They are also discussed in this chapter in reference to indefinite articles.) Here are some examples of the definite article with singular count nouns, plural count nouns, and noncount nouns:

Singular Count Nouns	Plural Count Nouns	Noncount Nouns
the car	*the* cars	*the* traffic
the fight	*the* fights	*the* violence
the orange	*the* oranges	*the* fruit
the suitcase	*the* suitcases	*the* luggage

The only problem with the definite article is knowing when to use it. Use the definite article if *both* of the following statements about the noun being modified are true (especially the second):

1. You have a specific person, place, thing, or idea in mind, *and*

2. You can reasonably assume that the listener or reader will know which specific person, place, thing, or idea you mean.

In practice, there are four situations that dictate the use of the definite article:

1. **Previous mention.** Use the definite article if you have already introduced the noun. For example:

   > I just got a new camera. *The* camera has an image-stabilization feature.

   The definite article is used in the second sentence because the noun *camera* was introduced in the first sentence, and thus we can reasonably assume that the listener or reader will know which camera we are talking about.

2. **Defined by modifiers.** Even if the noun has not been previously mentioned, use the definite article if the noun is followed by modifiers that serve to uniquely identify it. Here are two examples:

> Did you see *the* movie that is showing at the Roxie?

The noun *movie* is uniquely defined by the modifier *that is showing at the Roxie*.

> *The* assignment that I just got in calculus is a real killer.

The noun *assignment* is uniquely defined by the modifier *that I just got in calculus*.

3. **Normal expectations.** Use the definite article if the noun is something that we can reasonably expect from the context of the sentence even if there has been no previous mention of the noun. This important use of the definite article is often not understood by nonnative speakers. Here are several examples:

> I opened a book and checked *the* index. (We expect books to have indexes.)

> *The* screen on my new computer is flickering. (We expect computers to have screens.)

> A storm far out to sea was making *the* waves higher than normal. (We expect the sea to have waves.)

> I love my new car, but *the* brakes are pretty squeaky. (We expect cars to have brakes.)

English has an unexpected usage of the definite article with the names of places that you expect to find in a particular environment. Here are some examples grouped by environment:

At a university

I have to go to *the* bookstore.

the dean's office

the library

the registrar's office

We expect to find these places at a university.

In a city

I have to go to *the* post office

the bank

the airport

the drugstore

We expect to find these places in a city.

On a ranch or farm

I have to go to *the* barn

the stables

the chicken coop

the vegetable garden

We expect to find these places on a ranch or farm.

What is so odd about this use of the definite article is that it seems to violate the second rule that governs the use of the definite article: you can reasonably assume that the listener or reader knows *which* specific noun you have in mind. For example, consider the following sentence:

I'll be a few minutes late; I have to get to *the* bank.

Here the definite article is used even though the speaker is aware that the listener could not possibly know *which* bank the speaker is talking about. Nevertheless, this usage of the definite article with expected places is firmly established.

The meaning would change slightly if the speaker of the example sentence were instead to use the indefinite article:

I'll be a few minutes late; I have to get to *a* bank.

This sentence could have the implication that the speaker does not have any bank location in mind either. Perhaps the speaker is from out of town.

4. **Uniqueness.** Use the definite article with nouns that everybody already knows about. For example:

The sun was just dropping below *the* horizon.

Unless you are writing a science-fiction novel, there is only one sun and only one horizon. Therefore, the definite article is appropriate.

Using the Definite Article with Proper Nouns. We do not normally associate the definite article with proper nouns, but it is used in a limited way with names of people and places.

People. Typically, we do not use the definite article with the names of individual people unless there is a post-noun modifier that provides some special information about that person. For example, compare the following sentences:

John went on vacation last week.
The *John* who works in my office went on vacation last week.

The use of the post-noun modifier *who works in my office* tells us which of two or more people named John the speaker is talking about. In this case, the use of the definite article becomes obligatory. There is a similar use of the indefinite article with proper nouns (see the following section).

One of the few instances in which we regularly use the definite article with names is for titles—both royal titles and organizational titles. For example:

Royal titles:	the Duke of York, the Prince of Wales, the prime minister
Organizational titles:	the president, the treasurer, the CEO, the secretary

Places. By far the most common use of *the* with proper nouns is for place names. Plural place names are typically preceded by *the*. Two especially common categories are the names of mountain ranges and island chains. For example:

Mountain ranges:	the Alps, the Andes, the Himalayas, the Rockies
Island chains:	the Aleutians, the Azores, the Philippines, the Shetlands

The use of *the* with singular place names is much more inconsistent. Here are some categories of singular place names that are typically used with the definite article:

Bodies of water

Rivers:	the Columbia, the Mississippi, the Potomac, the Thames
Seas and oceans:	the Atlantic, the Bay of Bengal, the Gulf of California
Canals:	the Erie Canal, the Hood Canal, the Panama Canal

Public facilities, monuments, buildings, and the like (especially if well known)

Hotels:	the Days Inn, the Marriott, the Ritz
Theaters:	the Apollo, the Globe, the Met, the Roxie
Bridges:	the Brooklyn Bridge, the Golden Gate Bridge
Monuments:	the Lincoln Memorial, the Tomb of the Unknown Soldier
Libraries:	the British Museum, the Getty, the Library of Congress

The Indefinite Articles

Unlike the definite article, which can be used with all types and numbers of common nouns, the use of the indefinite articles, *a/an* and *some*, is determined by the nature of the common noun being modified—whether the noun is a singular countable noun, a plural countable noun, or a noncount noun.

Using *a/an* and *Some* with Countable Nouns. We use the indefinite article *a/an* when we first mention a singular countable noun. The use of *a/an* signals that the writer or speaker does not expect the audience to have any prior knowledge of the noun being modified—just the reverse of the function of the definite article, *the*. Notice the shift in articles in the following sentence:

> I have *a* response, but I'm not sure that it is *the* response you want to hear.

The first time the noun *response* is mentioned, it is used with the indefinite article *a*. After the first mention, all subsequent mentions of the noun *response* are used with *the*.

The indefinite article *a* has a second form, *an*, which is used before vowels; for example: *a banana* but *an apple*. The rule governing the use of *an* pertains to vowel pronunciation, not vowel spelling. For example, the following words use *a* where the spelling would seem to require *an*, because the pronunciation of the nouns actually begins with a /y/ consonant sound:

a unicorn   *a uniform*

a unit   *a usage*

Both *a* and *an* are normally unstressed. *A* is pronounced to rhyme with *duh*. *An* is pronounced to rhyme with *bun*.

The reason for the two forms *a* and *an* is historical. Both *a* and *an* come from the word *one*. Over the years, the pronunciation of *one* used as a noun modifier (as opposed to the use of *one* as number) became contracted: the *n* in *one* was preserved before words beginning with vowels and lost before words beginning with a consonant sound. So, today, we have the two forms of the indefinite article: *a* and *an*.

The origin of the indefinite article from the number *one* deeply affects the way the word is used in modern English. To begin with, as with the number *one*, *a/an* is inherently singular. Thus, we cannot use *a/an* to modify plural nouns:

X a books
X an oranges

What, then, do we use as an indefinite article for plural nouns, since *a/an* is unavailable? The answer is *some*. We need to think of *some* as functioning as the plural indefinite article, the plural counterpoint of the singular indefinite article *a/an*. Notice that the shift from *some* to *the* in the following sentence is exactly like the shift from *a* to *the* in the previous example:

I have *some* responses, but I am not sure that they are *the* responses
    you want to hear.

When used as an indefinite article, *some* is always unstressed. We need to distinguish this use of *some* from the completely unrelated use of *some* as a word conveying emphasis in informal spoken language. For example:

That was *some* party last night!

The stressed *some* is used here to emphasize the unique nature of last night's party. (The use of stressed *some* does not tell us whether the party was good or bad. The party could have been either, but in any case, it was memorable.)

Using *Some* with Noncount Nouns. Noncount nouns represent a unique category of nouns. They are called "noncount" because they cannot be used with number words. For example:

X one bacon   X two bacons
X one electricity X two electricities
X one luck   X two lucks
X one luggage   X two luggages
X one violence   X two violences

As you can see from these examples, another important feature of noncount nouns is that they cannot be used in the plural.

When we try to use the singular indefinite article *a/an* with a singular noncount noun, we run into a problem. As noted, the indefinite article *a/an* is derived from the word *one*. Since *one* is a number word, *a/an* is also going to be incompatible with noncount nouns:

X a bacon	X an electricity
X a luck	X a luggage
X a violence	

What, then, do we use as the indefinite article for noncount nouns? The answer again is unstressed *some*. Here are examples of *some* used as an indefinite article for the same five noncount nouns previously listed:

I would like *some* bacon, please.
After the storm, there was still *some* electricity in a few
   neighborhoods.
After many disappointments, we have finally had *some* luck.
Did you know that there is *some* luggage stacked in the hall?
Unfortunately, there was *some* violence associated with the recent
   rioting.

Using the Zero Article for Generalizations. We expect common nouns to be modified by some kind of article or other pre-adjective modifier. There is one important exception: using plural nouns or noncount nouns without any article or other pre-adjective modifier (also called a zero article), to signal that we are making a generalization about the noun. For example, compare the impact of the presence or absence of *some* on the meaning of the plural noun *bananas* in the following two sentences (using $\emptyset$ to indicate a zero article):

Generalization:	$\emptyset$ Bananas are high in potassium.
Nongeneralization:	There are *some* bananas on the shelf in the kitchen.

In the first sentence, the absence of any article (that is, a zero article) tells us that the sentence is making a generalization about all bananas. That is, bananas, as a category of fruit, are high in potassium. In the second sentence, the use of the expected *some* tells us that this is an ordinary sentence about a bunch of actual bananas. The sentence is not a generalization about all the bananas in the world.

Here is a similar example using the noncount noun *luggage*:

Generalization: Ø <u>Luggage</u> must be checked before boarding the aircraft.
Nongeneralization: We saw *some* <u>luggage</u> stacked out in the hall.

The zero article in the first sentence tells us that the sentence is a generalization about luggage as an entire category of objects. The use of *some* in the second sentence tells us that the sentence is about several actual pieces of luggage.

With plural count nouns and noncount nouns, it is sometimes hard to tell whether they are being used to make a generalization. There are two clues in the nature of the sentence that help identify when a generalization is intended: the use of the present tense and the use of adverbs of frequency.

Present-tense forms. Sentences that make generalizations are usually in the present-tense form—either the simple present, the present progressive, or the present perfect. In the following examples, the noun being used to make a generalization is underlined, and the present-tense verb is in italics:

Present: <u>Textbooks</u> *are* really expensive.
Present progressive: <u>Textbooks</u> *are being* priced out of students' reach.
Present perfect: <u>Textbooks</u> *have become* too expensive.

Adverbs of frequency. Sentences that make generalizations often contain adverbs of frequency (for example, *always, often, generally, frequently, usually*). In the following sentences, the noun being used to make a generalization is underlined, and the adverb of frequency is in italics:

<u>Japanese movies</u> *often* have ghosts in them.
<u>Olives</u> are *usually* too salty for me.

Generally, <u>political speeches</u> are nothing but empty platitudes. <u>Elections</u> are *rarely* fair and *never* free.

The most common error nonnative speakers make with nouns that are generalizations is to modify the noun with *some* because the speaker feels that every noun must have an article. For example:

X The barn is always full of *some* mice.

The speaker is not talking about specific, actual individual mice. The speaker is making a generalization about the kind of creatures found in the barn.

The use of the present tense and the adverb of frequency *always* signals that this sentence is making a generalization about what is happening in the barn—it is being overrun with mice. Therefore, the sentence is incompatible with the use of *some* to modify *mice*. The inappropriate use of *some* makes the sentence say something very strange:

X? Our barn is always full of one kind of mice (but not other kinds of mice).

The correct version of the sentence would use the noun *mice* without modifiers:

Our barn is always full of *mice*.

We can summarize the use of the indefinite articles, *a/an* and *some*, and the zero article through the following diagram:

INDEFINITE ARTICLE

Countable Nouns		Noncount Nouns
Singular	Plural	
a/an	some ∅	some ∅

Using the Indefinite Article with Proper Nouns.   We can use the indefinite article *a/an* with proper nouns, but only in special circumstances. One use (normally in spoken language) is to signal that the speaker is aware that the listener does not know *which* person the speaker is talking about. For example, here is what a receptionist might say to a fellow company employee on the office phone:

John, there is *a* Mr. Smith here to see you.

The receptionist uses the indefinite article to avoid saying this:

John, Mr. Smith is here to see you.

This second sentence would imply that John should know who Mr. Smith is. The use of the indefinite article is a warning to John that Mr. Smith is a stranger (as far as the receptionist knows).

A second use is to signal the reader or listener that the proper noun is being used as a kind of temporary common noun. For example:

There is *a* New York that tourists never see.

There are two New Yorks: a New York for tourists and a New York for nontourists. There is a similar use of the definite article with proper nouns (discussed earlier in the chapter).

Possessives

There are two types of possessives that function as noun modifiers: **possessive nouns** and **possessive pronouns**.

Possessive Nouns

The formation of possessive nouns is treated in detail in Chapter 1. It is important to realize that a possessive noun is not just the noun by itself but also all the words that modify that possessive noun, taken as a unit. Here is an example:

My father's sister was born in India.

Think of the phrase *my father* as being a single unit. Inside that unit, *my* modifies *father*. *My* cannot jump outside its own phrase and modify *sister*. The sister who was born in India is my father's sister, not my sister.

Possessive Pronouns

The term *possessive pronoun* is misleading, because there are actually two possessive forms for each pronoun. One form functions as an adjective, and the other functions as a true pronoun. To see the difference, compare the two possessive pronouns *my* (adjective) and *mine* (pronoun):

Adjective function: That is *my* book.
Pronoun function: That book is *mine.*

The two forms are not interchangeable:

X That is *mine* book.
X That book is *my.*

There is no standard terminology for distinguishing between the two different possessive pronoun functions. In this book we will refer to possessive pronouns functioning as adjectives as **adjectival possessive pronouns**. We will call possessive pronouns functioning as pronouns **pronominal possessive pronouns**. Here is a complete list of both types of possessive pronouns:

SINGULAR

	Adjectival Possessive Pronouns	Pronominal Possessive Pronouns
First person:	my (book)	(that book is) mine
Second person:	your (book)	(that book is) yours
Third person:	his (book)	(that book is) his
	her (book)	(that book is) hers
	its (book)	(that book is) its

PLURAL

	Adjectival Possessive Pronouns	Pronominal Possessive Pronouns
First person:	our (book)	(that book is) ours
Second person:	your (book)	(that book is) yours
Third person:	their (book)	(that book is) theirs

Notice that the possessive pronoun form *his* is used for both adjectival and pronominal functions. For example:

Adjectival possessive pronoun: That is *his* book.
Pronominal possessive pronoun: That book is *his*.

Demonstratives

There are four demonstratives: *this, that, these,* and *those.* As with posses-sive pronouns, the demonstratives can be used either as adjectives or as pronouns. Here is an example of *this* used both ways:

Adjective: I really liked *this* book.
Pronoun: I really liked *this.*

In this section we are concerned only with the use of demonstratives as adjectives.

This and *that* are singular; *these* and *those* are plural. For example:

Singular	Plural
Do you like *this* hat?	Do you like *these* hats?
Do you like *that* hat?	Do you like *those* hats?

The difference between *this/these* on the one hand and *that/those* on the other is much more complicated. Generally speaking, *this* and *these* have a sense of "closeness," and *that* and *those* have a sense of "distance." The "closeness"/"distance" distinction can be either in space or in time. Here are some examples of each type:

Space

This house (the closer of two houses) has a blue roof.

That house (the more distant of two houses) has a red roof.

I took *these* pictures (the closer ones), but not *those* pictures (the more distant ones).

Time

I was able to finish the project *this* week because I had more time than I did *that* week (a week at some more distant time in the past).

Did you like *these* movies (the ones that we just saw) better than *those* movies (the ones we saw earlier)?

In informal conversation, *this* and *these* can be used to introduce a new topic. For example:

There was *this* guy at the party last night . . .

Here the use of *this* signals two things to the listener: that the speaker has a specific person in mind but is aware that the listener does not know yet who the speaker is talking about, *and* that the speaker is introducing this person as a new topic of conversation. Accordingly, we would expect the speaker to elaborate on what was so interesting about that person.

Here is a similar sentence with *these*:

Ralph's boss said that he had *these* concerns.

Again, the use of *these* signals that Ralph's boss has specific concerns in mind, *and* that the concerns have now been introduced as a new topic of conversation.

Quantifiers

The term *quantifier* refers to a number of noun modifiers that express amount or degree. This section focuses only on the quantifiers that pose problems for nonnative and native speakers alike.

Quantifiers Affected by the Count/Noncount Distinction

Count nouns are nouns that have both singular and plural forms. Non-count nouns cannot be used in the plural or with *a/an* (see Chapter 1).

Many/Much. *Many* is used only with plural count nouns. *Much* is used only with noncount nouns. Compare the following sentences, with the noun being modified underlined:

Plural count: There are *many* concerns about the project.
Noncount: There is *much* debate about the project.

Trying to use *many* with a noncount noun or *much* with a plural count noun results in ungrammatical sentences:

Noncount: X There is *many* debate about the project.
Plural count: X There are *much* concerns about the project.

While the use of *much* in the noncount statement is grammatical, it has a slightly artificial or overly formal tone. In spoken language, we would probably choose a quantity phrase with *of* instead of *much*:

Noncount: There is *a lot of* debate about the project.
Noncount: There is *plenty of* debate about the project.
Noncount: There is *lots of* debate about the project.

(A) Few/(a) Little/Any. *Few* is used only with plural count nouns. *Little* is used only with noncount nouns. Compare the following sentences, with the noun being modified underlined:

Plural count: I have had *few* problems with the system.
Noncount: I have had *little* information about the system.

Few and *a few* are nearly identical in meaning, but there are differences in implications. Compare the following sentences:

few:	We have had *few* <u>complaints</u>.
a few:	We have had *a few* <u>complaints</u>.

The use of *few* implies that we have been virtually complaint-free. The use of *a few* is an acknowledgment that we have indeed had complaints, though not a huge number of them. In this context, *few* and *a few* are significantly different.

There is a similar distinction between *little* and *a little*. Compare the following sentences:

little:	There was *little* <u>confusion</u> about the new rules.
a little:	There was *a little* <u>confusion</u> about the new rules.

The use of *little* implies that the new rules were understood perfectly by nearly everybody. The use of *a little* concedes that there was some difficulty (and maybe a lot of difficulty) in people's understanding of the new rules.

In questions and negative sentences, we would normally use *any* rather than either *few* or *little*. For example:

Plural count:	Have you had *any* <u>problems</u> with the system? (question)
Noncount:	Do you have *any* <u>information</u> about the system? (question)
Plural count:	We haven't had *any* <u>problems</u> with the system. (negative)
Noncount:	We don't have *any* <u>information</u> about the system. (negative)

Fewer/Less. *Fewer* is used with plural count nouns. *Less* is used with non-count nouns. For example:

Plural count:	The children had *fewer* <u>colds</u> this year.
Noncount:	The kids had *less* <u>illness</u> this year.
Plural count:	I took *fewer* <u>suitcases</u> with me this year.
Noncount:	I took *less* <u>luggage</u> with me this year.

Some/Any. *Some* is used with both plural nouns and noncount nouns in statements. However, in questions, *some* is replaced by *any*. For example:

Plural count: We have *some* apples. (statement)
Plural count: Do you have *any* apples? (question)
Noncount: We have *some* fruit. (statement)
Noncount: Do you have *any* fruit? (question)

Likewise, in negative sentences, *some* is replaced by *any*. For example:

Plural count: We have *some* apples. (statement)
Plural count: We don't have *any* apples. (negative)
Noncount: We have *some* fruit. (statement)
Noncount: We do not have *any* fruit. (negative)

Agreement with *a Lot Of*

Normally, nouns inside a prepositional phrase do not affect subject-verb agreement. In the following sentence, the prepositional phrase is underlined:

The decisions of the committee are final.

The verb *are* is plural, in agreement with the noun *decision*. *Committee*, a singular noun, is locked up inside the prepositional phrase *of the committee* and thus cannot determine subject-verb agreement.

The quantifier *a lot of* is unusual in that the noun that follows the preposition *of* can enter into subject-verb agreement. In the following sentences, the subject is underlined, and the verb is in italics:

A lot of the committee *is* appointed by the board.
A lot of the committees *are* appointed by the board.

As you can see, the verb agrees with what is technically the object of a preposition.

All /All (of) The

When *all* is used by itself, *all* makes an unrestricted generalization about something. For example:

All trains leave from the lower level.

However, *all (of) the* narrows the scope of the generalization to a particular subclass. For example:

All (of) the trains for New York leave from the lower level.

All (of) the (unlike *all*) can be used to modify singular count nouns. For example:

All of the tree was damaged by insects.
X All the tree was damaged by insects.

Comparative and Superlative Forms of *Few, Little, Much*, and *Many*

Few, little, much, and *many* are unique among quantifiers in that they have comparative and superlative forms, many of them irregular:

Quantifier	Comparative	Superlative
few	fewer	fewest
little	less	least
many	more	most
much	more	most

Here are some example sentences that illustrate these quantifiers:

few
We have made *few* mistakes.
We have made *fewer* mistakes than we did last quarter.
We have made the *fewest* mistakes of any comparable period.

In informal conversation, *less* is sometimes used instead of *fewer*, but this is only marginally acceptable. For example:

X? We have made *less* <u>mistakes</u> this year.

little
It was only a *little* <u>money</u>.
It was *less* <u>money</u> than we had expected.
It was the *least* <u>money</u> that we have ever earned.

many
It took *many* <u>dollars</u> to buy that.
It took *more* <u>dollars</u> than we had expected.
It took the *most* <u>dollars</u> of any transaction we have ever had.

much
We don't have *much* <u>money</u>.
We have *more* <u>money</u> than they do.
We have the *most* <u>money</u> of any company.

Post-Noun Modifiers

This chapter delves into the noun modifiers that follow the nouns that they modify. There are five main types of post-noun modifiers: **adjectival prepositional phrases**, **adjective (relative) clauses**, **appositive phrases**, **participial phrases**, and **infinitive phrases**. Here is an example of each of the five types of post-noun modifiers, with the noun being modified in bold and the modifier in italics:

Adjectival prepositional phrase:	The **car** *in the garage* belongs to a friend.
Adjective clause:	The **car** *that is parked in the garage* belongs to a friend.
Appositive phrase:	The **car**, *an old Ford*, belongs to a friend.
Participial phrase:	The **car** *parked in the garage* belongs to a friend.
Infinitive phrase:	The **decision** *to repair the car* was a costly one.

Adjectival Prepositional Phrases

Prepositional phrases consist of prepositions followed by noun phrase objects. The noun phrase objects are nouns (with or without modifiers), pronouns, gerunds (Chapter 6), or noun clauses (Chapter 7). Here are examples of adjectival prepositional phrases with various types of objects; the entire prepositional phrase is in italics, and the object is in bold:

Noun phrase:	We found a solution *to **the problem we were talking about***.
Pronoun:	The people *with **us*** are friends of the Johnsons.
Gerund:	The argument *about **my taking extra time off*** was resolved.
Noun clause:	An apartment *near **where we live*** is for rent.

Adjectival prepositional phrases are by far the most common type of post-noun modifier. One study found that adjectival prepositional phrases were three times as common as adjective clauses, the next most common type.

Many adjectival prepositional phrases provide spatial or temporal information about the nouns they modify. For example (the preposition is in bold, and the entire prepositional phrase is in italics):

Spatial Information
the house ***by** the river*
the book ***on** the table*
the wall ***behind** the piano*
the window ***over** the sink*
the road ***to** Chicago*
the lands ***beyond** the sea*

Temporal Information
the day ***before** yesterday*
the week ***after** next*
some afternoon ***during** the week*
every Sunday ***till** the holidays*

However, many other adjectival prepositions have a wide range of meanings that cannot be so easily classified. For example:

a play ***by** Shakespeare*
the man ***with** the red beard*
the causes ***of** the Civil War*
a friend ***of** the family*
a victory ***despite** all the odds*
everyone ***except** me*

Adjective Clauses (Relative Clauses)

Adjective clauses, also known as **relative clauses**, are the next most common form of post-noun modifier. Adjective clauses have their own internal subject-verb structure, but they cannot stand alone as independent sentences. Adjective clauses always immediately follow the nouns that they modify. Adjective clauses begin with a **relative pronoun** that must refer to and agree with the noun that the adjective clause modifies. We refer to this noun as the **antecedent** of the relative pronoun.

All languages have some form of adjective clause, but English is remarkable for the wide variety of types of nouns that can be modified by adjective clauses and for the complexity of the internal structure of its adjective clauses.

In some languages, adjective clauses can modify only nouns playing the basic roles of **subjects** and **objects**. In addition to these, English allows adjective clauses to modify nouns playing the roles of **objects of prepositions** and **predicate nominatives** (nouns following **linking verbs**, such as *be*). Here are examples of adjective clauses modifying nouns playing each of the four noun roles; the entire adjective clause is in italics, and the antecedent noun is in bold:

Subject:	The **computer** *that you use* has been disconnected.
Object:	They fixed the **computer** *that you use*.
Object of preposition:	We returned the computer to the **man** *who works in accounting*.
Predicate nominative:	She is a **person** *whom we can all look up to*.

Internal Structure of Adjective Clauses

All adjective clauses must begin with a relative pronoun that immediately follows and refers to the noun that the adjective clause modifies (the relative pronoun's antecedent). The determination of the form of the relative pronoun and the mechanisms by which the relative pronoun ends up at the beginning of the adjective clause are the focus of this section.

Adjective clauses can relate to the nouns they modify in two different ways. If the adjective clause significantly narrows or redefines the meaning of the noun being modified, the adjective clause is called **restrictive**. If the adjective clause merely renames the noun being modified but does not narrow or redefine its meaning, the adjective clause is called **nonrestrictive**. With a few exceptions that will be pointed out as we go along, there are few differences between the internal structures of restrictive clauses and nonrestrictive clauses. Since the distinction is largely irrelevant to describing how adjective clauses are built, all of the examples in this section contain only restrictive adjective clauses.

Relative Pronoun Forms.   The form of the relative pronoun is determined by two different considerations—one external to the adjective clause, and the other internal.

The **external consideration** is the nature of the noun being modified (the antecedent of the relative pronoun). The antecedent is, of course, *outside* the adjective clause. If the antecedent is human, we normally use one of these relative pronouns: *who, whom,* or *whose.* However, in casual spoken language *that* is often used to refer to humans in place of the more formal *who* or *whom*, in part to avoid making a choice between *who* and *whom*. If the antecedent is not human (i.e., a thing, an idea, or an abstraction), we use *that* or *which* as the relative pronoun. (The factors affecting the choice of *that* or *which* are complicated. For now, we will use *which* only when it is required. Otherwise, we will use *that* to refer to all nonhuman antecedents. We will discuss the differences between *that* and *which* when we discuss restrictive and nonrestrictive adjective clauses later in this section.)

The **internal consideration** is the role that the relative pronoun plays *inside* its own adjective clause. For the moment, let us assume that the antecedent is human. If the relative pronoun plays the role of subject inside the adjective clause, then we use *who*. If the relative pronoun is an object, we use *whom*. If the relative pronoun is a possessive, we use *whose*. Fortunately, we do not have to worry about *that* and *which*, because they do not change form no matter what role they play inside the adjective clause.

In addition to the conventional relative pronouns cited, we can use *where* and *when* as adverbial relatives to refer to nouns that have distinct spatial or temporal meanings.

The following chart summarizes the basic rules about how the external and internal considerations jointly determine the form of the relative pronouns:

RELATIVE PRONOUN'S ROLE INSIDE AN ADJECTIVE CLAUSE

External Antecedent	Subject	Object	Possessive Adverb
Human:	*who (that)*	*whom (that)*	*whose*
Nonhuman:	*that, which*	*that, which*	*whose*
Spatial noun:	*where*		
Temporal noun:	*when*		

Here are some examples that illustrate each of the relative pronouns (in bold), with the entire adjective clause in italics:

Human—subject:	She is a person **who (that)** *will listen to everybody.*
Human—object:	She is a person **whom (that)** *we all admired.*
Human—possessive:	She is a person **whose** *attitude everyone admires.*
Nonhuman—subject:	It is a book **that** *has influenced us all.*
Nonhuman—object:	It is a book **that** *we have all admired.*
Nonhuman—possessive:	It is a book **whose** *title is known by everyone.*
Spatial adverb:	It is a place **where** *we could all meet.*
Temporal adverb:	It was a time **when** *we could all meet.*

Relative Pronoun as Subject. When the relative pronoun plays the role of subject inside the adjective clause, the relative pronoun is already at the beginning of its clause, so no movement of the relative pronoun is necessary. The adjective clause is correctly formed as it stands. Following are two examples, one with a human antecedent and one with a nonhuman antecedent. Here and in all following examples, the relative pronoun is in bold, and the entire adjective clause is in italics:

Human:	I met the man **who** *is interviewing for the new job.*
Nonhuman:	I found the switch **that** *turns on the power.*

Relative Pronoun as Object. When the relative pronoun plays the role of object of a verb, the relative pronoun must be moved forward from its normal object position, leaving behind a gap (underlined) immediately following the verb where the object had originally been:

Human:	I met the teacher **whom** *we discussed* _____.
Nonhuman:	We got the medicine **that** *the doctor prescribed* _____ *for us.*

After the relative pronoun that plays the role of object has been moved to the beginning of an adjective clause, we then have the further option of deleting that relative pronoun from the adjective clause. Deleting the relative pronoun from the two preceding example sentences would give us the following:

Human:	I met the teacher ~~**whom**~~ *we discussed* _____.
Nonhuman:	We got the medicine ~~**that**~~ *the doctor prescribed* _____ *for us.*

A deleted relative pronoun makes adjective clauses much more difficult for nonnative speakers to recognize, because the relative pronoun, the normal flag word that signals the beginning of an adjective clause, is now missing. Here are some more examples of this hard-to-recognize construction:

Human:	The company hired an accountant ~~**whom**~~ *we had used* _____ *before.*
Nonhuman:	We finally found the answer ~~**that**~~ *we had been looking for* _____.
Human:	I really like the new teacher ~~**whom**~~ *the school just hired* _____.
Nonhuman:	I didn't like the plan ~~**that**~~ *they were proposing* _____.

Relative Pronoun as Object of a Preposition. When the relative pronoun plays the role of the object of a preposition, the adjective clause can be formed in either of two ways. In Option 1, the preposition and its relative pronoun object are moved forward together as a unit, leaving a gap where the prepositional phrase had originally been. In Option 2, the relative pronoun is moved forward alone, leaving behind the preposition in its original position, but now without its object. Compare the following examples showing a human antecedent:

Option 1—Preposition and relative pronoun move together
We visited the children ***about whom*** *you had asked* _____.

Option 2—Relative pronoun moves alone
We visited the children ***whom*** *you had asked **about** *_____.

Here is an example with a nonhuman antecedent:

Option 1—Preposition and relative pronoun move together
I rented the movie ***about which*** *we had talked* _____.

Notice that when the preposition and the relative pronoun move together, we must use the relative pronoun *which*. The use of *that* is ungrammatical in Option 1:

X I rented the movie ***about that*** *we had talked* _____.

Option 2—Relative pronoun moves alone
I rented the movie ***that*** *we had talked **about*** _____.

In conversational English, Option 2, with the preposition left at the end of the sentence, is strongly preferred over Option 1 for both human and nonhuman antecedents. In formal, written English, however, the reverse is true: writers prefer to move the preposition along with the relative pronoun, as in Option 1. The preference for Option 1 probably reflects a schoolroom grammar bias against ending sentences with prepositions in formal, written English.

In Option 2, we have the additional option of deleting the object relative pronoun from the beginning of the adjective clause. Here are both Option 2 examples again, but now with the object relative pronoun deleted:

We visited the children **whom** *you had asked* **about** _____.
I rented the movie **that** *we had talked* **about** _____.

We cannot delete the relative pronoun when we use Option 1, because the object relative pronoun is locked up inside a prepositional phrase:

X We visited the children **about whom** *you had asked* _____.
X I rented the movie **about that** *we had talked* _____.

Relative Pronoun as Possessive. When the relative pronoun is the possessive pronoun *whose*, both the possessive pronoun and the noun that the possessive pronoun modifies must be moved forward as a unit. Here are some examples with both human and nonhuman antecedents:

Human: We talked to the man **whose firm** *you so admired*

_____.

Nonhuman: We enjoyed the play **whose script** *we read*
_____ *last night.*

Notice that *whose* can be used to refer to nonhuman antecedents.
Even though the relative pronoun *whose* has been moved to the first position of the adjective clause, we cannot delete *whose*, because it is locked together with the noun it modifies:

Human: X We talked to the man **whose firm** *you so admired*

_____.

Nonhuman: X We enjoyed the play **whose script** *we*
read _____ *last night.*

Relative Pronoun as Adverb. When the noun being modified has a strong sense of place or time, we can use the appropriate adverb as a relative pronoun instead of *that* or *which* + a preposition:
Where *as a relative pronoun of place*. Here is an example using the antecedent noun *office*, a noun with a strong sense of place. In addition to the

standard relative pronouns *that* and *which*, we can use *where* as a relative pronoun:

that: I know the office **that** he works **in** _____.
which: I know the office **in which** he works _____.
where: I know the office **where** he works _____.

Where, unlike *that*, cannot be deleted:

X I know the office ~~where~~ she works _____.

Here are some more examples of *where* used as a relative pronoun of place:

They were searching in a remote canyon **where** *the hikers were last seen*

_____.

The suburb **where** *they lived* _____ was miles from any public transportation.

I returned it to the store **where** *I had bought it* _____.

When *as a relative pronoun of time.* We have a similar set of alternatives with nouns that have a strong sense of time. In addition to the standard relative pronouns *that* and *which*, we can use *when* as a relative pronoun. For example:

that: I remember the day **that** *she was born on* _____.
which: I remember the day **on which** *she was born* _____.
when: I remember the day **when** *she was born* _____.

Here are some more examples of *when* used as a relative pronoun of place:

That is the time **when** *I have to be at work* _____.
I think 2003 was the year **when** *I got my first job* _____.
That was the moment **when** *I knew I was in trouble* _____.

Restrictive and Nonrestrictive Adjective Clauses

Adjective clauses have two different functions. One function, called **restrictive**, changes the meaning of the noun being modified (the relative pronoun's antecedent) by redefining it or by significantly limiting the scope of reference of the noun. All of the examples of adjective clauses in this chapter up to this point have been restrictive.

Here is a clear-cut example of a restrictive adjective clause (in italics):

All students *who have missed the final* will fail the course.

The relative clause significantly narrows the meaning of the antecedent *all students* to a small group of those students—namely, just those who have missed the final. Without the adjective clause, the sentence has a totally different meaning:

All students will fail the course.

The other function, called **nonrestrictive**, is to provide additional information about the noun that the adjective clause modifies. This information does not significantly alter or restrict the meaning of the noun.

Here is a clear-cut example of a nonrestrictive clause (in italics):

I bumped into my boss, *who was also doing some last-minute shopping.*

My boss is my boss, whether he was doing last-minute shopping or not. In other words, the additional information provided by the nonrestrictive adjective clause does not serve to limit or redefine who my boss is. If we delete the adjective clause, the basic meaning of the sentence is unchanged:

I bumped into my boss.

When we delete the nonrestrictive adjective clause, naturally we also lose the meaning contained in that clause. The point is that the loss of that meaning does not significantly alter the meaning of the noun it modified.

The distinction between restrictive and nonrestrictive is not trivial or merely academic. Arguments about whether an adjective clause is restrictive or nonrestrictive have caused more lawsuits and patent disputes than all other aspects of English grammar put together.

To see how important the distinction between restrictive and nonrestrictive is, compare the following sentences, with adjective clauses in italics:

Restrictive: Contract terms *that are approved by the board* are binding.

Nonrestrictive: Contract terms, *which are approved by the board,* are binding.

The restrictive adjective clause means that *only* those contract terms that are approved by the board are binding. Any contract term, even though legal in all other respects, is not binding *unless* and *until* it has been explicitly approved by the board.

The nonrestrictive adjective clause, on the other hand, asserts that *all* contract terms are binding. The fact that contract terms are approved by the board is (maybe) an interesting piece of information, but that information has nothing to do with determining which contract terms are binding. The terms of a contract are binding even if the board never approves them.

Since the distinction between restrictive and nonrestrictive can be so important, it is critical that we know how to tell the two functions apart. Only one feature absolutely distinguishes them: the presence or absence of commas. If an adjective clause is set off with commas, it is nonrestrictive. If an adjective clause is *not* set off with commas, it is restrictive. Nothing else really counts.

It is important to understand what the presence or absence of commas is signaling. The presence of the pair of commas signals that the adjective clause can be cut out of the sentence without changing the basic meaning of the noun that the clause modifies. The absence of commas tells us that the adjective clause is bound to the noun as an essential part of the meaning of that noun. If the restrictive adjective clause were to be removed from the sentence, the meaning of the noun being modified would be radically altered.

In your own writing, when you are trying to decide whether an adjective clause is restrictive or nonrestrictive, use this test: Remove the adjective clause to see the effect on the sentence. If the sentence still has the same basic meaning you intend, then the adjective clause is probably nonrestrictive and should be set off with commas. If the sentence no longer means what you want it to say, then the adjective clause is probably restrictive and should *not* be set off with commas.

Using *That* and *Which* to Distinguish Between Restrictive and Nonrestrictive Clauses. You may have noticed a second difference between the restrictive and nonrestrictive adjective clauses in the example sentences: the choice of relative pronouns. The restrictive clause used *that*; the nonrestrictive clause used *which*. In many grammar and style books (including most technical writing manuals), you will see the following statement as an absolute rule: Always use *that* with restrictive clauses and *which* with nonrestrictive clauses.

This is not a bad rule to follow in your own writing, especially if you are doing any kind of technical or legal writing. However, be aware that most native speakers of English do not actually follow this rule, especially in spoken language. The problem is that people often use *which* in restrictive clauses interchangeably with the more conventional *that*. Here are some examples:

Restrictive: I need the names ***that** you collected.*
Restrictive: I need the names ***which** you collected.*
Restrictive: The cars ***that** are already in line* get to go in first.
Restrictive: The cars ***which** are already in line* get to go in first.

However, the reverse is not true. We cannot use *that* in nonrestrictive clauses:

Nonrestrictive: Our first house, ***which** was on Elm Street*, still belongs to our family.
Nonrestrictive: X   Our first house, ***that** was on Elm Street*, still belongs to our family.

Since *that* and *which* can both be used in restrictive clauses, we cannot rely on *that* and *which* to signal the difference between restrictive and nonrestrictive clauses. It bears repeating that the only reliable way to distinguish the two types of clauses is by the difference in their use of commas. If a clause is set off with commas, it is nonrestrictive. If it is not set off with commas, it is restrictive. The choice of *that* or *which* is only supplementary information.

Vague *Which*. One final word of warning about using nonrestrictive adjective clauses: Be sure that *which* has a real antecedent. Here is an example that illustrates the problem:

> She went into the room and closed the shades, **which made the room dark.**

Ask yourself this question: What noun is the actual antecedent of *which*? At first glance, it appears that *which* refers to *shades*, but that is not really accurate. What made the room dark was the entire act of closing the shades. Compare that sentence with the following:

> She went into the room and closed the shades, **which were made of a light cream-colored fabric.**

In this second sentence, *shades* is truly the antecedent of *which*.

The antecedent-less use of *which* in nonrestrictive relative clauses is called a "vague *which*." A vague *which* is typically used for a nonrestrictive clause that makes a comment on or gives a reaction to the information in the first part of the sentence. Here are some more examples:

> Our team finally won the championship, **which made all the effort worthwhile.**
> I don't have to work on Fridays, **which is great for me.**
> We missed our sales quota, **which upset everyone.**
> I injured my knee, **which will cause me to miss the next few games.**

Sometimes in fiction writing, the author will set the antecedent-less adjective clause off in a separate sentence to capture the sound of spoken language. For example:

> Sarah rejected John's proposal. ***Which*** *caused his mother to stop*
>   *speaking to Sarah's family.*

Vague *which* is common in speech, but careful writers rarely use it. It is especially inappropriate in formal writing.

Restrictive and Nonrestrictive Clauses with Proper Nouns. To this point, we have talked about only common nouns. The situation with proper nouns is much simpler. Proper nouns are normally modified only by nonrestrictive nouns. That's because proper nouns already refer to specific persons, places, or things, and thus they cannot be further narrowed or defined by adjective clauses. Here are some examples of nonrestrictive clauses modifying proper nouns:

Person:	We met Dr. Edwards, ***who*** *is our director of research.*
Place:	We went to Berkeley, ***where*** *my brother lives.*
Thing:	The original Declaration of Independence, ***which*** *was signed on July 4, 1776,* is still on display in Washington.

The rare exception is the case in which we turn a proper noun into a kind of common noun by using *the.* For example:

We visited the Oakland ***that*** *is in Michigan,* not the one in California.
The San Francisco ***that*** *we knew in the 1960s* does not exist anymore.

Appositive Phrases

An **appositive** is a noun that identifies or explains another noun. For example:

John Booth, *a financial reporter,* will visit our office tomorrow.

The appositive *a financial reporter* explains who *John Booth* is. Technically speaking, the appositive in this example is just the noun *reporter*. The whole structure *a financial reporter* is an **appositive phrase**. However, since the distinction between appositive and appositive phrase is inconsequential for this discussion, we will use the term *appositive* broadly to refer to the appositive together with its modifiers (if any).

Nearly all appositives are derived from **nonrestrictive adjective clauses**. Nonrestrictive adjective clauses are always set off from the rest of the sentence with commas. Accordingly, the appositive phrases that are derived from nonrestrictive adjective clauses are also set off with commas. Following are some examples of appositives along with the adjective clauses from which they are derived. Those in the first group modify proper nouns, and those in the second group modify common nouns:

Proper Nouns

Appositive:	They moved to Olympia, *the capital of Washington.*
Adjective clause:	They moved to Olympia, *which is the capital of Washington.*
Appositive:	Judy, *the only child with perfect attendance,* smiled proudly.
Adjective clause:	Judy, *who was the only child with perfect attendance,* smiled proudly.

Common Nouns

Appositive:	His apartment, *a dingy little room in Soho,* costs him a fortune.
Adjective clause:	His apartment, *which is a dingy little room in Soho,* costs him a fortune.
Appositive:	I answered the final question, *a tough one about foreign trade.*
Adjective clause:	I answered the final question, *which was a tough one about foreign trade.*

An unusual feature of appositives is that they can be moved away from the nouns that they modify. We do this most commonly as a way of introducing subject nouns. Here are some examples:

Ruth, *a longtime family friend*, could be trusted to do the right thing.
A longtime family friend, Ruth could be trusted to do the right thing.

Our old truck, *a useless piece of junk*, finally quit working altogether.
A useless piece of junk, our old truck finally quit working altogether.

We normally shift appositives that modify personal pronouns to the beginning of the sentence. For example:

X? I, *a hopeless romantic*, always want movies to have happy endings.
    A hopeless romantic, I always want movies to have happy endings.

X? She, *the most popular actress in the 1950s*, appeared in dozens of films.
    The most popular actress in the 1950s, she appeared in dozens of films.

X? He, *a noted expert on the Middle East*, is often quoted on the BBC.
    A noted expert on the Middle East, he is often quoted on the BBC.

Another use of shifted appositives is moving appositives that modify objects to the end of the sentence for emphasis or surprise. In the following examples, the noun being modified is in bold:

We bought them a **present** in Mexico, *a beautiful ceramic vase*.
Noel Coward wrote his best-known **play** in 1930, *Private Lives*.
We got a wonderful **speaker** for the convention, *Senator Smith*.

So far, we have looked only at nonrestrictive appositives. Are there also restrictive appositives? The answer is that there are, but they are uncommon and are limited in their range of meaning, because they work against the idea of using appositives in the first place. Restrictive modifiers, by definition, significantly change the meaning of the nouns they modify, whereas the whole point of using an appositive is to give supplementary, nonredefining information. Thus, a restrictive appositive is almost a self-contradiction.

About the only time we find a restricted appositive is when a proper noun is used as an appositive to define a vague common noun. Here is a typical example:

My friend *Alice White* was visiting from London.

The proper noun *Alice White* is an appositive used to define the common noun *friend*.

Here are several more examples of restrictive appositives:

Shakespeare's play *Hamlet* is his most complex work.
His brother *Alfred* is going to MIT.
Our neighbor *Linda Lingle* is from the island of Maui.

Participial Phrases

Participial phrases act as adjectives modifying the nouns they follow. Participial phrases always contain a verb in either the **present-participle** or **past-participle** form. Here are some examples with the participle in bold and the entire participial phrase in italics:

Present-Participial Phrases
We got an apartment **facing** *the ocean.*
The New York office **being** *picketed* had already closed.
It is an occupation **requiring** *good technical skills.*

Past-Participial Phrases
One book **required** *for the course* is out of print.
I attended a lecture **presented** *by a famous economist.*
He had some french fries **smothered** *in ketchup.*

In all participial phrases, the noun being modified acts as the subject of the present-participle or past-participle verb. For example:

They tried to mop up the water *flowing out of the washing machine.*

Water is the subject of the present participle *flowing*.
   Here's another example:

The cloth **wrapped** *around his hand* stopped the bleeding.

Here *cloth* is the subject of the past participle *wrapped*.
   Participial phrases are like reduced adjective clauses. The most important point of similarity is that both participial phrases and adjective clauses have exactly the same kind relationship to nouns they modify—they are either **restrictive** or **nonrestrictive**. Here are some examples of restrictive and nonrestrictive participial phrases together with their corresponding adjective clauses (both types of modifiers are in italics):

Restrictive

Present-participial phrase:	The man *standing next to her* is her uncle.
Adjective clause:	The man *who is standing next to her* is her uncle.
Past-participial phrase:	Everyone knows the plays *written by Shakespeare.*
Adjective clause:	Everyone knows the plays *that were written by Shakespeare.*

Nonrestrictive

Present-participial phrase:	Susan, *returning my call*, gave me an update.
Adjective clause:	Susan, *who was returning my call*, gave me an update.
Past-participial phrase:	Our CEO, *worried about the news*, called a meeting.
Adjective clause:	Our CEO, *who was worried about the news*, called a meeting.

Let us now look at each type of participial phrase in more detail.

Present-Participial Phrases

Present-participial phrases must contain a verb in the **present-participle** form. The present participle is one of the few verb forms in English that are absolutely regular. The present participle is the base (or dictionary) form of a verb + -*ing*. Even the verb *be* is regular: *being*. The only variation is the result of normal spelling rules for final silent *e* and doubled consonant spellings. For example, the final *e* of *hope* is dropped when we add a suffix beginning with a vowel: *hope–hoping,* and the final consonant of *hop* doubles when we add a suffix beginning with a vowel: *hop–hopping.*

Present-participial phrases are so like adjective clauses in both their structure and meaning that it is easy to assume that the present-participle verb form is derived directly from the use of the progressive tense in the corresponding adjective clause. If this were the case, the present participle in the participial phrase would mean the same thing as the progressive tense in the adjective clause. For example, in the following set of sentences, the present participle *answering* would mean the same thing as *was answering* in the corresponding adjective clause:

Present-participial phrase:	The woman *answering the phone* took my name.
Adjective clause:	The woman *who **was answering** the phone* took my name.

The problem is that they do not mean the same thing. To see why not, we need to understand the difference in meaning between the progressive tenses (past, present, and future) and the present tense. Briefly, the progressive tenses describe action in progress (hence the name "progressive") at some moment of time (past, present, or future). The present tense, on the other hand, is literally "time-less." It is used to describe an ongoing state or permanent condition. For example, compare the following sentences:

Progressive:	The woman **was answering** the phone.
Present:	The woman **answers** the phone.

The progressive sentence describes what the woman was doing at some actual moment of time—when we came into the office, for example. It does not mean that answering the phone was her regular job. The present-tense sentence, on the other hand, does exactly that: it describes what the woman's usual job is. It does not necessarily describe what she is doing at the moment. In fact, she may not be on the phone at all; she might be out taking a break.

Now let's return to the sentence with the present-participial phrase:

The woman ***answering*** *the phone* took my name.

What does the participial phrase *answering the phone* mean? Does it describe what the woman is doing at that moment in time (progressive tense), or does it describe what the woman's normal job is (present tense). The answer is, of course, that we cannot tell. In other words, when we create a present-participial phrase, we destroy the distinction between the progressive and present tenses in the underlying adjective clause. Do not equate the present participle with the progressive tense, even though both end in *-ing*. They do not mean the same thing.

Past-Participial Phrases

Past-participial phrases must contain a verb in the **past-participle** form (see Chapter 8). The biggest problem working with past participles is not the irregular ones (though they are bad enough); it is the regular ones, because they look like past tenses—both end in *-ed*.

Past-participial phrases are derived from adjective clauses that contain verbs in the **passive** voice (see Chapter 18.) Here are some examples of past-participial phrases with their corresponding adjective clauses (modifiers are in italics; verbs are bold):

Past-participial phrase:	The statements ***made*** *by the defendant* were read in court.
Adjective clause:	The statements *that **were made** by the defendant* were read in court.
Past-participial phrase:	The confusion ***caused*** *by the misunderstanding* was soon cleared up.

Adjective clause:	The confusion *that **was caused** by the misunderstanding* was soon cleared up.
Past-participial phrase:	Scrooge, *always **depressed** at Christmastime*, went on a Caribbean cruise.
Adjective clause:	Scrooge, *who **was** always **depressed** at Christmastime*, went on a Caribbean cruise.

As you can see, the past-participial phrase is a reduced version of the underlying passive-voice adjective clause. The relative pronoun and the verb *be* have been deleted. What remains is the past-participial phrase.

Movable Participial Phrases and Dangling Participles

Nonrestrictive participial phrases, both present participial and past participial, have an unusual feature: they can be shifted away from the nouns they modify. Here are some examples, with the participial phrases first in their normal positions and then in various shifted positions:

Normal:	The campers, *picking their spot carefully*, unpacked their tents.
Shifted:	*Picking their spot carefully*, the campers unpacked their tents.
Shifted:	The campers unpacked their tents, *picking their spot carefully*.

Normal:	Uncle Robert, *worn out by the kids*, went to bed early.
Shifted:	*Worn out by the kids*, Uncle Robert went to be early.
Shifted:	Uncle Robert went to bed early, *worn out by the kids*.

The option of shifting is not open to restrictive participial phrases. For example:

Normal:		The cables *leading to the power source* had been disconnected.
Shifted:	X	*Leading to the power source*, the cables had been disconnected.
Shifted:	X	The cables had been disconnected, *leading to the power source*.

In most situations, shifting nonrestrictive participial phrases away from the nouns they modify is a stylistic option. However, when we modify pronouns, shifting the participial phrase is a virtual requirement:

Normal:	?	He, *waving to the crowd*, stepped onto the stage.
Shifted:		*Waving to the crowd*, he stepped onto the stage.
Shifted:		He stepped onto the stage, *waving to the crowd*.

Normal:	?	They, *exhausted by the long trip*, fell asleep immediately.
Shifted:		*Exhausted by the long trip*, they fell asleep immediately.
Shifted:		They fell asleep immediately, *exhausted by the long trip*.

When we shift a nonrestrictive participial phrase away from its normal position, we run the risk of creating a **dangling participle**. A dangling participle is a participial phrase that says something we do not mean to say. Here is an example of a dangling participle:

X *Having hiked all day*, my backpack was killing me.

To see what the problem is, shift the participial phrase back to its normal position—following the noun it is supposed to modify:

X My backpack, *having hiked all day*, was killing me.

What the unfortunate author of this sentence actually said was that the *backpack* had hiked all day. Compare that sentence with a similar sentence that has correctly shifted the nonrestrictive participial phrase:

Having hiked all day, I had to get out of my backpack.

Here is an example of a dangling modifier with a past-participial phrase:

✗ *Damaged beyond all repair,* Sam had to trash his hard drive.

When we try to shift the participial phrase back to the noun it modifies, we discover that the author has said something other than what was intended:

✗ Sam, *damaged beyond all repair,* had to trash his hard drive.

Of course, what is damaged is the hard drive, not Sam. Here is how we could fix the sentence so that the participial phrase has something to modify:

Damaged beyond all repair, Sam's hard drive had to be trashed.

Here is a second example, this one with a present-participial phrase:

✗ *Running across the uneven ground,* my ankle twisted.

We know what the writer means, but this is what he or she actually says:

✗ My ankle, *running across the uneven ground,* twisted.

We get the strange picture of an ankle, all by itself, running across the ground. We can repair the dangling modifier by supplying a subject pronoun for the participial phrase to modify:

Running across the uneven ground, I twisted my ankle.

Here is a much more subtle dangling participle:

✗ *Terrified by the loud noise,* there was panic among the animals.

The problem here is that there is no noun to serve as a subject for *terrified*. In other words, the participial phrase does not modify anything. Here is how we might repair the sentence:

> *Terrified by the loud noise*, the animals panicked.

Now the participial phrase modifies *animals*.

It is often comical when someone else writes a dangling modifier. However, it is not so funny when you write one. The lesson is that whenever you use a participial phrase shifted away from the noun it modifies, mentally shift it back to its normal position to see if it makes sense.

Infinitive Phrases

An **infinitive** consists of *to* + the base (or dictionary) form of the verb. For example:

> to be   to go
> to have   to sing

Infinitive phrases consist of the infinitive followed by whatever object or complement the verb in the infinitive phrase takes, together with any optional adverbs that may modify the verb. Infinitive phrases can be used as adjectives, nouns, and adverbs.

Adjective infinitive phrases always immediately follow the nouns they modify. Here are some examples with the infinitive verb in bold and the entire phrases in italics:

> I bought some magazines *to **read** on the trip.*
> She was the first woman *to **serve** as prime minister in her country.*
> There were important decisions *to **be** made.*

One of the disadvantages of using adjectival infinitive phrases is that they are inherently ambiguous. Unlike the case with participial phrases, in which the noun being modified is always the subject of the verb, the verbs in infinitive phrases have no automatically defined subject.

For example, consider the following sentence:

He is the best man **to choose.**

What is the relation of *man* to the verb *choose*? Is *man* the subject of *choose*—that is, the one doing the choosing? Or is *man* the object of *choosing*—that is, the one to be chosen? There is simply no way to tell.

A related problem is that we are often not aware of how ambiguous our adjectival infinitive phrases actually are. Here is an example:

Her doctor gave Susan a list of drugs **to avoid** *during pregnancy.*

We might think that the preceding sentence means that Susan is pregnant and concerned about what drugs to avoid. But it does not have to mean that at all. Compare that sentence with the following one:

Her doctor gave John a list of drugs **to avoid** *during pregnancy.*

Here it is clear that the list of drugs could be for anybody.

Probably the most common implied subject of an adjectival infinitive phrase is a vague universal *we/us/everybody.* For example:

Now is the time **to work** *together.*

There is one way to actually define what the subject of the infinitive is: use a prepositional phrase beginning with *for* immediately in front of the infinitive. The object of that preposition *must* be the subject of the verb in the infinitive. The noun that is the object of *for* in this kind of construction is sometimes called the **subject of the infinitive.** Let us go back to our sentence about the list of drugs and supply a prepositional phrase beginning with *for*:

Her doctor gave Susan a list of drugs **for Ann** *to avoid during pregnancy.*

Now the sentence is totally unambiguous: the list can only be for Ann. Here are some more examples, with the subjects of the infinitives underlined:

I bought a gift *for us* **to take** *to the reception.*
The books *for the children* **to read** are on the desk.
Noon would be a good time *for the guests* **to get** *there.*

Pronouns

In this chapter we discuss four types of pronouns: **personal, reflexive, indefinite,** and **demonstrative.** Two other types of pronouns—**relative** and **interrogative**—are used as parts of noun phrases. Relative pronouns are discussed in Chapter 4 in connection with adjective clauses, which must begin with relative pronouns. Interrogative pronouns are used in forming question-word questions, as explained in Chapter 17. Pronounlike words called ***wh-* words** are also used in forming *wh-* infinitives (Chapter 6) and *wh-* type noun clauses (Chapter 7).

Personal Pronouns

You are probably familiar with the traditional definition of **pronoun:** "a pronoun is a word that replaces one or more than one noun." The "one or more than one noun" part of the definition refers to **compound nouns** (two nouns joined by *and* or *or*). Here is an example:

John and Mary are coming to the party.

We can replace the compound nouns *John and Mary* with the third-person pronoun *they:*

<u>*John and Mary*</u> are coming to the party.
     They

However, if we were to take the definition literally, we'd have a problem. For example, consider the following sentence:

The young *man* in the yellow sweater asked who you were.

If we were to replace the noun *man* in this sentence with *he*, we would get the following nonsensical result:

X The young *he* in the yellow sweater asked who you were.

Clearly, what the pronoun *he* really replaces is the entire noun phrase *the young man in the yellow sweater*, not just the noun *man*:

The young **man** in the yellow sweater asked who you were.
          He

A **noun phrase** is a noun together with all of that noun's modifiers. In the preceding example, *he* replaces the noun *man* together with all of *man's* modifiers: the pre-noun modifiers *the* and *young* plus the post-noun adjectival prepositional phrase *in the yellow sweater*.

The noun in the noun phrase is still the most important part of the noun phrase, because the noun determines which pronoun to use, as we can see in the following examples:

The young **woman** in the yellow sweater asked who you were.
          She

The young **children** in the yellow sweaters asked who you were.
          They

Third-person pronouns are unique even among pronouns. The ability of third-person pronouns to substitute for noun phrases is not shared with first-person and second-person pronouns.

First-person and second-person pronouns do not replace anything. The first-person pronouns refer only to the speaker or writer of a sentence, and the second-person pronouns refer only to the real or imagined audience. For example, consider the following sentence:

I see *you*.

The first-person pronoun *I* and the second-person pronoun *you* do not substitute for other noun phrases. They are just themselves—speaker and audience, respectively.

Personal pronouns are the most important and complex family of pronouns. Personal pronouns have different forms depending on their **person** (first, second, and third), **number** (singular and plural), and **form** or **case** (subject, object, and possessive). The following chart represents all the personal pronouns.

CHART OF PERSONAL PRONOUNS

Form (Case)	Number	
	Singular	Plural
First-Person Pronouns		
Subject:	I	we
Object:	me	us
Possessive pronominal:	mine	ours
Possessive adjectival:	my	our
Second-Person Pronouns		
Subject:	you	you
Object:	you	you
Possessive pronominal:	yours	yours
Possessive adjectival:	your	your
Third-Person Pronouns		
Subject:	he, she, it	they
Object:	him, her, it	them
Possessive pronominal:	his, hers, its	theirs
Possessive adjectival:	his, her, its	their

Notice that the possessive pronouns have two different sets of forms. The pronominal forms (*mine, ours, yours, his, hers, its, theirs*) act as true pronouns in the sense that they can play the standard noun roles of subject, object, and complement of linking verbs. For example:

Subject:	*Mine* was the only correct answer.
	Ours didn't stand a chance.
Object:	Bob couldn't find his program, so I gave him *yours*.
	The children lost *theirs* again.
Complement:	The decision is *yours*.
	The missing purse was *hers*.

Adjectival forms (*my, our, your, his, her, its, their*) act as adjectives modifying nouns (Chapter 3). Here are some examples of this use:

My answer was the only correct one.
I gave him *your* program.
It was *your* decision to make.

Sexist Use of Pronouns

Using the masculine pronoun *he* to refer to males is perfectly normal. However, there is a problem when we use *he* to refer to people in general. Here is an example:

When a person first uses a computer, *he* tends to be completely overwhelmed.

Many people would find this sentence to be objectionable because it sends a message that males are the only kind of people who use computers.

There are two simple ways of rewriting this type of sentence to eliminate the generic *he*:

1. Replace *he* with the compound *he or she*. For example:

   When a person first uses a computer, *he or she* tends to be completely overwhelmed.

2. Replace *he* with the plural pronoun *they*. This solution will require the subject of the sentence to be rewritten as a plural so that *they* will have an appropriate plural antecedent:

   When **people** first use computers, *they* tend to be completely overwhelmed.

Of the two solutions, usually the second alternative is better, even though it usually requires more sentence revision. The option with *he or she* often seems clumsy.

Distinguishing Between *Its* and *It's*

The possessive pronoun *its* is often confused with *it's*, the contracted form of *it is*. There is a simple and highly reliable way to tell them apart: Expand the *its* to *it is*. If that expansion makes sense, then use *it's*. If the expansion does not make sense, then use *its*, the possessive pronoun. Here are two examples of the process:

> **Example 1**
> *Its* OK with me. **(?)**
> **Expansion test:**   *It is* OK with me.
> **Correction:**   *It's* OK with me.

The success of the expansion test in Example 1 shows that *its* is actually intended to be a contraction of *it is*, and thus it must be spelled with an apostrophe (or left as two separate words, which is actually a better alternative, especially in formal writing).

> **Example 2**
> Our company changed *it's* logo. **(?)**
> **Expansion test:**   X   Our company changed *it is* logo.
> **Correction:**   Our company changed *its* logo.

The failure of the expansion test in Example 2 shows that *it's* is not intended to be a contraction, and thus the word must be spelled without an apostrophe.

Reflexive Pronouns

Reflexive pronouns are a unique groups of pronouns that always end in either *-self* or *-selves*. Here is the complete list:

Person	Singular	Plural
First person:	myself	ourselves
Second person:	yourself	yourselves
Third person:	himself	themselves
	herself	themselves
	itself	themselves

Reflexive pronouns have no independent meaning; they must refer back to some noun (or pronoun) mentioned earlier in the same sentence. This earlier mentioned noun is called the **antecedent** of the reflexive pronoun. The word *reflexive* comes from a Latin word meaning to "bend back." Reflexive pronouns must "bend back" to their antecedents (the nearest appropriate noun—usually the subject of the sentence). Here are some examples, with the reflexive pronoun in italics and the antecedent in bold:

The **queen** smiled at *herself* in the mirror.
The **couple** had accidentally locked *themselves* out of their car.
The **computer** shut *itself* off.
I want to do it by *myself.*
Mary told **John** to help *himself* to some dessert.

Note that in the last example, the antecedent of the reflexive pronoun *himself* is not the subject of the sentence, *Mary*, but the object, *John*.

Reflexive Pronouns Used for Emphasis

Reflexive pronouns can also be added to a sentence for emphasis. For example:

I wouldn't do that *myself.*

The reflexive pronoun *myself* is valid in that it has the subject pronoun *I* as an antecedent. What is unusual about it is that *myself* is added to an already complete sentence just for emphasis. Whereas a normal reflexive pronoun plays the role of object of a verb or a pronoun, this pronoun has no grammatical role at all. We can delete it:

I wouldn't do that ~~*myself*~~.

Or we can move it:

I *myself* wouldn't do that.

Here are some more examples of reflexive pronouns added for emphasis:

He wouldn't do that *himself*.
He *himself* wouldn't do that.
They did not know the answers *themselves*.
They *themselves* did not know the answers.

In contrast, we cannot delete or move a reflexive pronoun used in the normal way, since it is the object of the verb or of a preposition. For example:

I cut *myself*.
X **I** cut ~~*myself*~~.
X **I** *myself* cut.

We wanted to finish it by *ourselves*.
X **We** wanted to finish it by ~~*ourselves*~~.
X **We** *ourselves* wanted to finish it by.

Misuse of Reflexive Pronouns

Reflexive pronouns are sometimes improperly used (especially in conversation) to avoid making the choice between subject and object pronouns. For example:

X The manager had to make a choice between Ralph and *myself*.

The speaker of this sentence uses the reflexive pronoun *myself* to avoid making the choice between *I* and *me*. This use of a reflexive pronoun is ungrammatical because there is no noun in the sentence that can serve as a grammatical antecedent. *Myself* cannot possibly refer to the object, *Ralph*, or to the subject, *manager*. If we did want to refer back to *manager*, we would have to use a third-person reflexive pronoun:

The **manager** had to make a choice between Ralph and *himself.*

Indefinite Pronouns

Indefinite pronouns refer to unspecified persons, things, or groups. Here are some examples:

Both were parked in the garage.
I wanted *another.*
Few would agree with that.
They found *several* in an online search.

Most indefinite pronouns can also be used as adjectives to modify a following noun. Here are some examples of the same word used both ways:

Pronoun: *Many* were not ready to go.
Adjective: *Many* children were not ready to go.

Pronoun: We found *some* in the drawer.
Adjective: We found *some* coins in the drawer.

In this chapter we are concerned only with their use as pronouns.

Indefinite pronouns, like definite and indefinite articles, pose special problems for nonnative speakers (and sometimes problems for native speakers, too). One problem is that indefinite pronouns are unstressed, so they are easily misheard or not heard at all.

A second problem is that indefinite pronouns convey a lot of meaning, sometimes in subtle ways. For example, compare the following two sentences:

My boss said that there were *few* concerns about my proposal.
My boss said that there were *a few* concerns about my proposal.

There is a world of difference between these two sentences. In the first sentence, your proposal is in good shape. In the second sentence, your proposal is in big trouble.

Here are the most common indefinite pronouns, organized by whether they are used in the singular only, in the plural only, or in either the singular or the plural (brief explanations accompany indefinite pronouns whose meanings are not self-evident).

Singular Only

another: *Another* is on the table.

either: *Either* is OK with me. (*either* = "one of two alternatives")

little: *Little* (work) is needed. (*little* = "hardly any"; *little* is used with noncount nouns)

a little: *A little* (work) is needed. (*a little* = not much, but definitely some; *a little* is also used with noncount nouns)

much: There isn't *much* (bread) left. (*much* usually refers to noncount nouns)

one: *One* is all you need.

Plural Only

both: *Both* are ready to go.

few: *Few* are chosen. (*few* = "almost none")

a few: *A few* are chosen. (*a few* = "not many, but definitely some")

many: *Many* (plates) were broken.

several: *Several* have been rejected.

Singular or Plural

all—singular: *All* is ready. (*all* = "everything")

all—plural: *All* are here. (*all* = "the whole group")

any—singular: *Any* is OK with me. (*any* = "single person or thing")

any—plural: *Any* are welcome to come (*any* = "all members of a group")

Other uses of *any* are discussed later in this section.

each—singular: *Each* has been carefully chosen. (*each* = "every individual")

each—plural: *Each* are excellent in their own way. (*each* = "all members of a group")

most—singular: *Most* (milk) is pasteurized. (singular *most* refers to noncount nouns)

most—plural: *Most* (companies) are unionized. (plural *most* refers to plural nouns)

neither—singular: *Neither* is ready. (*neither* = "one member of a pair")

neither—plural: Neither are ready. (neither = "both members of a pair")

none—singular: *None* is ready. (none = "not one")

none—plural: *None* are ready. (none = "no groups")

some—singular: *Some* (bread) has been eaten. (singular *some* refers to noncount nouns)

some—plural: *Some* (apples) have been eaten. (plural *some* refers to plural count nouns)

Other uses of *some* are discussed later in this section.

such—singular: *Such* is life. (*such* = "this" or "that")

such—plural: *Such* are the problems we face. (*such* = "these")

In questions, *any* and *some* can refer to either noncount nouns or plural count nouns. For example:

Do you have *any* (milk)?
Do you have *any* (peaches)?
Do you have *some* (milk)?
Do you have *some* (peaches)?

However, there is a difference in expectations between *any* and *some*. When we use *any*, we acknowledge that we may receive a negative answer. *Some* is neutral; we could get either a positive or a negative answer.

There is also a difference in answers. A positive answer requires *some*. A negative answer requires *any*. Compare the following questions and answers:

Question:	Do you have *any* (milk)/*some* (peaches)?
Answer:	Yes, we have *some* (milk/peaches).
Answer:	No, we do not have *any* (milk/peaches).

A second important group of indefinite pronouns comprises compounds of *any*, *every*, *no*, and *some* followed by *-body*, *-one*, or *-thing*.

	-body	**-one**	**-thing**
any-	anybody	anyone	anything
every-	everybody	everyone	everything
no-	nobody	no one	nothing
some-	somebody	someone	something

Note the spelling of the compound *no one*. In British English, the compound is often hyphenated: *no-one*.

Demonstrative Pronouns

Demonstrative pronouns are a small class of just four words: *this*, *that*, *these*, and *those*. As with indefinite pronouns, demonstrative pronouns can also be used as adjectives to modify a following noun:

Pronoun:	I want to buy *that*.
Adjective:	I want to buy *that* book.

Pronoun:	*Those* are mine.
Adjective:	*Those* books are mine.

For a discussion of demonstrative adjectives, see "Demonstratives" in Chapter 3.

This and *that* are singular; *these* and *those* are plural. For example:

Singular	Plural
Do you like *this*?	Do you like *these*?
Do you like *that*?	Do you like *those*?

The difference between *this* and *these* on the one hand and *that* and *those* on the other is more complicated. Generally speaking, *this* and *these* have a sense of "nearness," and *that* and *those* have a sense of "distance." Here are some examples:

This (the closer of two houses) has a blue roof.
That (the more distant of two houses) has a red roof.
I took *these* (the closer of two pictures), but not *those* (the more distant of two pictures).

Gerunds and Infinitives

Gerunds are verb forms used as nouns. **Infinitives** are used in a variety of ways, but this chapter is concerned only with infinitives that function as nouns.

Gerund and infinitive phrases (gerunds and infinitives together with their various subjects, objects, complements, and adverbs) are **noun phrases**. As with all noun phrases, gerund and infinitive phrases can be replaced by third-person pronouns. Since gerund and infinitive phrases are always singular, they can always be replaced by *it*.

Here are some examples with gerund and infinitive phrases playing the noun roles of subjects and objects. The gerund and infinitive verbs are in bold, and the entire gerund and infinitive phrases are in italics. Under each sentence is a second sentence in which *it* replaces the entire gerund or infinitive phrase.

Subject

Gerund: ***Answering** the question* was not an easy matter.
                It was not an easy matter.

Infinitive: ***To answer** the question* was not an easy matter.
                It was not an easy matter.

Object

Gerund: We like ***answering** easy questions.*
                We like *it*.

Infinitive: We like ***to answer** easy questions.*
                We like *it*.

Gerunds and Gerund Phrases

Gerunds are **present-participle** forms of verbs. The present participles are formed by adding -*ing* to the base (or dictionary) forms of verbs. Present participles are completely regular. The only variation is the result of normal spelling rules for final silent *e* and doubled-consonant spellings. For example, the final *e* of *hope* is dropped when we add a suffix beginning with a vowel: *hope–hoping*, and the final consonant of *hop* doubles when we add a suffix beginning with a vowel: *hop–hopping*.

Gerunds are verbs that function as nouns. Here are examples of gerunds playing the role of subject:

Smiling doesn't cost you anything.
Complaining won't get you anywhere.
Winning is our only option.

Since gerunds are verbs, those verbs can also have their own objects and modifiers. When this happens, the entire **gerund package** is called a **gerund phrase** (or a **gerundive phrase**, to use an older term). Here are the preceding gerunds now expanded to gerund phrases (gerunds in bold, and the entire gerund phrase in italics).

Smiling *at the customers* doesn't cost you anything.
Complaining *about the bad service* won't get you anywhere.
Winning *the game today* is our only option.

From this point on, we will use the plural term *gerunds* to refer collectively to both gerunds used by themselves and whole gerund phrases so that we do not have to constantly repeat both terms.

Gerunds can be used in all four of the main noun roles: subject, object, object of preposition, and **predicate nominative**. (A predicate nominative is the complement of a **linking verb**, such as *be*. See Chapter 11.) Here are examples of gerunds used in all four roles:

Subject
Answering *my e-mail* takes all morning.
Having *such a bad cold* ruined the weekend.
Making *a profit* is never easy.

Object

I love *going to New York.*
We began *cleaning out the garage.*
My job requires *working long hours.*

Object of Preposition

I am upset about *missing my appointment.*
Before *painting the room,* we removed the furniture.
I got my job by *working as an intern.*

Predicate Nominative

My concern is *finishing the project on time.*
The kids' main activity is *playing electronic games.*
My worry was *having to commute so far to work.*

Subjects of Gerunds

Gerunds, like all other verbs, must have subjects. Gerunds that play the role of subject of the sentence have no overt subjects of their own. There are two main ways of interpreting these gerunds. One interpretation is that the speaker of the sentence is the implicit subject of the gerund. For example:

Missing the train made me late for an important meeting.

We would interpret the speaker of this sentence as being the person who missed the train.

Another common interpretation of gerunds in the subject position is that the entire sentence is being used to make a broad generalization. For example:

Playing a musical instrument takes a big commitment.

We would interpret this sentence as a generalization about the difficulty that we all face when we try to learn to play musical instruments.

For all other, nonsubject uses of gerunds—that is, gerunds used as objects or complements—the subject of the main verb is automatically assigned to the gerund. Here are examples of gerunds playing the three nonsubject roles of object of verb, object of preposition, and predicate nominative:

Object of verb:	Jason tried **rewriting** *his paper again.* (Jason rewrote the paper.)
Object of preposition:	Jason was worried about **finishing** *on time.* (Jason was finishing on time.)
Predicate nominative:	Jason's job was **keeping** *a record of all payments.* (Jason kept the records.)

We can greatly expand the usefulness of gerunds by inserting a new subject of the gerund independent of the subject of the sentence. We do this in a rather peculiar way—by making the new subject into a possessive noun or possessive pronoun that immediately precedes the gerund. For example, first consider the following sentence:

Jane recalled **hearing** *a strange noise during the night.*

In this sentence, the person hearing the noise was Jane. The subject of the verb *recalled* has been automatically assigned to the gerund *hearing* in the normal way. Suppose, however, it was Tom, not Jane, who actually heard the noise. To make Tom the subject of the gerund *hearing*, we must insert the possessive form of the noun or pronoun into the gerund phrase immediately in front of the gerund. This possessive noun or pronoun then becomes the new subject of the gerund. In this case, we insert the possessive *Tom's* into the gerund phrase in front of the gerund:

Jane recalled **Tom's** *hearing a strange noise during the night.*

Now the person doing the hearing is Tom, not Jane. By inserting the possessive noun *Tom's* into the gerund phrase, we have blocked the automatic assignment of Jane, the subject of the sentence, to the gerund.

Here is the same example, but now with a possessive pronoun instead of a possessive noun:

Jane recalled **his** *hearing a strange noise during the night.*

Now *his* is the subject of the gerund, not Jane.

Notice what would happen if we were to use the pronoun *her* as the subject of the gerund:

Jane recalled **her** *hearing a strange noise during the night.*

To whom does the pronoun *her* refer? Does it refer back to Jane, or does it refer to somebody else? The answer is that it is completely ambiguous. It could refer back to the subject, Jane, or it could refer to somebody else. Possessive pronouns used as subjects of the gerund are not bound to any antecedent in the sentence and are thus free to refer to anybody, including the subject. Writers need to be aware of the risk of misinterpretation inherent in using possessive pronouns as subjects of gerunds.

Whenever you encounter the term "subject of the gerund," bear in mind that the term refers only to a possessive noun or pronoun that has been added to create a new subject independent of the subject of the main verb. The "subject of the gerund" does not include automatically assigned subjects from the main verb. This restriction of the term is misleading in that it incorrectly implies that gerunds without possessive nouns or pronouns do not have subjects at all. This, of course, is not true. Gerunds that do not have overt "subjects of the gerunds" have automatically been assigned the subject of the main verb as their subjects. Nevertheless, that is the way the term is used—a convention that we also follow in this book.

We can also supply possessive nouns or pronouns as subjects for gerunds that are playing the role of subject of the sentence. For example:

Bob's *adjusting the antenna* did not improve the reception.
The government's *imposing new deadlines* generated a lot of discussion.
The referee's *delaying the start of the game* allowed the field to dry.

As we would expect, the third-person possessive pronouns (*his, her, its, their*) will also be ambiguous, since they have no antecedent. For example:

Their *attempting to use chopsticks* greatly amused the Chinese waiters.

Their can refer to anybody, even including the Chinese waiters.

Here are some more examples of sentences with subjects of gerunds in all of the other gerund roles:

Object of Verb
Susan always hated **Larry's** *being late to meetings.* (Larry was late to meetings, not Susan.)
Thelma forgave **Louise's** *wrecking the car.* (Louise wrecked the car, not Thelma.)

Object of Preposition
He is always complaining about **his sister's** *getting the first turn.* (His sister, not he, got the first turn.)
Gary talked about **the company's** *proposing to relocate.* (The company proposed the relocation, not Gary.)

Predicate Nominative
The director's main worry is **the cast's** *getting such a late start.* (The cast got a late start, not the director.)
The advantage is **our** *getting our money back earlier.* (We are getting our money back.)

A number of verbs do not allow gerund objects to have their own subject of the gerund independent of the subject of the main verb. These verbs require that the subject of the main verb be passed along to the gerund. For example, the verb *quit* will allow a gerund as object, but only with an automatically assigned subject:

Automatically assigned subject:	John quit *playing basketball.*
Independent subject of gerund:	X John quit **Mary's** *playing basketball.*

In other words, the verb *quit* requires that the subject of the sentence be the one doing the action of the gerund. Here are some more examples of verbs with the same restriction:

admit

Automatically assigned subject:	The mayor admitted *taking a bribe.*
Independent subject of gerund:	X The mayor admitted **George's** *taking a bribe.*

avoid

Automatically assigned subject:	Sally avoided *working weekends.*
Independent subject of gerund:	X Sally avoided **her husband's** *working weekends.*

try

Automatically assigned subject:	I tried *rebooting the disk drive.*
Independent subject of gerund:	X I tried **my friend's** *rebooting the disk drive.*

Following is a summary listing of the more common verbs that permit gerund objects with assigned subjects but do not permit gerunds with independent subjects of the gerunds. The verbs are roughly grouped into semantic categories.

Group 1: ask, beg, decline, demand, offer, promise, refuse, swear, undertake

Group 2: attempt, begin, cease, continue, resume, start, stop, try

Group 3: avoid, endeavor, fail, learn, manage, neglect, omit

Group 4: admit, claim, confess, profess

Verbs That Do Not Allow Gerunds as Objects

Except for verbs that require concrete objects (for example, *smash* or *paint*), most verbs permit both gerunds and infinitives as objects. However, there are some verbs that will accept infinitives as objects, but not gerunds. For example, the verb *promise*:

| **Infinitive object:** | | Aunt Betsy promised *to take* the kids to the zoo this weekend. |
| **Gerund object:** | X | Aunt Betsy promised *taking* the kids to the zoo this weekend. |

Here are some more examples of verbs that will allow infinitives as objects, but not gerunds:

ask

| **Infinitive object:** | | We asked *to meet* them after lunch. |
| **Gerund object:** | X | We asked *meeting* them after lunch. |

help

| **Infinitive object:** | | After dinner, we helped *to do* the dishes. |
| **Gerund object:** | X | After dinner, we helped *doing* the dishes. |

wish

| **Infinitive object:** | | Mr. Johnson wishes *to return* to his hotel. |
| **Gerund object:** | X | Mr. Johnson wishes *returning* to his hotel. |

Following is a summary listing of the more common verbs that permit infinitives as objects, but not gerunds. The verbs are roughly grouped into semantic categories.

Group 1:	ask, beg, contrive, decline, demand, offer, promise, refuse, swear, vow
Group 2:	choose, hope, mean, need, want, wish
Group 3:	disdain, help, venture

Infinitives and Infinitive Phrases

Infinitives consist of *to* + the base (or dictionary) form of the verb. For example:

| to be | to go |
| to have | to sing |

Infinitive phrases are used four different ways: as nouns, as noun modifiers (Chapter 4), as complements of adjectives (Chapter 13), and as verb modifiers (Chapter 14). This section focuses only on their use as nouns. For example, here is the infinitive *to live* used as a noun playing various roles:

Subject:	*To live* is the goal of every living thing.
Object of verb:	We all want *to live*.
Predicate nominative:	Our greatest need is *to live*.

Notice that there is one noun role absent from this list: object of a preposition. Infinitives, unlike gerunds, cannot be used as objects of prepositions. The reason for this is historical. The *to* in an infinitive comes from the preposition *to*, and so the *to* blocks the infinitive from being the object of another preposition—prepositions cannot be the objects of other prepositions. (However, infinitives can be the objects of prepositions if the infinitive phrase does not actually begin with *to*—see "*Wh-* Infinitives" later in the chapter.)

Since infinitives come from verbs, those verbs can also have their own objects and modifiers. When this happens, the entire infinitive package is called an **infinitive phrase**. Here are some examples of infinitive phrases used in different noun roles (infinitives in bold, and the entire infinitive phrase in italics):

Subject
To do the right thing is not always easy.
To go to the movies with your family costs a fortune.

Object of Verb
I need *to get a new ink cartridge for my printer.*
The manager tried *to get some temporary help.*

Predicate Nominative
Everyone's goal should be *to do the right thing.*
My job is *to oversee the terms of all contracts.*

From this point on, we will use the plural term *infinitives* to refer collectively to both infinitives and whole infinitive phrases so that we do not have to constantly repeat both names.

Subjects of Infinitives

Infinitives are verbs, and so infinitives also must have subjects. When infinitives play the role of subjects of main verbs, there are two common interpretations: the infinitive's subject can be inferred from the context, or the sentence is being used to make a broad generalization, with "people in general" as an understood subject. Here are examples:

Context:	*To lose* the contract would be a disaster for our company. (Our company is the one losing the contract.)
Generalization:	*To live* abroad is a major commitment. (This is a generalization about everyone living abroad.)

When infinitives follow the main verbs of the sentence, the subjects of the main verbs are automatically assigned to the infinitives (just as they were with gerunds). For example:

Object:	Susan decided *to hire a new secretary*. (Susan was the person hiring the new secretary.)
Predicate nominative:	Susan's concern was *to find a person as soon as possible*. (Susan was the one doing the finding.)

We can greatly expand the usefulness of infinitives by inserting new subjects independent of the subject of the main verb. These new subjects are called "subjects of the infinitive." As with gerunds, the label "subject of the infinitive" does not apply to the subjects of the main verb that are automatically assigned to the infinitive.

We create these new subjects by inserting prepositional phrases beginning with *for* immediately in front of the infinitive. The nouns or pronouns that are the objects of *for* are now the new subjects of the infinitives that follow them. Here are some examples with the subject of the infinitive in bold:

Subject

*For **Smith** to turn down the job* was a big surprise. (Smith is the person turning down the job.)
*For **Jones** to return the favor* meant a lot to us. (Jones is the one returning the favor.)

Predicate Nominative

The main decision was *for **the union** to go on strike.* (The union is going on strike.)
The arrangement is *for **Sally** to pick us up at noon.* (Sally is picking us up at noon.)

Object of Verb

We pleaded *for **them** to accept the offer.* (They, not we, would accept the offer.)
Our office arranged *for **me** to go to the meeting.* (I am the one going to the meeting.)

Just as we saw with gerunds, certain main verbs will not permit independent subjects (subjects of the infinitive) to be used with infinitives that play the role of object. In other words, these main verbs require their own subjects to be assigned to the infinitives that follow them. Here are several examples, each with an infinitive that has an assigned subject (grammatical) and then the same verb with a new independent subject of the infinitive (ungrammatical):

forget
Assigned subject: I forgot *to bring my cell phone.*
Independent subject
   of the infinitive: X I forgot *for **my secretary** to bring my cell phone.*

learn

Assigned subject:	They learned *to speak English in college.*
Independent subject of the infinitive:	X They learned *for us* to speak English in college.

start

Assigned subject:	John started *to call the meeting to order.*
Independent subject of the infinitive:	X John started *for Mary* to call the meeting to order.

Following is a summary listing of the more common verbs that permit infinitives with assigned subjects as objects of the verb but do not permit independent subjects of the infinitive. The verbs are roughly grouped into semantic categories.

Group 1:	affect, ask, claim, decline, demand, offer, promise, refuse, swear, undertake
Group 2:	afford, attempt, endeavor, fail, learn, manage, neglect, omit, try
Group 3:	begin, cease, continue, start, stop
Group 4:	hope, propose, want, wish
Group 5:	disdain, help, scorn, venture
Group 6:	forget, remember, regret

Verbs That Do Not Allow Infinitives as Objects

Except for verbs that require a concrete object (for example, *smash* or *paint*), most verbs permit both gerunds and infinitives as objects. However, a number of verbs will allow gerunds as objects but not infinitives. An example is the verb *recommend*:

Gerund object:	Our consultant recommended **relocating** our plants.
Infinitive object:	X Our consultant recommended **to relocate** our plants.

Here are some more examples of verbs that will allow gerunds as objects, but not infinitives:

(can't) help

Gerund object:	My mother can't help ***worrying*** about how hard I work.
Infinitive object:	X My mother can't help ***to worry*** about how hard I work.

enjoy

Gerund object:	They really enjoyed ***visiting*** Singapore.
Infinitive object:	X They really enjoyed ***to visit*** Singapore.

quit

Gerund object:	I finally quit ***smoking***.
Infinitive object:	X I finally quit ***to smoke***.

Following is a summary listing of the more common verbs that allow gerunds as objects, but not infinitives. The verbs are roughly grouped into semantic categories.

Group 1: admit, avoid, confess, consider, deny, envision, escape, (can't) help, imagine, involve, justify, permit, recall, recommend, repent, require, risk, rue

Group 2: begrudge, detest, dislike, enjoy, (don't) fancy, mind, miss, regret, relish

Group 3: cease, quit, resume, save, stop

Wh- *Infinitives*

Wh- infinitives are infinitives that begin with what are called **wh- words**. *Wh-* words (with the exception of *how*) all happen to begin with *wh-*. *Wh-* words are a mixture of adverbs and relative pronouns. The *wh-* words used with infinitives follow:

Adverbs	Relative Pronouns
how	what
when	which
where	who
why (rarely used)	whom
	whose

(A slightly larger group of *wh-* words can be used in forming noun clauses, as discussed in Chapter 7.)

Wh- infinitive expressions are widely used. Here are some examples of *wh-* infinitives (in bold) in the various roles that infinitives can play:

Subject
What *to say* always stumped Roger.
Where *to go to dinner* was hotly debated.
Which *plan to adopt* provoked a split in the committee.

Object of Verb
I don't know ***which*** *choice to make.*
We couldn't decide ***when*** *to schedule the meeting.*
Louise learned ***how*** *to fix a flat tire.*

Predicate Nominative
Our biggest concern was ***whom*** *to trust.*
The issue was ***what*** *to do now.*
The problem will be ***how*** *to make the decision.*

Wh- infinitives can be the objects of prepositions. Since *wh-* infinitives begin with *wh-* words instead of the preposition *to*, *wh-* infinitives avoid the restriction against having the *to* directly follow another preposition. Here are examples:

Object of Preposition
I really worried about ***what*** *to say to her.*
We finally decided on ***where*** *to get the supplies.*
The discussion came around to ***how*** *to solve the conflict.*

Dummy It *for Infinitives Used as Subjects*

We have seen many examples of infinitives used as subjects. Often, how ever, we prefer to move longer infinitive phrases to the end of the sentence, putting an *it* in the subject position to act as a placeholder or marker. This use of *it* is called a "dummy" or "empty" *it* because the *it* does not actually refer to anything. For example, consider the following sentence, which has an infinitive phrase in the subject position:

> **To accept** *such a generous offer* made good economic sense.

We could shift the infinitive phrase to the end of the sentence and put a dummy *it* in the position vacated by the infinitive phrase:

> **It** made good economic sense **to accept** *such a generous offer.*

Here are some examples of subject infinitive phrases shifted to the end of the sentence and replaced by dummy *it:*

Original: *For Smith to turn down the job* was a big surprise.
Shifted: **It** was a big surprise *for Smith to turn down the job.*

Original: *For Jones to return the favor* meant a lot to us.
Shifted: **It** meant a lot to us *for Jones to return the favor.*

We normally shift infinitive subjects when the sentence contains a **predicate adjective**. (Predicate adjectives are adjectives that follow **linking verbs**—see Chapter 11.) Here are examples:

Original: *To complete the survey* seemed important.
Shifted: **It** seemed important *to complete the survey.*

Original: *To drive on the wrong side of the road* was very strange.
Shifted: **It** was very strange *to drive on the wrong side of the road.*

Original: *For Ralph to miss work like that* was totally out of character.
Shifted: **It** was totally out of character *for Ralph to miss work like that.*

Noun Clauses

Noun clauses are **dependent clauses** that function as **noun phrases**. (Dependent clauses have their own subjects and verbs, but they are not able to stand alone as complete sentences.) Noun clauses, like gerunds and infinitives used as nouns, are singular, and thus they can always be replaced by the third-person singular pronoun *it*. Following are examples of noun clauses (in italics) playing the three noun roles of subject, object of verb, and object of preposition. Underneath each example sentence is a second sentence in which the noun clause has been replaced by *it*:

Subject:	*What they don't know* can't hurt them.
	It can't hurt them.
Object of verb:	I know *what you did*.
	I know **it**.
Object of preposition:	We worried about *which one we should buy*.
	We worried about **it**.

There is one important additional restriction on the use of noun clauses: they can be used only where the verb in the sentence will permit an **abstract** noun as a subject or object. Abstract nouns are nouns such as *idea, answer, outcome,* and *plan.* Abstract nouns are one of three semantic categories of noun that are controlled by the main verbs of sentences. The other two categories are **concrete** and **human**. Concrete nouns refer to tangible, physical objects. Human nouns are nouns that reflect human agency. Some verbs are highly restrictive on the type of subject and/or object that they can be used with. For example, the verb *paint* requires a human subject that performs the action of painting and a concrete object that is the recipient of the action of painting:

Tom painted the *fence.*

The verb *paint,* in its usual literal meaning, cannot be used with abstract nouns as either subject or object:

X The *idea* painted the *outcome.*

Consequently, we cannot use noun clauses as subjects or objects of the verb *paint:*

X *What you said* painted *that we could go.*

Notice that all of the noun clauses in the examples at the beginning of this chapter are used with verbs that permit abstract nouns—such as *idea, answer, plan,* and *outcome*—in that same sentence position:

Subject:	*What they don't know* can't hurt them.
	The idea can't hurt them.
Object of verb:	I know *what you did.*
	I know *the answer.*
Object of preposition:	We worried about *which one we should buy.*
	We worried about *the plan.*

There are two types of noun clauses, classified according to the initial word of the noun clause:

that
wh- word, such as *who, when, where,* and *why*

That Clauses

That clauses (as opposed to *wh-* word clauses) are built in a very simple way. The *that* introductory word is followed by a statement in its normal statement word order. The formula looks like this:

That clause = *that* + statement

Following are examples of *that* clauses in the noun roles of subject, object of a verb, and predicate nominative. Here and in all related examples, the introductory word is in bold, and the entire noun clause is in italics:

Subject:	**That** *the game was canceled* surprised us.
Object of verb:	I fear **that** *you may be right*.
Predicate nominative:	The plan was **that** *we would make a new offer.*

Notice that object of preposition, the fourth common role that nouns play, is missing from the preceding list. *That* clauses (unlike *wh-* clauses) are not used as objects of prepositions.

Distinguishing That *Clauses from Adjective Clauses*

Noun clauses that begin with *that* superficially resemble adjective clauses that also begin with *that*. For example, compare the uses of *that* in the following pair of sentences:

Noun clause:	I know **that** *we can all accept the plans.*
Adjective clause:	I know plans **that** *we can all accept.*

The simplest way to distinguish between the two different types of clauses is to replace the noun clause with *it*:

Noun clause:	I know **it**. (where *it* = **that** *we can all accept the plans*)

We cannot use *it* to replace the adjective clause:

Adjective clause:	X I know plans **it**. (where *it* = **that** *we can all accept*)

Another simple way to tell the two uses of *that* apart is to see if you can replace *that* with *which*. *That* and *which* are usually interchangeable in adjective clauses, whereas we cannot ever replace the *that* in a noun clause with *which*. Here are examples:

Noun clause:	I know ***that*** *we can all accept the plans.*
Noun clause:	X I know ***which*** we can all accept the plans.
Adjective clause:	I know plans ***that*** *we can all accept.*
Adjective clause:	I know plans ***which*** we can all accept.

Dummy It *for* That *Clauses Used as Subjects*

It is perfectly grammatical to use *that* clauses as subjects. Usually, however, we prefer to move these noun clauses to the end of the sentence putting an *it* in the subject position to act as a placeholder or marker. This use of *it* is called a "dummy" or "empty" *it*, as noted in Chapter 6, because the *it* does not actually refer to anything. For example, consider the following sentence with a noun clause in the subject position:

> ***That*** *the restaurant was closed* came as an unpleasant surprise.

We would normally shift the *that* clause to the end of the sentence and put a dummy *it* in the position vacated by the *that* clause:

> **It** came as an unpleasant surprise ***that*** *the restaurant was closed.*

Here are some more examples of subject *that* clauses shifted to the ends of their sentences and dummy *its* being used as place markers in the empty subject positions:

| Original: | ***That*** *you would believe such a story* makes you look bad. |
| Shifted: | **It** makes you look bad ***that*** *you would believe such a story.* |

| Original: | ***That*** *they would behave so thoughtlessly* really upset me. |
| Shifted: | **It** really upset me ***that*** *they would behave so thoughtlessly.* |

Certain verbs *require* that we shift the *that* clause to a position after the verb and use a dummy *it* in the subject position. These verbs include *appear, happen, seem,* and *turn out.* Here is an example:

It appears ***that*** *the meeting was canceled after all.*

If we try to put the *that* clause back in the subject position, the resulting sentence is ungrammatical:

X ***That*** *the meeting was canceled after all* appears.

There is one odd feature of these verbs: the word *that* can be deleted from the *that* clause. Thus, we can choose between two forms of the sentence—one with an expressed *that*, and one with a deleted *that*—both meaning exactly the same thing:

It appears ***that*** *the meeting was canceled after all.*
It appears *the meeting was canceled after all.*

The optional deletion of *that* from object *that* clauses is discussed in detail in the following section.

Here are examples of sentences using the other three verbs in this group:

It happens ***(that)*** *we are going to be out of town that week.*
It seems ***(that)*** *we made a mistake.*
It turns out ***(that)*** *you were right all along.*

Deleting That *from* That *Clauses Used as Objects of Verbs*

When a noun clause beginning with *that* is used as an object of a verb, we often delete *that* from the beginning of the noun clause. Here are some examples, with the deleted *that* represented by Ø:

We know Ø *we are able to carry out the project.*
The company revealed Ø *it had unexpected losses in the last quarter.*
The manager said Ø *it would be more than a one-hour wait.*
I suggest Ø *you check out the cost of replacing it.*

The option of deleting the introductory *that* from the beginning of *that* clauses poses a special problem for nonnative speakers because the introductory *that* is one of the key signals on which we can rely for recognizing noun clauses. In light of this fact, all following examples of object *that* clauses will show the introductory *that* in parentheses as a reminder that the word can be (and often is) deleted.

Using That *Clauses as Objects with Verbs of Speech and Cognition*

A number of verbs of speech and cognition do not take abstract nouns as objects. Nevertheless, these same verbs are commonly used with *that* clauses as objects. Here is an example:

We agreed *(that) we would accept their offer.*

The verb *agree* does not normally take an abstract noun as its object. For example:

X We *agreed* the idea.
          the outcome.
          the plan.

However, if we change the verb *agree* to the phrasal verb *agree on*, then abstract nouns are perfectly acceptable objects:

We *agreed on* the idea.
          the outcome.
          the plan.

Many of the verbs of speech and cognition that take *that* clauses as objects have phrasal verb forms that do take abstract nouns as objects.

Verbs of Speech That Take *That* Clauses as Objects. The following is a comprehensive list of common verbs of speech that do not normally take abstract nouns as objects but do routinely take *that* clauses as objects:

agree	concede	promise
allege	confess	remark
argue	contend	reply
assert	declare	say
bet	exclaim	state
boast	forecast	swear
claim	hint	testify
comment	insist	warn
complain	object	

Here are some examples of *that* clauses with verbs of speech:

The defense argued *(that)* their client was innocent
He said *(that)* he would be late.
They complained *(that)* they did not have enough time.

Verbs of Cognition That Take *That* Clauses as Objects. The following is a comprehensive list of common verbs of cognition that do not normally take abstract nouns as objects but do routinely take *that* clauses as objects:

assume	fear	note
conclude	feel	presume
deduce	find	prove
dream	gather	realize
ensure	hear	signify
establish	hope	suppose
estimate	learn	suspect
expect	mean	think

Here are some examples of *that* clauses with verbs of cognition:

We concluded *(that)* we should go ahead as we had planned.
I expected *(that)* I would feel better by now.
Let's hope *(that)* you are right.

Subjunctive That *Clauses as Objects*

In older forms of English, the subjunctive was a separate set of verb endings that were used to express wishes and commands and to make hypothetical statements. Probably the best-known surviving application of the subjunctive in Modern English is the use of *were* in adverbial *if* clauses. For example:

> If I *were* you . . .
> If I *were* running this company . . .

Another common use of the subjunctive is in *that* clauses following the verb *wish*. For example:

> I wish **(that)** I **were** *going too.*
> I wish **(that)** I **were** *there.*

Another form of the subjunctive is commonly used in *that* clauses with verbs that express requests or commands. Here is an example:

> I insist **(that)** he **remain** *silent.*

Except for the verb *be*, this form of the subjunctive is apparent only when the subject is in the third-person singular form. Instead of the expected third-person singular -s form, we use the base form. In the case of the preceding example, we get *he* **remain** *silent* rather than the expected *he* **remains** *silent*. Here are some more examples:

> The government demands **(that)** he **be** *released immediately.*
> We would prefer **(that)** *she* **stay** *where she is.*
> I insist **(that)** he **receive** *all back pay.*

This use of the subjunctive is formal. It is most likely to be found in official meetings or legal proceedings. Here are examples:

> Mr. Chairman, I move **(that)** *the motion* **be** *adopted.*
> The court decrees **(that)** *the defendant* **refund** *the entire amount owing.*
> We rule **(that)** *the motion* **be** *accepted.*

Since the verb *be* has distinctive forms throughout the present-tense system, we can recognize the subjunctive in the first and second persons. For example:

I request *(that)* I **be** *permitted to speak.*
They are recommending *(that)* you **be** *promoted.*
I suggest *(that)* they **be** *fully compensated for their losses.*

Here are the most common verbs that can (but do not have to) use subjunctives in object *that* clauses:

ask	insist	recommend
beg	instruct	request
command	move	require
decide	ordain	resolve
decree	order	rule
demand	pledge	stipulate
desire	pray	suggest
determine	pronounce	urge
entreat	propose	vote

Wh- Clauses

The second type of noun clauses comprises those that begin with a *wh-* word. The term "*wh-* word" refers to a special group of words, most of which happen to begin with the letters *wh-*. Here are the most common *wh-* words that begin noun clauses, classified by their parts of speech:

NOUNS

what	whichever	whom
whatever	who	whomever
which	whoever	whose

ADVERBS

---

how	when	where	why
however	whenever	wherever	

Here are some examples of *wh-* clauses playing the four noun roles of subject, object of verb, object of preposition, and predicate nominative:

Subject: *Whatever you want* is OK with me.
Object of verb: I wonder *why they did it that way.*
Object of preposition: We argued about *where we should go.*
Predicate nominative: The outcome was *what we expected it to be.*

In discussing *wh-* clauses, we must be careful to distinguish the *internal structure* of a noun clause from the *external role* that the whole noun clause plays in the main sentence. For example, in the following sentence, which is correct—*whoever* or *whomever?*

> They will give the contract to **whoever** *can make the best presentation.* **(?)**

or

> They will give the contract to **whomever** *can make the best presentation.* **(?)**

At first glance, it looks as if it should be *whomever,* because *whomever* appears to be the object of the preposition *to.* However, this initial analysis is wrong. The object of the preposition *to* is the entire noun clause, not just the *wh-* word. Inside the noun clause, *whoever* is the subject of the verb *can make.* This example points out how easy it is to confuse the internal structure and external role of *wh-* clauses. Accordingly, we will discuss the internal structure and external roles separately.

Internal Structure of wh- *Clauses*

Wh- clauses have a much more complex internal structure than *that* clauses do. Nevertheless, both types of noun phrases share one fundamental characteristic: they must begin with a special kind of introductory word. In the case of *wh-* clauses, obviously the introductory words are what are called "*wh-* words."

The label "*wh-* word" has become standard in modern grammars of English because there is no conventional term in traditional grammar for these introductory words. *Wh-* words are similar in form and function to the **interrogative pronouns** that are used in forming information questions. As with interrogative pronouns, *wh-* words are a mixture of nouns and adverbs, and they are moved to the front of the sentence from their normal positions. In fact, the similarity of *wh-* words and interrogative pronouns leads to one of the most common errors that nonnative speakers make with *wh-* clauses: they mistakenly use the word order of information questions in *wh-* clauses. (See the following discussion.)

Inside the noun clause, the *wh-* words that are nouns can play all four noun roles of subject, object of verb, object of preposition, and predicate nominative. The *wh-* words that are adverbs can play the standard adverb roles of denoting time, place, manner, and reason. In the following examples, note that all of the noun clauses play the same external role of subject of the verb in the main sentence:

Wh- words used as nouns inside wh- clauses

Subject:	***Whoever*** *finishes first* wins the prize.
Object of verb:	***Whatever*** *I said* must have been a mistake.
Object of preposition:	***What*** *they agreed to* is OK with me.
Predicate nominative:	***Who*** *they were* is still unknown.

Wh- words used as adverbs inside wh- clauses

Adverb of time:	***When*** *you called* was not a good time for me.
Adverb of place:	***Where*** *you work* is very important.
Adverb of manner:	***How*** *you use your leisure time* tells a lot about you.
Adverb of reason:	***Why*** *they said that* remains a complete mystery to us.

It is important to understand that noun clauses beginning with *wh-* words that are adverbs are just as much noun clauses as noun clauses beginning with *wh-* words that are nouns.

All *wh-* clauses are built in the same way: the *wh-* word must play the role of a noun or adverb inside the noun clause. That *wh-* word must then be moved forward to the first position inside the noun clause, leaving a gap in the noun clause where the *wh-* word was. (If the *wh-* word already plays the role of subject, then it cannot move; it is already in the first position, and thus no gap is created.) Following are examples of noun clauses with an underline showing the gap where the *wh-* word came from. Again, all noun clauses play the role of subject of the verb in the main sentence.

Wh- words used as nouns inside *wh-* clauses
Subject of Verb
What *goes around* comes around.
Who *laughs last* laughs best.
Whoever *answers the phone* will take a message.

Note: There is no gap when the *wh-* word plays the role of subject; the *wh-* word is already in the first position and therefore cannot be moved.

Object of Verb
Whatever *Lulu wants* _____ is what she gets.
Whichever *team I pick* _____ always seems to lose.
Whomever *they selected* _____ *for the job* is still a secret.

Object of Preposition
What *they argued about* _____ is unimportant now.
Whatever solution *they arrived at* _____ will be challenged.
Whomever *they relied on* _____ *to do the job* turned out to be a big disappointment.

Predicate Nominative
Who *they are* _____ changes everything.
What *it will be* _____ is anyone's guess.
Whatever *their answer is* _____ will come as a surprise.

Wh- words used as adverbs inside *wh-* clauses
Adverb of Time
Whenever you are ready _____ will be fine with us.

When the concert starts _____ isn't clear.

When the time is right _____ will be obvious to everyone.

Adverb of Place
Where I live _____ costs me a fortune in rent.

Where we would get the supplies _____ remains an ongoing concern.

Wherever we go _____ is a new experience for them.

Adverb of Manner
How you explain it _____ could change everything.

However well we do the job _____ makes no difference.

How you do _____ *in the interview* will determine whether you get the job.

Adverb of Reason
Why they want to do that _____ defies explanation.

Why we did it _____ is really none of their business.

Why the earth is getting warmer _____ is a big topic of debate nowadays.

External Role of wh- *Clauses*

Wh- clauses can play all four noun roles in the main sentence: subject, object of verb, object of preposition, and predicate nominative. *Wh-* clauses can be used in any of the noun positions that will accept an **abstract noun**. (Abstract nouns are words such as *outcome* and *idea*.)

Following are examples of noun clauses in each of the four roles. The examples also illustrate several different uses of the *wh-* word inside the noun clause, with an underline showing the gap where the *wh-* word has been moved from.

Noun clause as subject of verb in the main sentence

Whatever *house we looked at* _____ was outside our price range. (*Whatever* is the object of the preposition *at*.)

Who *started the fight* is not really important. (*Who* is the subject of the verb *fight*.)

Why *the computers crashed* _____ is the subject of an investigation. (*Why* is an adverb of reason that follows the verb *crashed*.)

Noun clause as object of the verb in the main sentence

We wondered **what** *was causing the problem*. (*What* is the subject of the verb *was causing*.)

I'll have **whatever** *you are having* _____. (*Whatever* is the object of *having*.)

I don't know **why** *you would think that* _____. (*Why* is an adverb of reason modifying the verb *think*.)

Noun clause as object of a preposition in the main sentence

We relied on **what** *we had been told* _____. (*What* is the object of the verb *had been told*.)

They argued about **who** *should take the lead in the new project*. (*Who* is the subject of the verb *should take*.)

I was very surprised at **how** *they responded* _____ *to our offer*. (*How* is an adverb of manner modifying the verb *responded*.)

Noun clause as predicate nominative in the main sentence

The problem was **what** *we should wear* _____. (*What* is the object of the verb *should wear*.)

The solution was **where** *we least expected it to be* _____. (*Where* is an adverb of place that is the complement of the verb *to be*.)

The new CEO wasn't **who** *called the press conference* after all. (*Who* is the subject of the verb *called*.)

Dummy It *for* wh- *Clauses Used as Subjects*

We sometimes prefer to move *wh-* clauses to the end of the sentence, putting a dummy *it* in the subject position to act as a placeholder or marker.

For example, consider the following sentence with a noun clause in the subject position:

What *will happen next* remains to be seen.

We can shift the noun clause to the end of the sentence and put a dummy *it* in the position vacated by the noun clause:

It remains to be seen **what** *will happen next.*

We don't shift subject *wh-* clauses as often as we do noun clauses beginning with *that.* We are more likely to shift *wh-* clauses when the main verb is a linking verb. Here are some more examples of subject noun clauses shifted to the end of the sentence and replaced by dummy *it.*

Original: *How the pictures turned out* was quite disappointing.
Shifted: It was quite disappointing **how** *the pictures turned out.*

Original: **Whom** *she meant* was obvious.
Shifted: It was obvious **whom** *she meant.*

Original: **When** *she will announce his candidacy* is a closely held secret.
Shifted: It is a closely held secret **when** *she will announce his candidacy.*

Using wh- *Question Word Order in* wh- *Clauses*

Probably the most common error that nonnative speakers make with *wh-* clauses is using the inverted word order of *wh-* questions. (Questions are discussed in Chapter 17.) *Wh-* questions are questions that begin with *wh-* words, such as *who, where, when,* and *why. Wh-* questions (unless the *wh-* word happens to be the subject of the sentence) require that the verb (abbreviated V) be moved in front of the subject (abbreviated S). For example:

Where <u>are</u> <u>you</u> going?
   V   S

What <u>can</u> <u>I</u> do?
   V   S

Whom <u>should</u> <u>I</u> give the announcement to?
     V   S

Why <u>have</u> <u>they</u> called a meeting at such short notice?
    V   S

Both *wh-* questions and *wh-* clauses use essentially the same set of *wh-* words. Since *wh-* questions are much more common than *wh-* clauses, it is natural that many nonnative speakers come to associate all *wh-* words with the inverted word-order pattern of *wh-* questions. Accordingly, these speakers will overgeneralize the inverted word order of *wh-* questions and extend the same inverted word order to *wh-* clauses. Here are some examples of this extension, first with a *wh-* question and then with a *wh-* clause, using the same question word order:

***Wh-* question:**	**Who** is that man?
***Wh-* noun clause:**	X I know **who** *is that man.*
***Wh-* question:**	**Where** are we?
***Wh-* noun clause:**	X I know **where** *are we.*
***Wh-* question:**	**Why** will they do that?
***Wh-* noun clause:**	X I know **why** *will they do that.*
***Wh-* question:**	**What** is the problem?
***Wh-* noun clause:**	X I know **what** *is the problem.*

The mistake is more likely to happen in speaking than in writing. It is more likely to occur in rapid conversation or when the situation is stressful. Nonnative speakers who tend to make this mistake need to be aware of their tendency and consciously monitor themselves for the error.

PART II

Verb Phrases

Basic Verb Forms

This chapter surveys the basic verb forms that are used as the raw material to make up the tense system of English. There are six verb forms that can be used with all verbs (except for a special group called the **modal auxiliary verbs**, whose tense forms are utterly unique). The six verb forms are the **base**, the **present tense**, the **past tense**, the **infinitive**, the **present participle**, and the **past participle**. The formation and meaning of the tenses created from these six verb forms and from the modal auxiliary verbs are the subject of the next chapter.

All verbs (with the important exceptions of *be* and the modal auxiliary verbs *can, may, must, shall,* and *will*) have all six of the forms. The six forms are illustrated in the following table by the regular verb *talk* and the irregular verb *sing.*

VERB FORMS

Base Form	Present Tense	Past Tense	Infinitive	Present Participle	Past Participle
talk	talk/talks	talked	to talk	talking	talked
sing	sing/sings	sang	to sing	singing	sung

We will now look at the formation of each of these six forms in detail.

Base Form

The base form is the dictionary-entry form of all verbs. For example, if you were to look up *sang* in the dictionary, it would refer you to the base form *sing.* Since the base form is identical in nearly all cases to the present tense, it is difficult at first to see how one could tell the base form and present tense apart. Fortunately, there is one verb in which the base form and present-tense forms are different—the verb *be*:

Base form: *be*
Present: I *am*
       you *are*
       he/she/it *is*
       we/you/they *are*

We can use the fact that the base form of *be* is different from all of its present-tense forms to determine when base forms are used. There are four places in which the base form is used: to form infinitives, to form the future tense, in imperative sentences (commands), and as part of the complement of some verbs.

Infinitives

All infinitives are formed by putting *to* in front of the base form. For example:

to *have*   to *go*
to *talk*   to *sing*

We can show that these verbs are indeed in the base forms by using the verb *be*. If we substitute any of the present-tense forms, the results are ungrammatical:

      to *be*   X to *am*
   X to *are*   X to *is*

Future Tenses

The future tense is formed by using a base form after the helping verb *will* (and other modal auxiliary verbs, too):

will *have*   can *go*
must *talk*   should *sing*

We can show that these verbs are in the base forms by again using the verb *be*. If we substitute any of the present-tense forms, the results are again ungrammatical:

will *be*   X will *am*
X will *are*   X will *is*

Imperatives (Commands)

Imperative sentences use the base form of the verb. Here are some examples:

Go away!
Oh, *stop* that!
Answer the question, please.

When we use the verb *be*, we again see that present-tense forms are ungrammatical:

Be careful what you wish for!
X *Am* careful what you wish for!
X *Are* careful what you wish for!
X *Is* careful what you wish for!

Verb Complements

Some verbs use base forms as part of their complements:

We made them *walk* to school.
I let them *finish* early.
John will have the office *send* you a copy.

When we use the verb *be*, we again see that the present-tense forms are ungrammatical:

> I made them *be* quiet.
> X I made them *am* quiet.
> X I made them *are* quiet.
> X I made them *is* quiet.

Present Tense

Again, with the exception of the verb *be* and the modal auxiliary verbs, the present tense of all verbs is derived directly from the base form.

However, the present tense differs significantly from the base form in that all verbs in the present tense must enter into a **subject-verb agreement** relationship with their subjects (something that base-form verbs can never do). This agreement is most easily seen in the unique use of the **third-person singular** -*(e)s* when the subject is a singular noun or noun phrase or a third-person singular pronoun (*he, she, it*). Here are some examples with subjects in bold and present-tense verbs in italics:

> **Mary** *refuses* to answer the phone. (singular noun subject)
> **The book on the desk** *has* to be returned. (singular noun phrase
>   subject)
> **She** *seems* upset about something. (third-person singular pronoun
>   subject)

The third-person singular -*(e)s* is regular in both pronunciation and spelling.

If the base ends in a sibilant (an /s/ or /z/ sound) sound, the ending is pronounced as a separate syllable rhyming with *buzz*. The ending is spelled -*es* (unless the present-tense verb already ends in an *e*, in which case just the *s* is added). For example:

Base	Third-Person Singular
box	box<u>es</u>
budge	budg<u>es</u>
buzz	buzz<u>es</u>
catch	catch<u>es</u>
glass	glass<u>es</u>
wish	wish<u>es</u>

If the verb ends in a voiceless consonant sound other than a sibilant, the ending is pronounced /s/ and is spelled *s*. The voiceless consonants are usually spelled with a *p, t, k, ck, f,* or *gh* (if pronounced /f/). Here are some examples:

back	back<u>s</u>
cough	cough<u>s</u>
cut	cut<u>s</u>
hop	hop<u>s</u>
walk	walk<u>s</u>

If the verb ends in a voiced consonant sound (other than a sibilant) or a vowel, the ending is pronounced /z/ and is spelled with an *s*. For example:

call	call<u>s</u>
come	come<u>s</u>
read	read<u>s</u>
rob	rob<u>s</u>
row	row<u>s</u>
see	see<u>s</u>
snow	snow<u>s</u>

If the verb ends in a consonant + *y*, change the *y* to *i* and add *-es*. For example:

cry	cries
fly	flies
reply	replies
spy	spies
try	tries

However, if the final *y* is part of the spelling of the vowel, then just add an *s*:

buy	buys
enjoy	enjoys
obey	obeys
play	plays

There are a few verbs with irregular third-person singular forms. The most common, of course, is *be*:

be	is

The verb *have* is irregular in the third-person singular:

have	has

Two other verbs have irregular pronunciations in the third-person singular:

do (rhymes with *two*)	does (rhymes with *buzz*)
say (rhymes with *gay*)	says (rhymes with *fez*)

Past Tense

There are two types of past-tense forms: **regular** and **irregular**. The regular verbs form their past tense by adding -*ed* (or -*d* if the word already ends in *e*) to the base form.

Regular Past Tenses

Base	Past Tense
answer	answered
cough	coughed
pass	passed
smile	smiled
walk	walked

The -*ed* has three different but completely predictable pronunciations. If the base ends in either *t* or *d*, the -*ed* is pronounced as a separate syllable rhyming with *bud*. Here are some examples:

fainted	kidded
mended	parted
raided	sighted
skidded	slighted

If the base ends in a voiceless consonant except for *t*, the -*ed* is pronounced /t/. The final voiceless consonants are usually spelled with a *p*, (*c*)*k*, *s*, *sh*, (*t*)*ch*, *x*, *f*, or *gh* (when pronounced /f/). For example:

boxed	capped
coughed	kissed
packed	pushed
tipped	wished

If the base ends in a vowel or voiced consonant except for *d*, the -*ed* is pronounced /d/. For example:

annoyed	bored
called	fanned
played	slammed
snowed	waved

If the base ends in a stressed syllable with a short vowel, a single final consonant will usually double, according to the normal spelling rules. For example:

Base	Past Tense
hop	hopped
rob	robbed
rot	rotted
sin	sinned
star	starred

Irregular Past Tenses

The irregular verbs preserve older ways of forming the past tense. In earlier forms of English, the irregular verbs fell into well-defined patterns. By modern times, the historical patterns had collapsed together, so that today it is not practical to learn irregular verbs according to their historical patterns.

However, one particular pattern is worth learning because it is actually fairly easy to identify, *and* it probably causes as many errors among nonnative speakers as all other patterns put together. Verbs that follow this pattern are all one-syllable words with short vowels that end in a *t* or *d*. Verbs that follow this pattern are unique in that the past-tense form is identical to the base form. In other words, the past tenses of these verbs look exactly like present tenses. Here are two examples, one ending in *t* (*bet*) and the other in *d* (*spread*):

Present tense:	I *bet* that you can't guess who is coming to dinner tonight.
Past tense:	I *bet* against the Yankees last week and lost as usual.
Present tense:	They always *spread* mustard on their sandwiches.
Past tense:	They *spread* mustard on my sandwich yesterday.

As you can see, we have to depend entirely on adverbs and other verbs in these sentences to tell whether these verbs are present tense or past tense. Nonnative speakers are especially likely to misinterpret the past tense of these verbs as present tenses. A second mistake that nonnative speakers make is to turn these verbs into regular verbs. That is, they tend to add an -*ed*, producing such incorrect forms as *costed*, *ridded*, and *shutted*.

Here is a list of all commonly used verbs that follow this pattern:

VERBS ENDING IN *T*

---

bet	fit	put	split
burst	hit	quit	sweat
cast	hurt	set	thrust
cost	let	shut	wet
cut			

VERBS ENDING IN *D*

---

bid	shed	wed
rid	spread	

Adding to the misery of this type of past tense is the fact that exactly these same forms can also be used as past participles. So, for example, the verb form *put* can be a present tense, a past tense, or a past participle:

Present:	I always *put* the mail on the desk.
Past:	I *put* the mail on the desk this morning.
Past participle:	I have always *put* the mail on the desk.

The past tense of *be* is doubly remarkable in that *be* is the only verb in English that has two past forms: *was* and *were*. Moreover, the past tense of *be* preserves an ancient way forming subject-verb agreement:

• *Was* is used when the subject is either the first-person pronoun *I* or a third-person singular form—that is, a singular noun or noun phrase or a third-person singular pronoun (*he, she, it*).
• *Were* is used with all other subjects—plural nouns and noun phrases, as well as all other pronouns (the second-person singular pronoun *you* and all plural pronouns). Here is a representation of this peculiar form of subject-verb agreement:

PRONOUNS

I	**was**
you (singular)	were
he/she/it	**was**
we	were
you (plural)	were
they	were

NOUNS

Singular nouns and noun phrases:	**was**
Plural nouns and noun phrases:	were

Infinitive

Mercifully, the infinitive is completely regular (even the verb *be*). The infinitive consists of *to* followed by the base form of the verb. Here are some examples:

Base Form	Infinitive
be	to be
do	to do
have	to have
sing	to sing
talk	to talk

Present Participle

The present participle is also completely regular. It is formed by adding -*ing* to the base form. Here are some examples:

Base Form	Present Participle
be	being
do	doing
have	having
sing	singing
talk	talking

The rules of spelling sometimes cause the present participle to be spelled differently from the base form. The most common changes are those concerning the final silent *e* and doubled consonants.

Final Silent e

If the base form ends in a final silent *e*, the *e* will drop:

Base Form	Present Participle
enlarge	enlarging
lose	losing
save	saving
use	using

Doubled Consonant

If the base ends in a single consonant preceded by a short vowel, the consonant will double:

Base Form	Present Participle
hit	hitting
hop	hopping
rub	rubbing
run	running
swim	swimming

Past Participle

There are two types of past participles: **regular** and **irregular**. The regular forms are exactly the same as the past tense—that is, they are the base + -(e)d. The rules for spelling and pronunciation are exactly the same as for the past tense.

If the forms of the regular past participle and the past tenses are identical in all respects, how can we tell them apart? The answer is in the way they are used. The past participle must follow either the helping verb *have* or the verb *be*. (These helping verbs can be in any tense form.) Here are some examples with the verbs in italics and the past participle in bold:

> *have*
> John *has* **requested** a meeting with his manager.
> Some problems *have* **forced** the meeting to be moved to Chicago.
> A schedule conflict *had* **caused** the meeting to be postponed.
> The committee *will have* **decided** by now.
>
> *be*
> He *is* **discouraged** by what has happened.
> The accident *was* **reported** on the radio.
> Several people *were* **injured**.
> The meetings *will be* **continued** next week.

(As you may have noticed, all the examples of past participles following *be* are **passives**—see Chapter 18.)

Irregular Past Participles

In older periods of English, most irregular past participles ended in -(e)n. Today only about one-third of irregular past participles still end in -(e)n. About the only generalization we can make now is that if an irregular verb has an -(e)n ending, then it is likely a past participle. Here are some examples:

Base	Past Participle
choose	chosen
eat	eaten
fall	fallen
fly	flown
freeze	frozen
hide	hidden
rise	risen
see	seen
speak	spoken
swear	sworn
tear	torn
wake	woken

As you can see from these examples, the changes in vowels from base form to past-participle form are unpredictable.

Two common past participles have unpredictable pronunciations: *been* rhymes with *sin* in American English, but it rhymes with *seen* in British English. *Done* rhymes with *sun*, rather than *soon* as might be expected.

Modal Auxiliary Verbs

There are five modal auxiliary verbs: *can, may, must, shall,* and *will.* These verbs have an utterly unique history. These verbs have no base form, no infinitive form, no present-participle form, and no past-participle form. The modal auxiliary verbs can be used only in the present-tense and past-tense forms (though, as discussed in Chapter 9, their present and past forms almost never actually mean present or past time). Here is the complete list of forms:

Present Tense	Past Tense
can	could
may	might
must	—
shall	should
will	would

Notice that the present-tense form *must* has no corresponding past-tense form. This is the only instance in English in which there is a present-tense form with no equivalent past-tense form.

The modal auxiliary verbs are also unique in that that they do not add an -*s* in the third-person singular form. For example:

Correct Third-Person Singular	Incorrect Third-Person Singular
He *can* go.	X He *cans* go.
He *may* go.	X He *mays* go.
He *must* go.	X He *musts* go.
He *shall* go.	X He *shalls* go.
He *will* go.	X He *wills* go.

The reason for this odd exception to the normal rule is historical. All of the present-tense modal auxiliary verbs are actually derived from past-tense forms, and so they cannot be used with a present-tense ending.

Verb Tenses and Modals

This chapter addresses the way the basic verb forms discussed in Chapter 8 are used to construct the tense and modal verb system of English *and* what these various tenses and modals mean and how they are used. Talking about the English verb system is made difficult by the confusing Latin-based terminology that evolved in the nineteenth century. There are two main problems: the multiple and inconsistent meanings of the term *tense*, and the lack of any standard terminology for talking about what are called the **modal verbs**.

We will begin by exploring what the terms *tense* and *modal* mean, and then we'll examine in detail each of the traditional nine tense constructions (present, past, future, present perfect, past perfect, future perfect, present progressive, past progressive, and future progressive). We will focus on what meanings are expressed by each construction and when it is appropriate to use the construction, paying special attention to the features that are most likely to confuse nonnative speakers.

The Meaning of *Tense*

The term *tense* is commonly used in four different ways:

• *Tense* can refer to the only two verb forms that can enter into subject-verb relationships—the present-tense form and the past-tense form. This is the way the term *tense* was used in Chapter 8. The present tense and past tense are collectively called **finite tenses**. Originally the term *finite* meant that the present and past tense could stand alone (without helping verbs) to make complete sentences. The implication is that all the other tenses (called **nonfinite tenses**) need a finite verb acting as a helping verb to make a complete sentence. For example, consider the following sentence:

Jason *has* been working all afternoon.

The helping verb *has* here is a finite verb; it is the present tense of the verb *have*. *Been* is a nonfinite verb; it cannot enter into a subject-verb relationship.

• *Tense* can refer to the logical threefold division of time into **present**, **past**, and **future**.

• *Tense* can refer to the three categories of verbs that we will call **simple**, **perfect**, and **progressive**.

• Finally, *tense* can refer to any of the nine different "tense" constructions that are at the intersections of the three time divisions (present, past, and future) and the three aspect categories of verbs (simple, perfect, and progressive). These nine constructions (with examples) are given in the following table:

THE TRADITIONAL NINE TENSE CONSTRUCTIONS

	Simple Category	Perfect Category	Progressive Category
Present Time	I *talk*	I *have talked*	I *am talking*
	I *sing*	I *have sung*	I *am singing*
Past Time	I *talked*	I *had talked*	I *was talking*
	I *sang*	I *had sung*	I *was singing*
Future Time	I *will talk*	I *will have talked*	I *will be talking*
	I *will sing*	I *will have sung*	I *will be singing*

The Meaning of *Modal*

This book uses the terms *modal* and *modal verb* as collective terms for two historically distinct groups of verbs that function identically: **modal auxiliary verbs** and **quasi-modal verbs**. There are (present + past tense forms) helping verbs called "modal auxiliary verbs." These verbs and the numerous peculiarities of their forms are discussed in Chapter 8.

Present-Tense Form	Past-Tense Form
can	could
may	might
must	—
shall	should
will	would

The terms *present tense* and *past tense* when applied to the modal verbs are historically accurate, but they are misleading in all other respects. For example, the past-tense modals are normally used for talking about future time:

> We **might** *miss* the last flight tonight.
> I **could** *meet* with you tomorrow.
> We **would** *love* to get together with you later this week.

Quasi-modal verbs are helping verbs that function much like historical modal auxiliary verbs but that have normal verb forms (unlike modal auxiliaries). The four most important quasi-modal verbs are *am going to, have to, have got to,* and *ought to.* Here are examples:

> We **are going to** *leave* soon.
> I **have to** *pack* this afternoon.
> We **have got to** *get* this in the mail as soon as possible.
> They **ought to** *be* ready to go by now.

Present Tense

One of the most confusing features of the present tense for nonnative speakers is that the present tense does not actually mean present time. In roughly descending order of frequency, the five most common uses of the present tense are for making time-less factual statements, describing habitual actions, writing reports or reviews, forming adverb clauses when the main clause is in the future tense, and describing present plans for future action.

Making Time-Less Statements

The present tense is used to state time-less (that is, not bound or limited by time) objective facts. For example:

In the Fahrenheit scale, water *boils* at 212 degrees.

This statement is not tied to any moment of time. It is a universal generalization that is valid forever. Here is an example in which the time-less nature of the factual statement is not so obvious:

My grandmother *lives* with me.

The use of the present tense signals that for the foreseeable future, the speaker's grandmother is expected to stay with the speaker. The meaning would change if the speaker had used the present-progressive tense:

My grandmother *is living* with me.

The sentence is now tied to the present moment. The grandmother is with the speaker now, but there is no implication that she is expected to stay there indefinitely. Here are more examples of time-less factual statements in the present tense:

Christmas *falls* on Sunday this year.
The moon and the earth *rotate* around a common center of gravity.
Cucumbers *make* my skin itch.

The present tense is also used for making time-less generalizations, assertions, and observations:

Smoking *causes* cancer.
Everyone *hates* Mondays.
My kids *watch* too much TV.

Stative verbs (see Chapter 10), with their inherent meaning of ongoing, time-less condition, are commonly used in making time-less statements of various kinds:

My friends *hate* rap music.
Today *is* the first day of the rest of your life.
I *know* what you mean.
Apartments in New York *cost* a fortune.

Describing Habitual Actions

The present tense is used to describe habitual or repeated actions. For example:

Alice *checks* her e-mail first thing when she gets into the office.

The use of the present tense here signals that the sentence is describing Alice's habitual or normal activity. The sentence does not mean that Alice is checking her e-mail now. The sentence would still be valid even if Alice has been on vacation and hasn't looked at her e-mail for a month. We typically use adverbs of frequency (such as *usually, always, every day,* and *normally*) in present-tense sentences to refer to habitual actions. Here are some more examples of this use of the present tense:

I *have* oatmeal for breakfast every morning.
He always *returns* his calls promptly.
They usually *stay* at the Marriott.
We *don't* eat out very often.

Writing Reports or Reviews

When we comment on the works of others, we often write in the present tense. Reviews of plays, books, movies, and other performances often use the present tense, particularly when the writer is evaluating or commenting on the performance. For example, a movie review might contain sentences that begin like this:

The movie *is* set in . . .
Hugh Grant *plays* the role of . . .
His character *enters* into . . .
The plot *seems* . . .

If you were asked to review a proposed policy manual at work, much of what you write would probably be in the present tense, especially when you were evaluating or commenting on ideas or recommendations in the manual. For example, many of your sentences might begin like this:

The manual *recommends* that we . . .
The policy *requires* us to . . .
The proposed policy *means* that . . .

Forming Adverb Clauses When the Main Clause Is in the Future Tense

When the main clauses of sentences are in the future tense (abbreviated FT), we often put subordinate **adverb clauses** in the present tense (abbreviated PT) to show a present-time/future-time relationship between the two clauses. Here is an example:

When she *gets* to work, I *will give* her a call.
    PT   FT

In this example, the subordinate adverb clause comes first. However, one of the characteristics of adverb clauses is that they can either precede or follow the main clause. (See Chapter 14.) Here is the same example, but now with the clauses in the opposite order:

I *will give* her a call when she *gets* to work.
   FT   PT

Here are some more examples of adverb clauses in the present tense:

After I *finish* work, I *will go* grocery shopping.
    PT   FT

I *will give* you a call if I *am* free this evening.
   FT   PT

Describing Present Plans for Near-Time Future Actions and Events

We can use the present tense for near-time future actions and events. One use is for stating present plans to carry out future-time actions in the near future:

We *leave* at ten tomorrow morning.
I *go* to Los Angeles next week.
Mrs. Jones *returns* on Tuesday.
Tomorrow, the kids *get* out of school at noon.

We can easily stretch the idea of near time as far as a year:

Next year, we *vacation* in Hawaii.

We often use the present tense for predictable events. For example:

The plane *leaves* at 5:45.
The movie *is* at seven.
Your presentation *begins* at 3:30 tomorrow.

We would not use the present tense for talking about actions or events beyond our control. For example, we would not use the present tense for future weather:

X It rains tomorrow.

We often use the present tense in asking questions about the future, especially for present plans and events. For example:

When *does* the movie start?
How soon *can* you get here?
When *are* they coming back?

Past Tense

The past tense is used to refer to events that were completed in the past. The key point to keep in mind is that the use of the past tense emphasizes that the events are over and done with; they occurred *before* the present moment. Often the use of the past tense implies that what was true then is not true now. For example:

When I was a little boy, I *hated* girls.

The use of the past tense here tells us that the speaker's childhood attitude toward girls is confined to the past.

The past tense can be used to refer to a single moment in past time. For example:

I *graduated* in 2004.

The past tense can refer to events that occurred repeatedly in the past. For example:

It *rained* every day during my vacation in Spain.

The implication is that the vacation was over with at some time prior to the present.

The past tense can refer to a span of time in the past. For example:

I *worked* for that company for six years.

The use of the past tense also tells us that the speaker no longer works for that company today. If the speaker were still working for that company today, the speaker would have used the present-perfect tense:

I *have worked* for that company for six years.

We can use stative verbs in the past tense, but even those normally timeless verbs are strictly bound to the past. For example:

The children *loved* visiting Uncle Horace.

The use of the past tense tells us that the children do not love visiting Uncle Horace today. Either Uncle Horace is no longer with us or, for whatever reason, the children never visit Uncle Horace now—maybe nobody can stand Uncle Horace anymore.

There are two other uses of the past tense that have quite different meanings: hypothetical statements and polite requests.

Hypothetical Statements

The past tense in Modern English has inherited some of the functions of the subjunctive from older periods of English. One of the most common uses of the subjunctive was to signal that a speaker was talking hypothetically or even contrary to fact. The past tense in Modern English can be used to express this subjunctive meaning. It is important to remember that this use of the past tense does *not* signal past time. It is used for present or (less commonly) future time.

We see the hypothetical subjunctive most commonly in clauses that begin with *if*. For example:

If I *were* you, I would be careful what I *said* to the boss.

Notice that all the verbs in this sentence, not just the verb inside the *if* clause, are in the hypothetical past tense. The sentence is hypothetical because, of course, I am not actually you, and I am not dumb enough to say anything to the boss.

Here are some more examples with *if* clauses:

If it *snowed* tomorrow, we would be in real trouble.

In this sentence, we use the past tense to refer to future-time possibilities. The sentence is in the past tense because the speaker is talking hypothetically about tomorrow's weather. The speaker doesn't actually know whether it will snow tomorrow.

If we *missed* our sales target, the manager will be really upset.

Again, the sentence is in the past tense because the speaker is talking hypothetically. The speaker does not actually know whether they have missed
their sales target.

Hypothetical past tenses can be used without an *if*. For example:

> Unless Paul *took* better care of himself than he did before, he is going
> to end up in the hospital.

The speaker uses the past tense *took* to signal that the speaker does not
actually know how well Paul is taking care of himself.

A final word of warning: Using the hypothetical past in questions can
be taken as criticism. For example, the following question in the present
tense could be reasonably neutral:

> *Are* you wearing that dress to the party?

However, the same question in the hypothetical past definitely conveys
criticism:

> *Were* you wearing that dress to the party?

The hypothetical past tense signals disbelief—I can't believe my eyes; I
thought you had better taste than to choose to wear that awful dress to
the party.

Polite Requests

The past tense also inherits another function of the subjunctive—deference or polite indirectness, especially in asking questions. In Modern English, we use the past tense to show that the person to whom we are talking
has no obligation to agree to or approve our request. In other words, the
use of the polite past tense signals that we are not acting as a superior who
is ordering a subordinate to answer our questions. For example, if you were
talking to a friend, a social equal, you would probably issue an invitation
in the present tense:

> *Do* you want to go to a movie tonight?

However, if a boy asked out a girl he did not know well, he would probably use the polite past tense:

Did you want to go to a movie tonight?

If you wanted to know if a colleague would read a report you had written, you would probably use the present tense *will*:

Will you take a look at my report?

However, if you asked your boss the same question, you would probably use the polite past-tense form *would*:

Would you take a look at my report?

If you were asking a friend about his or her plans, you would use the present tense. For example:

Are you going to the reception this evening?

If you asked the manager of the company the same question, you would probably use a polite past-tense form to indicate that you are not demanding an answer:

Were you going to the reception this evening?

Tense Shifting Between Past and Present

A standard piece of advice that all English-language writers get is "Don't switch tenses." On the whole, this is very good advice. Here is an example of the problem the advice is trying to prevent:

X Whenever we *went* to a restaurant, my uncle always *makes* a fuss about ordering the best wine.

The hitch with this sentence is that the writer is trying to do two things at once: tell a story about what happened (a past-tense narrative) *and* make a generalization about the way his uncle behaves (a present-tense generalization). The solution is to write the entire sentence either as a past-tense narrative or as a present-tense generalization:

Past-tense narrative:	Whenever we *went* to a restaurant, my uncle always *made* a fuss about ordering the best wine.
Present-tense generalization:	Whenever we *go* to a restaurant, my uncle always *makes* a fuss about ordering the best wine.

There is one important exception to this otherwise valid rule: when you are delivering a past-tense narrative, you need to shift to the present tense for time-less statements and generalizations. Here are some examples of errors created by *not* shifting tenses:

X My family *lived* in Southern California when I *was* growing up. I *went* to Pomona College, which **was** in a small town east of Los Angeles.

The problem is that the use of the past tense *was* makes it sound as though Pomona College is no longer in a small town east of Los Angeles. The use of the past tense to describe something ties the narration to past time. The past tense always has a strong implication of over and done with—what was true in the past is not true now. This is an implication we do not want to apply to a time-less statement or generalization. Thus, we need to shift those kinds of statements or generalizations to the time-less present tense:

My family *lived* in Southern California when I *was* growing up. I *went* to Pomona College, which **is** in a small town east of Los Angeles.

Here is an example of the reverse problem—a sentence that fails to shift from present tense to past tense:

X Artists today *are* still deeply influenced by the art styles that ***originate*** in prewar Germany.

Generalizations are in the present tense; historical events are in the past tense. The art styles of prewar Germany are a historical event, tied to that period. Therefore, we need to describe them in the past tense:

> Artists today *are* still deeply influenced by the art styles that ***originated*** in prewar Germany.

Future Tense

In traditional grammar, the future tense consists of the helping verb *will* followed by the main verb in the infinitive form. For example:

> I *will see* them at the meeting this afternoon.

Will is indeed used to talk about the future, but only a small fraction of sentences that talk about the future actually use *will*. The basic problem is that English has not had a true future tense for some two thousand years. At one point in the distant past, the ancestral language of English did have a true future tense—a verb ending that meant future time. This future-tense ending was comparable to the future-tense endings in Latin, Greek, Sanskrit, and the other languages related to English. At some later point in the prehistory of English, however, this future-tense ending disappeared. The future tense in English was probably driven into extinction by the development of a remarkable set of helping verbs, called the **modal auxiliary verbs**, that provided much greater flexibility in talking about the future.

Using Modals for Future Time

We customarily use modals for talking about future time. Modals (the nine historical modal auxiliary verbs plus a few quasi-modals) are always followed by a verb in the base form. Modals used for expressions of future time are always followed by the main verb in the base form. Here are some examples, first with several modal auxiliary verbs and then with several quasi-modal verbs.

Modal Auxiliary Verbs. In the following examples, the modal auxiliary verbs are underlined.

> We *should see* them in London next week.
> We *will see* them in London next week.
> We *could see* them in London next week.

Quasi-Modal Verbs. In the following examples, the quasi-modal verbs are underlined.

> I *am going to see* them in London next week.
> I *have to see* them in London next week.
> I *have got to see* them in London next week.
> I *ought to see* them in London next week.

While each of the modals has its own range of meanings, we can roughly sort them into five main groups:

- **Prediction** of future activities and events

- **Obligation** to carry out future activities

- **Necessity** of the occurrence of future events

- **Requests** to carry out future activities

- **Capability** of engaging in future activities

Note: Some verbs appear in more than one group because they can be used with more than one meaning.

Prediction. By far the most common use of modals is for making predictions about the future. We can rank these modals from high to mid to low probability:

High probability:	be going to, will
Mid probability:	may, ought to, should
Low probability:	could, might

To give some sense of the range of meaning of the modal verbs, following are two sets of examples—one with an impersonal subject, and one with a human subject:

Impersonal Subject

High probability:	It *is going to* rain tomorrow.
	It *will* rain tomorrow.
Mid probability:	It *may* rain tomorrow.
	It *should* rain tomorrow.
Low probability:	It *could* rain tomorrow.
	It *might* rain tomorrow.

Human Subject

High probability:	I *am going to* leave this evening.
	I *will* leave this evening.
Mid probability:	I *may* leave this evening.
	I *should* leave this evening.
Low probability:	I *could* leave this evening.
	I *might* leave this evening.

Obligation. Five modals express the obligation of individuals to carry out future activities: *have got to, have to, must, ought to,* and *should.* All of these verbs are roughly equivalent in meaning. Here are examples with a human subject:

I *have got to* go to the office tomorrow.
I *have to* go to the office tomorrow.
I *must* go to the office tomorrow.
I *ought to* go to the office tomorrow.
I *should* go to the office tomorrow.

Necessity. The same five modals—*have got to, have to, must, ought to,* and *should*—express the perceived necessity of the occurrence of an event in the future. Here are some examples:

We *have got to* arrange a meeting as soon as we can.
We *have to* arrange a meeting as soon as we can.
We *must* arrange a meeting as soon as we can.
We *ought to* arrange a meeting as soon as we can.
We *should* arrange a meeting as soon as we can.

We could also add the modal *shall* to this list. For example:

We *shall* meet again.
I *shall* certainly consider what you said.
I *shall* return.

The problem with *shall* is that Americans generally feel uncomfortable using it. They have a vague notion that *shall* and *will* are somehow different and that *shall* is more formal than *will* and signals a higher degree of commitment. About the only time *shall* is actually used in this perceived meaning is in formal or legalistic writing. For example:

The company *shall* be informed ninety days prior to any amendments
    to this contract.
The defendant *shall* post a bond of $100,000.
This court *shall* be reconvened tomorrow morning at ten A.M.

(A different use of *shall*, for making polite requests, is discussed under the next heading.)

Requests. Four modals—*can, could, may,* and *shall*—are commonly used for making requests (usually framed as questions) to carry out a future activity. *Can, could,* and *may* are used for direct questions.

May is preferred when the speaker is making a request in a formal situation or of someone who holds clearly defined authority. For example:

May I have this dance?
May I see you for a moment, Sir?

However, outside these somewhat special situations, Americans normally use *can* or *could* instead of *may*. For example, most Americans would use *can* or *could* in talking to an immediate superior:

Can/could I see you sometime this afternoon?

The distinction between *can* and *could* is one of politeness. In this context, *could* is functioning as the historical past-tense polite form of *can*. Nonnative speakers generally tend to use *can* or *may* in situations in which native speakers would use *could*. (Perhaps this is a result of the overemphasis on the distinction between *can* and *may* in most ESL grammar books.)

Shall is often used in questions as a polite way of making a request. For example:

Shall we go in to dinner?
Shall we dance?
Shall I get us some coffee?

Shall has the implication that the person being addressed has the right to refuse the request.

Shall is not the same as *let's*. *Let's* is much more informal. *Let's* is also less of a question and more of a statement of the speaker's intention (with the expectation that the listener will agree). For example:

Let's sit down.

This sentence really means "I want us to sit down."

Capability. Two modals, *can* and *could*, express the capability of the subject's carrying out a future action. For example:

I *can* finish the job tomorrow.
I *could* finish the job tomorrow.

Could is more hypothetical than *can*. In the preceding examples, the use of *can* is somewhat more of a commitment to finishing the job tomorrow than *could*. The use of *could* has an implied *if*—if you really want me to; or if it doesn't rain; or if I can find the time.

Other Tenses Used for Future Time

There are two other tenses that we often use for talking about future time: the present tense and the present progressive tense.

Present Tense. As we saw in the main discussion of the present tense earlier in the chapter, we often use the present tense to state present plans for future action and to talk about predictable future events. Here are some examples of present plans to carry out future-time actions:

We *leave* on the next flight.
I *go* to Florida tomorrow.
They *get* back some time this week.

Likewise, we often use the present tense for predictable events. For example:

The plane *leaves* at 5:45.
The movie *is* at seven.
Your presentation *begins* at 3:30 tomorrow.

In addition, we frequently use the present tense for asking questions about both present plans and predictable events. For example:

When *does* the meeting start?
When *is* breakfast?
When *are* they planning to come back?

There is a subtle but real difference between sentences that use *will* and sentences that use the present tense. Here is an example:

will
We *will* start at 9:30.
Present tense: We *start* at 9:30.

In the first sentence, the use of *will* conveys a presumption that the meeting time is new information—perhaps there has been a change of time, or perhaps the information is new to the people being addressed. In the second sentence, the use of the present tense conveys a presumption of old information—perhaps the sentence is merely a reminder of what has already been scheduled.

Present Progressive. The present progressive consists of the helping verb *be* in the present-tense form followed by a verb in the present-participle form. Here are some examples:

We *are getting* ready to go.
My eyes *are burning* from all the smoke.
We *are wondering* if you would like to join us.

The present-progressive tense is covered in detail in a later section.

We can use the present progressive much like the present tense to refer to plans for the immediate future and to predictable future events. For example:

Present Plans for Future Events
I'*m leaving* for the office around 7:30.
They *are calling* a meeting for next Wednesday.
The director *is making* the announcement tomorrow.
I'*m* not *answering* any calls this afternoon.

Predictable Future Events
The train *is arriving* on track 4 in fifteen minutes.
The moon *is rising* after midnight tonight.
DC United *is playing* at home this week.
I *am working* from home Friday.

The present progressive differs from *will* in much the same way that the present tense does: *will* has the implication of new information, while both the present and present progressive imply old or previously established information. For example, compare the following sentences:

will
We *will* have coffee and dessert on the deck.
Present progressive: We *are having* coffee and dessert on the deck.

Both sentences mean the same thing, but the sentence with *will* has the feeling of an announcement of new information, while the sentence with the present progressive has the feeling of an established and normal routine.

Perfect Tenses

The perfect tenses all consist of some form of the helping verb *have* followed by a verb in the past-participle form. The **present perfect** uses the present tense (*has* or *have*). The **past perfect** uses the past-tense form, *had*. The **future perfect** uses the future-tense form, *will have*.

What's so "perfect" about the perfect tenses? Nothing. The term is related to the Latin phrase *per fectus*, which means "completely done." The key idea of the perfect tenses is that they allow us to talk about actions or events that span a period up to some final limiting time or other limiting event. The action or event ended (it was "perfected") at or before that limiting time or event. The **present perfect** is used for past-time actions or events whose action or consequences continue up to the present moment. The **past perfect** is for past-time actions or events that were finished ("perfected") before some more recent time or event. The **future perfect** is for future-time actions or events that will be finished ("perfected") before some later time or event.

Present Perfect

The present perfect is formed by the present tense of *have* (*has* or *have*) followed by a verb in the past-participle form. Here are some examples:

I *have known* him all my life.
We *have* always *shopped* at Ralph's.
He *has* just *returned.*
That faucet *has been* leaking for weeks.

To understand the meaning of the present perfect, we must contrast it with the meaning of the past tense. Compare the following examples:

Past tense: I *lived* in Tampa for five years.
Present perfect: I *have lived* in Tampa for five years.

The use of the past tense in the first example signals that the speaker no longer lives in Tampa. The action was completed at some point in the past that no longer touches the present. The use of the present perfect tells us just the opposite—that the speaker is still living in Tampa today.

In general, the past tense emphasizes that the actions or events described through the use of the past tense are well and truly over with; they do not directly impact the present. The present perfect is just the opposite: it emphasizes the ongoing connection between the past and the present. In the preceding example of the past perfect, the speaker has lived in Tampa continuously for the last five years, right up to the present moment. Here are some more examples of the present perfect for events that have spanned an unbroken period up to the present moment:

She *has studied* English since she came to the university.
They *have shown* that same cartoon for the last three weeks.
As long as I can remember, I *have* always *hated* broccoli.
The company *has* never *missed* paying a dividend in its history.

A less obvious use of the present perfect is for single events, even unique ones, that continue to directly impact the present. For example, compare the use of the past tense (abbreviated PT) and the present perfect (abbreviated Present P) in the following sentence:

Last year, John <u>*had*</u> an accident that <u>*has*</u> totally *changed* his life.

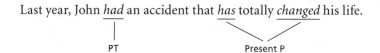

PT   Present P

The accident was a onetime-only event in the past. The accident is over and done with, so it is reported in the past tense. However, the consequences of the accident are not tied to that past moment of time; they have continued on to the present. Therefore, the present perfect is appropriate to describe the ongoing nature of the consequences.

Stative verbs (see Chapter 10), with their sense of ongoing states, are often used in the present perfect. For example:

I *have heard* that you weren't feeling well.
He *has owned* several pickup trucks.
It *has cost* us a fortune.
They *have* always *been* good friends.

Past Perfect

The past perfect consists of *had,* the past tense of *have,* followed by a past participle. Use of the past perfect requires the completion of a past-time action or event *prior* to some more recent past-time action or event.

The more recent past-time event can be expressed in an adverb of time. The past perfect is in italics in these examples:

He *had lived* in Montana before the war.
Sometime before 1996, they *had traveled* in Europe.

The more recent past-time (abbreviated P) action or event can also be in a separate clause, which can either precede or follow the past-perfect (abbreviated Past P) clause. Here are some examples showing both orders, with all verbs in italics:

They *had* already *left* by the time I *got* back.

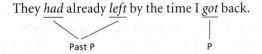

Past P   P

By the time I *got* back, they *had* already *left*.

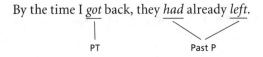

PT   Past P

They *got* engaged before they *graduated*.
    Past P   P

Before they *graduated*, they *had gotten* engaged.
              P   Past P

My sister *called* after I *had returned* home.
         P   Past P

After I *had returned* home, my sister *called*.
      Past P   P

Future Perfect

The future perfect consists of *will have* (the future tense of *have*) followed by a verb in the past-participle form. The action or event described by the future perfect tense must be completed *prior* to some other future time or event. The future time can be expressed as an adverb of time. The future perfect is shown in italics in these examples:

I *will have finished* everything by noon.
By then, we *will have* already *left*.

The future time or future perfect (abbreviated FP) can also be expressed in another clause, which can be in the present tense (abbreviated PT) or present perfect (abbreviated Present P). For example:

By the time you *get* this note, I *will have* already *called* the police.
                PT   FP

By the time you *have decoded* this, I *will have* already *left* the country.
                  Present P   FP

The two clauses can occur in either order:

He *will have packed* all the boxes before she *has printed* all the labels.
       FP   Present P

Before she *has printed* all the labels, he *will have packed* all the boxes.
           Present P   FP

Stative verbs are commonly used in the future perfect. For example:

By the time his investments *mature,* he *will have become* rich.
                             PT   FP

His car payments *will have cost* him a fortune by then.
                 FP

Modals + the Perfect Tense

We can easily combine modals with the perfect tense. Recall that the grammatical requirement for using modals is that they must be immediately followed by a base-form verb. When we use the modal for talking about the future, the verb that follows the modal is the main verb of the clause. When we use a modal with the perfect, the base-form verb that follows the modal is the helping verb *have* from the perfect tense. Here are some examples; the two-part perfect-tense construction is underlined:

Susan *must have been* very worried.

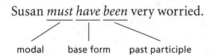

modal   base form   past participle

They *might have told* us.

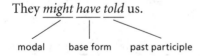

modal   base form   past participle

She *may have balanced* the accounts by now.

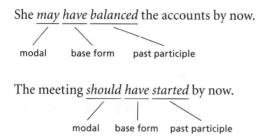

The meeting *should have started* by now.

One problem that nonnative speakers have with this construction in speech is that *have* is normally contracted either to a nearly inaudible sound that rhymes with *love* or to an "uh" sound. In newspaper cartoons, this latter contracted form of *have* is often written with an -*a*, like this:

You *shoulda* seen him.
I *gotta* go.
I don't *wanna* do it.

As you can see from these examples, modals used with the perfect typically do *not* mean future time. There are two main uses of the modals with the perfect tense: **speculation** and **regret for lost opportunities**.

Speculation. By far the most common use of the modal + perfect combination is to speculate about the outcome of actions or events that are ongoing or have recently been completed. To see how the different modals are used with the perfect, we will use the following perfect-tense sentence as a frame of reference:

John *has scheduled* the meeting.

The use of the perfect (without any modal) is a statement of fact. In this case, the speaker is asserting that John has indeed scheduled the meeting.

Each of the eight modals (except *shall*, which Americans would rarely use with the perfect) puts a different interpretation on the perfect-tense sentence. Since most nonnative speakers are unaware of the sometimes significant implications of using one modal rather than another, we will briefly discuss the meaning of each one.

Can + *perfect*. We do not normally use *can* with the perfect unless *can* is used in the negative:

John *can't have scheduled* the meeting.

Can't denies the possibility that the statement is true. In this case, perhaps the speaker knows that John lacks the information necessary to do the scheduling or was somehow prevented from doing the scheduling.

We also use *can't* (with extra stress) in an ironic way to express surprise, even astonishment. For example:

Bob ***can't*** *have refused* to meet with the chairman.

The speaker here is not denying what Bob actually did; the speaker is expressing utter amazement at what Bob has chosen to do.

May + *perfect*. By using *may*, the speaker is stating the possibility in a neutral, fifty-fifty way:

John *may have* scheduled the meeting.

Maybe John did, or maybe he didn't. However, consider the effect if the speaker stresses *may*:

John ***may*** *have* scheduled the meeting.

This sentence indicates that the speaker strongly doubts that John actually did schedule the meeting (though still admitting the possibility).

Must + *perfect*. The use of *must* signals a strong assumption:

John *must have* scheduled the meeting.

In this case, although the speaker does not know for a fact that John has scheduled the meeting, he or she has good reason for believing that John actually has done it.

Will + *perfect*. The use of *will* with the perfect tense is not just a simple statement about the future. It is an expression of confidence on the speaker's part that something the speaker has no direct control over has actually happened. For example:

John *will have* scheduled the meeting.

In this case, the speaker is confident that John has actually gone ahead and scheduled the meeting, even without the speaker's direct control or supervision.

Could + *perfect*. The use of *could* signals capability:

John *could have* scheduled the meeting.

John is able to schedule the meeting, though we do not know if he did or not. However, suppose *could* were stressed:

John **could** *have* scheduled the meeting.

This example implies that the speaker doubts that John actually did schedule the meeting.

Might + *perfect*. The use of *might* signals a fifty-fifty possibility:

John *might have* scheduled the meeting.

Again, if *might* were stressed, it would imply that the speaker doubts that John actually did schedule the meeting:

John **might** *have* scheduled the meeting.

Should + *perfect*. *Should* has two different meanings: John was expected to have scheduled the meeting, though we do not know if he actually did:

John *should have* scheduled the meeting.

And, John failed to schedule the meeting (a more likely interpretation if *should* is stressed). This second use of *should* is strongly negative. This use of *should* to express disapproval is quite common:

You ***should*** *have been* more careful!
They ***should*** *have watched* where they were going.
I ***shouldn't*** *have eaten* the whole thing!

Would + *perfect*. This use of *would* signals what we expect somebody to do:

John *would have* scheduled the meeting.

In this case, it tells us that the speaker expected John to schedule the meeting. We do not know if John actually scheduled the meeting.

Lost Opportunity. The past-tense modal auxiliaries *could*, *might*, and *should* have another meaning with the perfect: the expression of regret for a lost opportunity. Here is an example of this meaning using *could*. It is one of the most famous lines in American movies:

"I *coulda been* a contender. I *coulda been* somebody, instead of a bum, which is what I am." —Marlon Brando, *On the Waterfront* (1954)

In the movie, Brando plays a broken-down boxer. In this scene, his character laments the fact that he did not take advantage of his skills to become a challenger (a "contender") for the championship in boxing. The use of *could* emphasizes the fact that the speaker had the capacity to succeed, but he did not. None of the other modals used to express regret at lost opportunities have the same sense of personal responsibility for failure that *could* has. This is one reason why Brando's line is so effective.

Might + *perfect*. This construction recognizes the existence of an opportunity that failed to materialize through no particular fault of the subject. *Might* does not convey as deep a sense of loss or misfortune as the other modals. For example:

I *might have been* a star.
The company *might have won* the contract.
The sale *might have led* to a promotion for Jim.

Should + *perfect*. *Should* emphasizes the fact that the subject let the opportunity for success slip away through carelessness, bad judgment, or ineptitude. It can also convey a sense of looking back and commenting on past actions with the benefit of hindsight.

> I *should have quit* when I was ahead.
> They *should have taken* a chance.
> The Cubs *should have won* the World Series.

Progressive Tenses

The progressive tenses are all constructed by the helping verb *be* (in some form) immediately followed by a verb in the present-participle form. The **present progressive** uses a present-tense form of *be*, the **past progressive** uses a past-tense form of *be*, and the **future progressive** uses the future tense of *be*. The progressive tenses are all used to describe an action **in progress** (hence the name **progressive**) at some present, past, or future moment.

Present Progressive

The present progressive consists of the present tense of the verb *be* (*am*, *are*, or *is*) followed by a verb in the present-participle form. The present progressive is always tied to some present (or future) time. The present can mean an action in progress at the actual moment of uttering the sentence. For example:

> Can you turn the TV down? I'*m talking* on the phone.
> The doctor *is seeing* another patient now.
> I'*m returning* your call.

Or the present can mean some larger span of present time. For example:

> She *is working* on her M.B.A.
> The waves *are* gradually *eroding* away our beach.
> Global warming *is causing* climate change.

The present progressive often conveys a sense of temporariness. For example, compare the following pair of sentences—the first in the present tense and the second in the present progressive:

Present tense: They *fly* first-class.
Present progressive: They *are flying* first-class.

In the first sentence, the use of the present tense signals that it is their normal custom to fly first-class. It does not mean that they are flying first-class at the moment. The use of the present progressive in the second sentence means that they are flying first-class on the particular flight we are talking about at the moment. We do not know whether they regularly fly first-class.

Future Plans and Events. In the previous discussion of the future tense, we saw that we often use the present progressive for future plans and for scheduled future events.

Future Plans
I'*m leaving* at four today.
We'*re meeting* for a drink tonight.
Who'*s coming* to dinner?

Scheduled Future Events
The taxi *is coming* in ten minutes.
That movie *is showing* at 7:15.
Hurry, the office *is closing* in fifteen minutes.

Comments on Behavior. There is an odd use of the present progressive where we would normally expect the present tense. The present progressive (typically with the adverb *always*) is used to comment (usually negatively) on someone's behavior. Here are some examples:

He'*s* always *coming* in late to meetings.
She *is* always *interrupting* me.
Our neighbors *are* always *leaving* their trash on our lawn.
The mayor *is* always *blaming* somebody else for his mistakes.

Past Progressive

The past progressive consists of the past tense of the verb *be* (*was* or *were*) followed by a verb in the present-participle form. The present progressive is always tied to some past time. It can be a specific moment or period in the past. For example:

By 9 A.M., I *was working* at my desk.
At noon, we *were fixing* lunch.
During the afternoon, we *were having* drinks on the terrace.

Or the past time can be defined by some other event as expressed in a past tense (abbreviated PT) subordinate clause, such as the past progressive (abbreviated PProg.). For example:

We *were watching* TV when the lights *went* out.
   PProg.   PT

When you *called*, we *were working* in the garden.
        PT   PProg.

They *were driving* to Richland when they *had* the accident.
     PProg.   PT

The past progressive can also be used for a past-time action or event that spans a defined period of past time. For example:

All last week, my boss *was meeting* with the sales reps.
From noon on, I *was raking* leaves in the backyard.
All the time he *was talking*, I *was looking* at my watch.

The past progressive can be used to express polite deference in making requests:

I *was hoping* you could give me a ride home.
I *was wondering* if you would put a good word in for me.
I *was thinking* that we could eat out tonight.

Future Progressive

The future progressive consists of the future tense of the verb *be* (*will be*) followed by a verb in the present-participle form. The present progressive describes some activity that will be carried out at some future time. The future time can be a specific moment or period. For example:

> At noon, I *will be flying* to Houston.
> Next week, the kids *will be staying* with their grandparents.
> During the school year, she *will be living* in a dorm.

Or the future time can be defined as taking place during some future-time event that is expressed in a present-tense (abbreviated PT) subordinate clause, such as the future progressive (abbreviated FProg.). For example:

> While you <u>are</u> in California, I <u>*will be working*</u> on my thesis.
>   PT   FProg.

> He <u>*will be arranging*</u> more interviews while you <u>enter</u> the data.
>   FProg.   PT

> I <u>*will be working*</u> from home when they <u>repaint</u> my office.
>   FProg.   F

Modals + the Progressive Tense

We can easily combine modals with the progressive tense. Recall that the grammatical requirement for using modals is that they must be immediately followed by a base-form verb. When we use a modal with the progressive, the base-form verb that follows the modal is the helping verb *be*. Here are some examples with the two-part progressive tense construction underlined:

> We <u>*might be eating*</u> dinner out tonight.
>   / | \
> modal base form present participle

John *is going to be doing* his paperwork today.

modal   base form   present participle

You *ought to be thinking* about new plans for the office.

modal   base form   present participle

As is true of modals used for talking about future time, by far the most common use of modals with the progressive is for predicting future actions and events. We can rank the various modals used for prediction by their degree of probability:

High probability: be going to, will
Mid probability: may, should
Low probability: could, might

Here are some examples with the modal underlined:

High probability: John *is going to be working* late tonight.
They *will be cleaning* the rugs tomorrow.

Mid probability: It *may be raining* by the time we get to Detroit.
They *should be finishing up* by now.

Low probability: The children *could be sleeping*.
He *might be playing* golf this afternoon.

Special Verbs

This chapter examines three types of verbs with unique properties. The major emphasis is on **phrasal verbs**. These verb + preposition compounds are the chief source of new verbs in English. The second topic is a large group called **stative verbs**, whose meaning makes them incompatible with the progressive tenses. The third topic is a small group called **causative verbs**.

Phrasal Verbs (Two-Word Verbs)

All languages have ways of making new words. Most new verbs in English are created by compounding verbs with prepositions. The oldest form of verb compounding fuses the preposition onto the front of the verb. Here are some examples with the preposition in italics:

*by*pass	*down*play
*over*throw	*under*stand
*up*set	*with*draw

Beginning in the early Middle Ages, English developed a second way of forming verbs—by compounding the verb with a following preposition. These verb + preposition compounds are called **phrasal verbs** or **two-word verbs**. Over time, phrasal verbs have evolved to become the principal source of new verbs in English. The best reference work on phrasal verbs is the *Longman Dictionary of Phrasal Verbs*. (Nonnative speakers who want to develop a near-native fluency in conversational English need to have this book.) To give you an idea of how common phrasal verbs are, the *Longman Dictionary of Phrasal Verbs* has more than twelve thousand entries (though not all are phrasal verbs in the narrow sense in which we are using the term). Phrasal verbs are probably more numerous than nonphrasal verbs, especially in informal, spoken language.

The key characteristic of a phrasal verb is that the verb + preposition unit acts exactly like an ordinary, single-word verb. An example of an **intransitive** phrasal verb follows. (*Intransitive* means that the verb does not require an object—see Chapter 11.) Here and in all related examples, both the verb and the preposition are in italics:

Alfred *passed out*.

The phrasal verb *passed out* means "fainted." The fact that we can find a single-word verb that substitutes for the phrasal verb is strong evidence in itself that *passed out* is a single verb made with two components.

The only other possible interpretation of *passed out* is that *out* is an ordinary adverb. If that were the case, then we could ask an adverb question beginning with *where* that would give us back the adverb as the answer. To demonstrate this test, here is an example of a sentence containing a verb with a true adverb:

Verb + adverb: Alfred *went* out.
Adverb question: Where did Alfred go?
Adverb answer: Out.

When we apply the same test to the sentence with a phrasal verb, the test and the answer are nonsensical:

Phrasal verb: Alfred *passed out*.
Adverb question: X Where did Alfred pass?
Adverb answer: X Out.

Here is a more complicated example, using a **transitive** phrasal verb. (*Transitive* means that the verb requires an object—see Chapter 11.)

Susan *turned down* the offer.

We can see that *turned down* is acting like a one-word verb by substituting a one-word verb paraphrase for it:

Susan *rejected* the offer.

The biggest problem in identifying transitive phrasal verbs is that they look exactly like verbs followed by prepositional phrases. To see the difference, compare the following sentences:

Phrasal verb: Susan *turned down* the offer.
Verb + prepositional phrase: Susan *turned* down the road.

Prepositional phrases (abbreviated PP) that follow verbs function as adverbs that modify the verb. We can see the difference between the two sentences when we try to use them to answer the adverb question *where*. When we apply the adverb test to the verb + prepositional phrase sentence, the adverb question and answer are both perfectly normal:

Verb + prepositional phrase: Susan *turned* down the road.
Adverb question: Where did Susan turn?
Answer: Down the road.

This test shows that the sentence has the following structure:

Susan *turned* down the road.
       V   A   PP

When we apply the same test to the phrasal-verb sentence, the adverb question and answer are both nonsensical:

Phrasal verb: Susan *turned down* the offer.
Adverb question: X Where did Susan turn?
Answer: X Down the offer.

The failure of the test shows that the phrasal-verb sentence must have the following structure:

Susan *turned down* the offer.
       V   O

As the two phrasal verbs *pass out* and *turn down* illustrate, the meaning of phrasal verbs cannot necessarily be determined by adding together the meaning of the verb and the meaning of the preposition. Why does *pass + out* = "faint"? Why does *turn + down* = "reject"? The fact that phrasal verbs are highly idiomatic, together with fact that there are thousands of them, means that phrasal verbs are a formidable obstacle for nonnative speakers.

Adding to the difficulty is the fact that most bilingual English dictionaries and student dictionaries do not give adequate coverage to phrasal verbs. All but the most common verb + preposition combinations are ignored. At the least, nonnative speakers need to use a standard English desk dictionary such as *Webster's Collegiate*.

To this point, we have looked only at the immense vocabulary problem that phrasal verbs pose for nonnative speakers. An additional grammatical complication arises with transitive phrasal verbs. There are two types of transitive phrasal verbs, each having somewhat different grammatical properties.

In one type, called **separable phrasal verbs**, the preposition can actually move to a position after the object. Here is an example:

The students *turned **in*** their papers.
The students *turned* their papers ***in***. (*turn in* = "submit")

In the other type, called **inseparable phrasal verbs**, the preposition cannot move. For example:

The company will *go **after*** new markets.
X The company will *go* new markets ***after***. (*go after* = "aim for" or "pursue")

So, as you can see, in addition to learning what all the phrasal verbs mean, nonnative speakers need to know which transitive phrasal verbs are separable and which are inseparable.

Finally, there is an issue of terminology. Nobody is happy with the term *preposition* for the words that join together with verbs to form phrasal verbs (even though the term is historically correct). The reason is that we then end up with two kinds of prepositions: the kind that is used in phrasal verbs and the normal kind, which is used in prepositional phrases. Grammar books and textbooks have not yet evolved a single standard terminology that everyone agrees on, though most books adopt one of the two following approaches:

- Use the term *particle* for all second elements in phrasal verbs.
- Distinguish between **adverbs** and **prepositions**. If the second element in a phrasal verb is always followed by a noun phrase (as is the case with inseparable phrasal verbs), it is called a **preposition**. If the second element is *not* always followed by a noun phrase (as is the case with separable phrasal verbs and intransitive phrasal verbs), it is called an **adverb**. As the following diagram shows, this is simpler than it sounds:

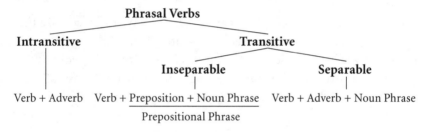

Both approaches are perfectly logical and consistent. Both give exactly the same analysis of phrasal verbs. *Longman's Dictionary of Phrasal Verbs* uses the second approach, with its distinction between adverbs and prepositions. In this book we will adopt the first approach and simply use the term *particle*. The only reason for choosing this approach is that life is short and grammar books are long.

There is actually a fourth use of phrasal verbs: as a prepositional phrase that follows a noun phrase. In keeping with the preceding diagram, this fourth type would look like this: verb + noun phrase + **preposition** + noun phrase. We will analyze this type after discussing the more common phrasal verbs given in the diagram.

We now turn to a more detailed description of the three common types of phrasal verbs: **intransitive**, **inseparable transitive**, and **separable transitive**.

Intransitive Phrasal Verbs

Intransitive verbs are verbs that do not take objects. Some examples of nonphrasal intransitive verbs are *die, sleep,* and *smile*:

The flowers *died.*
The children *were sleeping.*
The waiter *smiled* politely.

Intransitive phrasal verbs consist of a verb (V) and a particle (P) acting as a single unit. For example:

The patient <u>*pulled*</u> <u>*through.*</u>
            V   P

The phrasal verb *pull through* means to "survive." We can recognize that *pull through* is a phrasal verb because it has an idiomatic meaning that can be paraphrased by a single-word verb (i.e., *survive*). It also has a distinctive grammatical structure. If *through* were not part of the verb, it would be an optional adverb that could be used to answer an adverb question:

Adverb question: X Where did the patient pull?
Answer: X Through.

Since both the adverb question and the answer are nonsensical, we can tell that *through* is not an ordinary, optional modifying adverb. It is part of the verb itself.

The number of intransitive verbs that can be used as phrasal verbs is so large that there is no practical way to list them. However, the list of prepositions that can be used as particles to form intransitive phrasal verbs is sufficiently limited. Here is a list of the most commonly used ones: *apart, around, away, back, by, down, in, off, on, out, over, together, up.*

Here are sentences that illustrate the use of these prepositions in intransitive phrasal verbs, arranged alphabetically by the preposition:

Sometimes couples *grow **apart**. (grow apart* = "become estranged")
They were *fooling **around**. (fool around* = "act silly or improperly")

He was *running **away**.* (*run away* = "flee" or "escape")
The Empire *struck **back**.* (*strike back* = "retaliate" or "avenge")
Some old friends *dropped **by**.* (*drop by* = "visit")
Our car *broke **down**.* (*break down* = "fail" or "quit operating")
They need help, so we *chipped **in**.* (*chip in* = "contribute")
The kids were *showing **off**.* (*show off* = "exhibit oneself")
The idea was *catching **on**.* (*catch on* = "become successful")
Time *ran **out**.* (*run out* = "expire")
The baby *turned **over**.* (*turn over* = "flip" or "rotate")
The tourists *kept **together**.* (*keep together* = "stay close")
Something *came **up**.* (*come up* = "happen")

Inseparable Transitive Phrasal Verbs

Inseparable phrasal verbs are **transitive** verbs (see Chapter 11). Transitive verbs require objects (O)—noun phrases or other constructions that can play the role of noun phrases. Here is a typical example of an ordinary nonphrasal transitive verb:

The children *ate* the pizza.
            O

The only thing that is different about transitive phrasal verbs is that the verb is a compound of a verb + a particle. Here is an example:

Everybody *talked about* the meeting.
        V + P   O

This type of phrasal-verb construction is called "inseparable" because the particle cannot be separated from the verb. (The next section discusses a type of phrasal verb in which the particle can move away from the verb.)

The simplest way in which we can tell that *talk about* is a phrasal verb is that we can easily find a one-word paraphrase for it:

Phrasal verb: Everybody *talked about* the meeting.
Nonphrasal verb: Everybody *discussed* the meeting.

The problem with inseparable phrasal verbs is that they look much like ordinary, nonphrasal verbs followed by prepositional phrases. Compare the following sentences:

Everybody *talked about* the meeting.
Everybody *walked* about the gardens.

Despite their apparent similarity (subject noun phrase + verb + preposition + noun phrase), the two sentences have different internal structures:

| **Phrasal verb + object:** | Everybody *talked about* the meeting. |
| | S   V   O |

| **Verb + adverb prepositional phrase:** | Everybody *walked* about the gardens. |
| | S   V   APP |

We can confirm that *talk about* is a verb and that *the meeting* is the object of that verb by ruling out the only other possible interpretation. If *talked* is the verb, then *about the meet*ing must be an adverb prepositional phrase. If this were the case, then *about the meeting* would answer an adverb question:

Sentence:	Everybody *talked about* the meeting.
Adverb question:	X Where did everybody talk?
Answer:	X About the meeting.

As you can see, the adverb question and answer are nonsensical. The only possible interpretation remaining is that *talked about* is a phrasal verb and *the meeting* is an object.

In the case of the ordinary verb sentence, the corresponding adverb question and answer will be perfectly grammatical:

Ordinary verb sentence:	Everybody *walked* about the garden.
Question:	Where did everybody walk?
Answer:	About the garden.

As is the case with intransitive phrasal verbs, it is not practical to try to list the verbs that can be used as inseparable phrasal verbs. However, we can list the limited number of prepositions that can be used as particles. Here are the most common ones: *about, after, against, at, by, for, from, into, of, on, through, to, with.*

Here are sentences that illustrate the use of these prepositions as particles in inseparable phrasal verbs, arranged alphabetically by the preposition:

Verb	Preposition	Example/Meaning
know	*about*	She *knows about* the meeting. (*know about* = "be informed of")
look	*after*	Please *look after* my plants. (*look after* = "take care of")
guard	*against*	You must *guard against* overconfidence. (*guard against* = "avoid" or "be careful of")
hint	*at*	They *hinted at* the problem. (*hint at* = "indirectly suggest")
stand	*by*	She will *stand by* her man. (*stand by* = "support")
ask	*for*	They all *asked for* you. (*ask for* = "request")
abstain	*from*	They *abstain from* smoking. (*abstain from* = "don't engage in or do")
bump	*into*	He *bumped into* her yesterday. (*bump into* = "encounter by accident")
hear	*of*	I just *heard of* your new appointment. (*hear of* = "learn about")
bet	*on*	You can *bet on* it. (*bet on* = "be assured that it will happen")
work	*through*	I finally *worked through* the problem. (*work through* = "complete a difficult task")
talk	*to*	She *talked to* the president of the company. (*talk to* = "directly address")
consult	*with*	He *consulted with* his staff. (*consult with* = "seek advice from")

Compound Inseparable Phrasal Verbs. A few inseparable phrasal verbs are compounded with a second particle. (*Longman's Dictionary of Phrasal Verbs* describes these verbs as adverb + preposition compounds.) Here is an example:

Senator Fogg *looks down on* his opponents.

Look down on is a compound phrasal verb that means something like "hold in contempt" or, in modern slang, "disrespect." Inseparable compound phrasal verbs are much like ordinary, uncompounded inseparable phrasal verbs in that very few prepositions can be used to form the compound. The most common ones are *against, from, of, on, to,* and *with.* If you examine the preceding list of prepositions that can be used as particles with ordinary, uncompounding inseparable verbs, you will notice that these six—*against, from, of, on, to,* and *with*—are drawn from the same list.

Here are some examples of compound phrasal verbs, arranged alphabetically by the second preposition:

Verb	Preposition	Example/Meaning
bring up	**against**	His bad grades were *brought up against* him. (*bring up against* = "raise an issue to someone's disadvantage")
keep away	**from**	Alice *kept away from* dark alleys. (*keep away from* = "avoid")
get out	**of**	We decided to *get out of* retail sales. (*get out of* = "quit" or "withdraw from")
check up	**on**	The nurse *checked up on* her patients. (*check up on* = "monitor" or "investigate")
face up	**to**	You must *face up to* your fears. (*face up to* = "confront")
put up	**with**	We had to *put up with* all his boring jokes again. (*put up with* = "tolerate")

Separable Transitive Phrasal Verbs

Separable phrasal verbs are transitive verbs just like inseparable phrasal verbs. There is one key difference, though: with separable verbs, the particle can (and in certain circumstances, *must*) move away from the verb. The rules governing when the particle moves depend on the nature of the object. There is one set of rules for when the object is a noun phrase and a second set of rules for when the object is a pronoun.

Noun Phrase Objects. An example of the separable phrasal verb *call off* (meaning "cancel") with a noun phrase object follows. Here and in all related examples, the phrasal verb is shown in both of its forms: first in the verb's normal position, with the particle immediately following the verb, and then in its shifted form, with the particle moved after the object noun phrase:

Normal position:	The CEO *called off* the talks.
Shifted:	The CEO *called* the talks *off.*

There is no difference in basic meaning between the two versions. However, shifting the particle definitely gives the meaning of the entire verb extra emphasis, especially if the particle is stressed. The shifted sentence can express surprise or even indignation at the fact that the CEO canceled the talks.

The example is misleading in one respect: it looks as if the particle is simply moved to the end of the sentence. That is not correct. When we add an adverb, as in the following sentence, we can see that the particle must immediately follow the object:

Normal position:	The CEO *called off* the talks abruptly.
Shifted:	The CEO *called* the talks *off* abruptly.

Shifting the particle to the end of the sentence, makes it ungrammatical:

Shifted:	X The manager *called* the meeting abruptly *off.*

We do not shift the particle when the object noun phrase is long and/or complicated. Here are some examples:

Normal position: The CEO *called off* the talks about the new product.

Shifted: X? The CEO *called* the talks about the new product *off*.

Normal position: The CEO *called off* the talks scheduled for Monday.

Shifted: X? The CEO *called* the talks scheduled for Monday *off*.

Here are some more examples of separable phrasal verbs with noun phrase objects:

Normal position: John *called up* his girlfriend last night.
Shifted: John *called* his girlfriend *up* last night.
                       (*call up* = "telephone")

Normal position: She *passed around* the picture to everyone.
Shifted: She *passed* the pictures *around* to everyone.
                       (*pass around* = "distribute" or "show something to people")

Normal position: The kids *nailed together* some boards in the basement.
Shifted: The kids *nailed* some boards *together* in the basement.
                       (*nail together* = "attach using nails")

Pronoun Objects.   The real problem for nonnative speakers arises when the object is not a noun phrase and is instead a pronoun. To explore the issue, let's return to our original example, but this time we will replace the noun phrase *the talks* with the pronoun *them*. The version in the normal position is now ungrammatical:

Normal position: X   The CEO *called off* them.

The shifted position is the only grammatical possibility:

Shifted: The CEO *called* them *off.*

When the object is a pronoun (instead of a noun or any type of noun substitute other than a pronoun), the particle in a separable phrasal verb *must* be shifted. Since moving the particle is obligatory with pronoun objects, there is no sense of extra emphasis resulting from shifting the particle.

The rule for shifting the particle also holds for pronouns: the particle is shifted to a position immediately following the pronoun and in front of any adverbs. For example:

The CEO *called* them *off* abruptly.

Here are some more examples of separable phrasal verbs with pronoun objects:

John's expensive habits finally *did* him *in*. (*do in* = "ruin" or "kill")
We *took* them *back* to the station after dinner. (*take back* = "return")
You can't *rule* them *out* of the race. (*rule out* = "eliminate"—often
     used with *of* + noun phrase)

Prepositions Used as Particles with Separable Phrasal Verbs. The number of prepositions that can be used as particles with separable phrasal verbs is relatively limited. Here is a list of the most common ones: *apart, away, back, down, in, off, on, out, over, up.*

Following are sentences that illustrate the use of these prepositions as particles in separable phrasal verbs, arranged alphabetically by the prepositions. Notice that in these examples, all ten prepositions are used with a single verb. These examples illustrate how the use of phrasal verbs has greatly increased the number of verbs in English. Each example shows both a noun-phrase object and a pronoun object:

Verb	Preposition	Example/Meaning
take	**apart**	We *took* **apart** the bicycle.
		We *took* it **apart**.
		(*take apart* = "disassemble")
take	**away**	The police *took* **away** the intruders.
		The police *took* them **away**.
		(*take away* = "remove")
take	**back**	I *take* **back** what I said.
		I *take* it **back**.
		(*take back* = "retract")
take	**down**	He *took* **down** the minutes of the meeting.
		He *took* them **down**.
		(*take down* = "record")
take	**in**	Susan *took* **in** all the plays in town.
		Susan *took* them **in**.
		(*take in* = "attend")
take	**off**	Thomas *took* **off** his wet shoes.
		Thomas *took* them **off**.
		(*take off* = "discard" or "remove")
take	**on**	The ship *took* **on** the whole enemy fleet.
		The ship *took* them **on**.
		(*take on* = "fight against" or "engage")
take	**out**	We *took* **out** my wife's parents.
		We *took* them **out**.
		(*take out* = "entertain")
take	**over**	Ralph *took* **over** the failing restaurant.
		Ralph *took* it **over**.
		(*take over* = "assume control of")
take	**up**	We *took* **up** the matter with the accountant.
		We *took* it **up** with the accountant.
		(*take up* = "discuss" or "contest")

Distinguishing Inseparable and Separable Phrasal Verbs

For nonnative speakers, distinguishing between inseparable and separable phrasal verbs seems a nearly impossible task. It is certainly difficult, but there is one feature that minimizes the problem somewhat: inseparable and separable phrasal verbs (with one exception) use different prepositions as their particles. Here is a rundown of the prepositions that are most commonly used as particles with the two different types of phrasal verbs:

Inseparable Prepositions	Separable Prepositions
about	apart
after	away
against	back
at	down
by	in
for	off
from	**on**
into	over
of	up
on	
through	
to	
with	

What is striking about these two lists is that there is only one preposition that the two lists have in common: *on*. There also seems to be a general pattern in each of the lists. The separable prepositions all have a sense of motion or movement, while only four of the inseparable prepositions—*from, into, through,* and *to*—have that same sense. Most of the remaining inseparable prepositions have no sense of motion at all: *about, after, against, at, by, for, of, with.*

It is probably useful for nonnative speakers to simply memorize the nine prepositions used as particles with separable verbs and then make the working assumption that any other prepositions used as particles with transitive verbs are going to be inseparable. Sometimes this rule of thumb (a "rule of thumb" is an English idiom meaning an imperfect but helpful guide) will be wrong, but it will be right far more often; without it, nonnative speakers have only a fifty-fifty chance of being correct.

Noun Phrase + Prepositional Phrase Phrasal Verbs

Grammar textbooks often ignore this final type of phrasal verb. This omission is unfortunate given that the construction is fairly common. Noun phrase is abbreviated NP; prepositional phrase is abbreviated PP. Here is an example:

John *blames* <u>his problems</u> ***on*** <u>everybody else.</u>
     NP   PP

The preposition, as one would expect, cannot be moved:

X John *blames* his problems everybody else ***on***.

As we have seen with the other types of phrasal verbs, it is impractical to list the verbs that enter into this construction. However, we can list the prepositions. The more common ones are the following: *about, against, for, from, in, into, of, on, to, with*. Again, as we would expect, all the prepositions in this list are also on the list of inseparable prepositions in the preceding section.

Here is an example arranged alphabetically by preposition:

Verb	[NP]	Preposition	Example
ask		*about*	We *asked* the clerk ***about*** our order.
			(*ask* [NP] *about* = "make inquiries of ")
stack		*against*	They *stacked* the jury ***against*** us.
			(*stack* [NP] *against* = "bias someone against")
thank		*for*	We *thanked* them ***for*** their support.
			(*thank* [NP] *for* = "express appreciation to someone")
take		*from*	The school *took* the cell phones ***from*** the students.
			(*take* [NP] *from* = "remove" or "confiscate")
engage		*in*	We *engaged* them ***in*** a lengthy debate.
			(*engage* [NP] *in* = "interact with someone")

talk	*into*	They *talked* us *into* their stupid plan. (*talk* [NP] *into* = "persuade somebody to agree to something")
deprive	*of*	The car accident *deprived* us *of* our transportation. (*deprive* [NP] *of* = "cause somebody to lose something")
blame	*on*	They always *blame* their problems *on* us. (*blame* [NP] *on* = "assign blame to someone")
leak	*to*	He *leaked* the information *to* the press. (*leak* [NP] *to* = "give private information to someone")
provide	*with*	Our garden *provides* us *with* lots of lettuce. (*provide* [NP] *with* = "give supplies to someone")

Stative and Nonstative Verbs

Not all verbs can be used in all nine tense categories. Of particular importance is a group of verbs called **stative** verbs. All stative verbs share a common meaning: they depict a time-less state or condition. This meaning of stative verbs makes them completely incompatible with the progressive tenses, since the progressive tenses always describe action that is in progress at some moment of present, past, or future time. For example:

X I *am hating* spinach.
X They *are doubting* the truth of what you say.
X He *was having* a laptop at the time.
X We *were liking* your proposal.
X She *will be loving* that.

Stative verbs tend to fall into distinct categories based on meaning:

Emotions:	appreciate, desire, dislike, doubt, feel, hate, like, love, need, prefer, want, wish
Measurement:	consist of, contain, cost, entail, equal, have, measure, weigh
Cognition:	believe, doubt, know, mean, think, understand
Appearance:	appear, be, look, resemble, seem, sound
Sense perception:	feel, hear, see, seem, smell, taste
Ownership:	belong, have, own, possess

(Note that some verbs appear twice because they can be used with different meanings.)

Many of these same verbs can be used as regular verbs, but with a definite shift in meaning. Here are some examples of the same verb used first as a stative verb and then as an action verb:

| **Stative verb:** | The lamb chops *weigh* four pounds. |
| **Action verb:** | The butchers always *weigh* the lamb. |

| **Stative verb:** | You *are* stubborn. |
| **Action verb:** | You *are being* stubborn. (= "You are acting in a stubborn manner.") |

| **Stative verb:** | I *have* a problem. (= "A problem exists.") |
| **Action verb:** | I *am having* a problem. (= "I am experiencing a problem at the moment.") |

The fact that stative verbs all depict time-less states or conditions means that they can be freely used in the present tense without the limitations that nonstative verbs encounter. For example, compare the stative verb *own* with the nonstative verb *fix*:

| **Stative:** | John *owns* a car. |
| **Nonstative:** | X? John *fixes* a car. |

(See the treatment of present tense in Chapter 9 for more details.)

Causative Verbs: *Rise-Raise*; *Sit-Set*; *Lie-Lay*

These three pairs of verbs—*rise-raise, sit-set,* and *lie-lay*—are frequently confused, even by native speakers. In fact, native speakers have such trouble with these verbs that they often avoid using them at all.

To make a brief digression: At an early stage of English, there was a special ending that could be attached to nearly any intransitive verb. This ending later disappeared, though its effects live on today. This ending is what linguists call a **causative**. A causative ending means to "cause the action of the verb to which it is attached." For example, if we added this ending to the verb *sneeze,* we would create a new verb with the meaning of to "cause someone to sneeze." If we added the ending to the verb *sleep,* we would create a new verb meaning to "cause someone to sleep."

The suffix was always attached to an intransitive verb. The new verb that resulted was always **transitive**—that is, it required an object. Also, when the causative suffix was attached to the original intransitive verb, the resulting new transitive verb had a different vowel. In other words, the causative suffix caused a vowel change in the base form of the word to which it was attached. We will see this same pattern in two of the pairs of causative verbs.

The newly created transitive causative verb is always regular.

Rise-Raise

The intransitive verb *rise* means to "go up" or "get up." For example:

The sun *rises* in the east.
The farmers *rise* before dawn.

As you would expect, the causative verb *raise* is a transitive verb that means to "cause someone or something to rise" (virtually synonymous with *lift*). For example:

The company *will raise* their wages.
The tide *is raising* the boats.

Over the years, the meaning of *raise* has broadened to mean, among other things, to "rear" (children or animals) and to "grow" (crops or plants). For example:

She *raised* three children on her own.
The farmer *is raising* wheat and barley.

For the verbs *rise* and *raise*, the original intransitive verb is irregular, while the newer transitive causative verb is regular:

Intransitive Verb *Rise*

Base/present tense:	*rise/rises*
Past tense:	*rose*
Past participle:	*risen*
Present participle:	*rising*

Transitive Causative Verb *Raise*

Base/present tense:	*raise/raises*
Past tense:	*raised*
Past participle:	*raised*
Present participle:	*raising*

Sit-Set

The intransitive verb *sit* means to "be seated" or "be situated." For example:

Please *sit* down.
The house *sits* on a hill overlooking the valley.

Historically, the transitive causative verb *set* meant to "cause someone or something to sit." For example:

The teacher *set* the children down at the table.
The masons *will set* the stones into the wall.

Over time, the meaning of *set* has broadened to also mean to "arrange" or "assign":

We *will set* the table for six people.
The committee *will set* the date for the next meeting.

The original intransitive verb *sit* is irregular:

Intransitive Verb *Sit*
Base/present tense: *sit/sits*
Past tense: *sat*
Past participle: *sat*
Present participle: *sitting*

The transitive causative verb *set* is one of those odd one-syllable verbs ending in a *t* or *d* (like *hit* and *rid*) that use the same form for the present tense, the past tense, the past participle, and the present participle:

Transitive Causative Verb *Set*
Base/present tense: *set/sets*
Past tense: *set*
Past participle: *set*
Present participle: *setting*

Greatly adding to the confusion of *sit* and *set* is the fact that *set* developed a second use as a noncausative, intransitive verb meaning to "descend." For example:

The sun rises in the east and *sets* in the west.

This second use of *set* has tended to undercut the use of the historical intransitive verb *sit*.

Lie-Lay

This verb is the most difficult of the causative group of verbs. The difficulty stems from a historical accident: the past tense of the irregular intransitive verb *lie* happens to be *lay*, which is also the present-tense form of the regular transitive causative verb *lay*. Outside of this confusion of identities, the difference between *lie* and *lay* is what we have seen with the other pairs of verbs.

The original intransitive verb meant to "recline." The meaning has broadened over time to mean "spread out" and "be placed." For example:

Lie back and relax.
The business district *lies* along the west bank of the river.

As we would expect, the transitive causative verb *lay* means to "cause to lie"—that is, to "place." For example:

Please *lay* your papers on the desk.
I had to *lay* my head down.
The movers *will lay* the rugs in the living room this afternoon.

In casual conversation, there is a tendency to use *lay* as a noncausal, intransitive verb, meaning something like "hang out." For example:

X?   Don't just *lay* there. Do something!
X?   I got tired *laying* around the apartment all day.

The fact that we frequently hear *lay* used as an intransitive verb means that we need to be especially careful to monitor our use of *lay* in formal writing, where this intransitive use of *lay* is not acceptable. If *lay* does not have an object, it is not correct in formal writing. If you have trouble with *lie* and *lay* (and we all do), it might be worthwhile to memorize the following sentence:

We *lie* around, but we *lay* something down.

The original intransitive verb *lie* is irregular:

Intransitive Verb *Lie*

Base/present tense:	*lie/lies*
Past tense:	*lay*
Past participle:	*lain*
Present participle:	*lying*

The transitive causative verb *lay* is regular. (The change of the final *y* in *lay* to *i* in *laid* is the result of normal spelling rules.)

Transitive Causative Verb *Lay*

Base/present tense:	*lay/lays*
Past tense:	*laid*
Past participle:	*laid*
Present participle:	*laying*

Verb Complements I: Simple Complements

A **complement** is any grammatical structure required by a verb to make a valid sentence. The scope of this chapter is verbs that take no complement at all (**intransitive verbs**) and verbs that take only single complements (**action verbs** and **linking verbs**). Chapter 12 addresses verbs that take multiple complements.

Nearly every verb can be used with more than one type of complement. For example, the verb *get* can be used with the following three different complements (among others):

Adjective complement:	I *got* angry. (*get* = "become")
Noun phrase complement:	I *got* an answer. (*get* = "receive" or "have")
Noun phrase + infinitive phrase complement:	I *got* him to finish the job. (*get* = "cause")

As you can see, the meaning of the verb *get* shifts with each different complement that it takes. There are really three *get* verbs: *get* that takes an adjective complement, *get* that takes a noun phrase complement, and *get* that takes a noun phrase + infinitive phrase complement.

The fact that nearly all verbs have multiple complements means that there are as many meanings for the verb as there are types of complements. The multiplicity of complements for most verbs poses a special problem for nonnative speakers because most bilingual and student dictionaries seldom give more than one or two meanings for each verb. When nonnative speakers find themselves unable to understand the meaning of a sentence, it is often because the verb in the sentence uses a complement type that their dictionaries do not provide.

Intransitive Verbs

Verbs that take no complement are called **intransitive** verbs. Here are some examples of sentences with intransitive verbs:

> The old cow *died*.
> My knee *hurts*.
> The kids *are sleeping*.

Most of the time, we use intransitive verbs with various kinds of optional adverbs. For example:

> The old cow finally *died* during the night.
> My knee *hurts* whenever it rains.
> The kids *are sleeping* at my cousin's house tonight.

Bear in mind that these adverb expressions are not part of the complement. In other words, these verbs do not require these adverb expressions for the sentences to be grammatical. That is not always the case, though. For example, consider this sentence:

> Philip *put* the pasta in the pot.

The adverb of place *in the pot* is required for the sentence to be grammatical. If we delete the adverb expression, the sentence becomes ungrammatical:

> X Philip *put* the pasta.

One of the complements that the verb *put* takes is noun phrase + adverb of place.

Intransitive Phrasal Verbs

Chapter 10 discusses a number of intransitive phrasal verbs. Intransitive phrasal verbs are verb compounds consisting of a verb and an adverb. These compounds act as a single unit, often with an idiomatic meaning. Here are some more examples:

> My taxi finally turned up. (turned up = "arrived")
> The driver *pulled over*. (*pull over* = "stop at the side of the road")
> The storm finally *died down*. (*die down* = "exhaust itself")

Since the particles *up, over,* and *down* are themselves part of a compound verb, they do not count as independent complements that follow the verb.

Transitive Verbs Used as Intransitives

Most transitive verbs can also be used without objects—that is, used intransitively—but with a special meaning: to engage in the action of the transitive verb. For example, the verb *rule* is normally a transitive verb:

> King George III *ruled* the American colonies.

However, we can use *rule* as an intransitive verb meaning to "engage in the act of ruling." This is a common use of the word among sports fans. For example:

> Manchester United *rules*!

Here are some slightly less slangy examples of normally transitive verbs used intransitively (that is, with no complement):

> When they came, Ralph *was painting*. (*paint* = "engage in the act of painting something")
> When the president is in public, the police always *protect*. (*protect* = engage in the act of protecting someone")
> You count the votes, and I *will record*. (*record* = "engage in the act of recording something")

Single-Complement Verbs

There are two main types of verbs that take a single complement: **action verbs** and **linking verbs**. **Action verbs** (AV), as their name suggests, typically express an actor (A)–action–recipient of action (RoA) relationship among the subject, verb, and object. Here is a typical example:

Thomas *kicked* the ball.
    A   AV   RoA

    Linking verbs (LV) typically describe the nature of the subject. The subject is not an actor performing any action. The complement is not the recipient of any action. Rather, the complement is used to describe some characteristic of the subject (CoS). The verb is called a "linking verb" because it links the complement to the subject. Here is an example:

Thomas *was* a football player.
    S   LV   CoS

Action Verbs

Action verbs are transitive verbs with single noun phrases or pronouns as their complements. (Compound nouns and pronouns are counted as single complements.) Action verbs are probably the most common of all types of verbs. Here are some examples with the noun phrase complement in bold:

John *saw* **Mary.**
Theo *washed* **his new car.**
Lois *cashed* **her check.**
The bright lights *frightened* **them.**

Phrasal Action Verbs. Many phrasal verbs function as action verbs as shown in Chapter 10. A phrasal verb is a compound consisting of a verb and a preposition or an adverb. Typically, phrasal verbs have idiomatic meanings. Transitive phrasal verbs are divided into two groups: **inseparable phrasal verbs** and **separable phrasal verbs**:

Inseparable Phrasal Verbs

We *pored over* our notes. (*pore over* = "examine thoroughly")
The union *pushed for* higher wages. (*push for* = "urge" or "demand")
The company *went with* her suggestion. (*go with* = "accept")

Separable Phrasal Verbs

We *headed off* the problem. (*head off* = "avoid")
They *turned down* our offer. (*turn down* = "reject")
The judge *let off* the defendants. (*let off* = "release")

Separable phrasal verbs are so-called because the second component of the phrasal verb can (and in some situations, must) move to a position immediately following the object:

We *headed* the problem *off.*
They *turned* our offer *down.*
The judge *let* the defendants *off.*

Because these prepositions and adverbs are actually the second components of verb compounds, these prepositions and adverbs do not count as independent verb complements.

Noun Clauses, Gerunds, and Infinitives as Complements. The complement of an action verb is a noun phrase or a pronoun. (The complement of an action verb is traditionally called an **object.**) The term *noun phrase* is an umbrella term that includes, in addition to nouns, three grammatical structures that function as nouns—noun clauses, gerunds, and infinitives.

The use of noun clauses, gerunds, and infinitives as complements (objects) of action verbs is controlled by the meaning of the verb. We can use noun clauses, gerunds, and infinitives only if the verb will permit **abstract nouns** as objects. Abstract nouns are nouns such as *idea, answer, outcome,* or *plan* (see also Chapter 7). If a verb can use these nouns as objects, that same verb can also use a noun clause, a gerund, or an infinitive as its object.

For example, the verb *like* can use the abstract nouns *idea, answer,* and *outcome* as the object:

We *like* the idea.
> > the answer.
> > the outcome.

Thus, we expect to be able to use noun clauses, gerunds, and infinitives as objects of *like*:

Noun clause: We like *what they suggested.*
                  We like *that we can get home early.*
Gerund: We like *getting home early.*
Infinitive: We like *to get home early.*

Linking Verbs

The term *linking* refers to the relation between the complement of the linking verb and the subject. In linking-verb sentences, the verb "links" the complement back to the subject. In other words, the complement gives some information about or describes in some way the nature of the subject.

There are three grammatical structures that can act as complements of linking verbs: predicate adjectives, noun phrases, and adverbs of place and time. Here is an example of each type; the linking verb is in italics, and the complement is in bold:

Complement Type
Predicate adjective: Donald *is* **funny.**
Noun phrase: Donald *became* **a writer.**
Adverb of place: Donald *is* **in New York.**

Each of the three complements refers back to and describes Donald.

Following is a summary of all commonly used linking verbs, roughly grouped into three categories based on meaning. All of these verbs can be used with predicate adjective complements. Only seven are commonly used with noun phrase complements; these seven verbs are marked with (N) to indicate that the verb can be used with both predicate adjective and noun phrase complements.

GROUP 1: APPEARANCE

appear (N)	smell
feel (N)	sound
look (N)	taste
seem (N)	

GROUP 2: CHANGE

become (N)	go
end up (N)	grow
get	turn

GROUP 3: STATE

be (N)	remain
keep	stay

Predicate Adjective Complements. Predicate adjectives are "true" adjectives that are the complements of linking verbs. (For the characteristics of adjectives see Chapter 2.) The most important feature of "true" adjectives for this discussion is that they have **comparative** and **superlative** forms. For example, the predicate adjectives *tall* and *beautiful* have the following comparative and superlative forms:

Adjective	Comparative	Superlative
tall	taller	tallest
beautiful	more beautiful	most beautiful

Predicate adjectives can be used with their own complements. The surprisingly large and diverse family of predicate adjective complements is discussed in Chapter 13.

Here are examples of sentences with predicate adjective complements (in bold):

The children *appeared* **happy**.
We *got* **ready** as soon as we could.

The new dress *looked* very **pretty** on her.
The weather *turned* bitterly **cold** last night.

Many predicate adjectives are derived from the **present-participle** form of verbs. Here are some examples: *alarming, amusing, charming, discouraging, failing, worrying.*

These predicate adjectives are sometimes difficult to distinguish from the same present participles used as part of the **progressive tense.** After all, the adjective and the verb forms are identical: they both end in *-ing*, and they can both follow the verb *be*. Compare the following sentences:

Predicate adjective: The movie was *amusing.*
Progressive: The movie was *amusing* the children.

There is a simple way to distinguish the predicate adjective from the progressive verb: see if you can put *very* in front of the *-ing* word. *Very* modifies adjectives but does not modify verbs. For example:

Predicate adjective: The movie was **very** *amusing.*
Progressive: X   The movie was **very** *amusing* the children.

Here are several more examples:

Predicate adjective: The report was **very** *discouraging.*
Progressive: X   The report was **very** *discouraging* everyone.

Predicate adjective: Their repeated failures were **very** *worrying.*
Progressive: X   Their repeated failures were **very** *worrying* us all.

Noun Phrase Complements. The only two linking verbs that are commonly used with noun phrase complements are *be* and *become*. For example:

His car *was* a **junky old Ford**.
She *became* **a tax expert**.

Most of the other verbs that can be used with noun phrase complements are verbs of appearance, such as *appear, feel, look, seem,* and *sound.* While it is perfectly grammatical to use these verbs with noun phrases, most speakers today prefer to use the verbs with the infinitive *to be* or the preposition *like.* For example, most people would not use the following construction:

Thomas *seems* **a pleasant young man.**

Instead, they would probably use either of the following alternatives:

Thomas *seems to be* **a pleasant young man.**
Thomas *seems like* **a pleasant young man.**

Here are some more examples of *to be* and *like* with linking verbs:

It *appears to be* **an eagle.**
I *felt like* **a complete fool.**
The car *looked to be* **a total wreck.**
The choir *sounded like* **angels.**

Adverbs of Place and Time Complements. The verb *be* is often used with adverbs of place or time as a complement. The term *adverb* here means either a single-word adverb or an adverb prepositional phrase. Here are several examples of each type:

Adverb of Place Complements
The picnic *is* **at the beach.**
Our apartment *was* **on Fifty-Third Street.**
We *were* **there.**

Adverb of Time Complements
The meeting *is* **at ten.**
The game *is* **Saturday afternoon.**
That *was* **then;** this *is* **now.**

Verb Complements II: Multiple Complements

A **complement** is any grammatical structure required by a verb to make a valid sentence. This chapter outlines eight different verb complements that contain two components.

Indirect Object + Direct Object Complement

A small but important group comprises verbs that take not one object but *two* objects. When there are two objects in a sentence, the objects are called the **indirect object** (abbreviated as IO) and the **direct object** (abbreviated as DO). The two objects occur in a fixed order: the indirect object always precedes the direct object. Here are two examples of sentences with this type of double complement:

Jane *gave* the boss her report.
$\underset{\text{IO}}{\underline{\hphantom{the boss}}}$ $\underset{\text{DO}}{\underline{\hphantom{her report}}}$

John *got* the kids a pizza.
$\underset{\text{IO}}{\underline{\hphantom{the kids}}}$ $\underset{\text{DO}}{\underline{\hphantom{a pizza}}}$

Paraphrasing the Indirect Object with *to* and *For*

Nearly all complements that have an indirect object + direct object complement have an alternative form that functions as a paraphrase of the original form. We can imagine this paraphrase taking place as a two-step process. First, the indirect object is turned into a prepositional phrase (abbreviated as PP) using *to* or *for,* and then the direct object is moved in front of the prepositional phrase. Here are examples of how this *to/for* paraphrase transforms the original indirect object + direct object complements:

Jane *gave* <u>the boss</u> <u>her report.</u> ⇒ Jane gave <u>her report</u> *to* <u>the boss.</u>
    IO   DO   DO   PP

John *got* <u>the kids</u> <u>a pizza.</u> ⇒ John got <u>a pizza</u> *for* <u>the kids.</u>
    IO   DO   DO   PP

A few verbs that take an indirect object + direct object complement do not permit the *to/for* paraphrase. The most common ones are *cost, fine,* and *wish.* Here are some examples:

The lessons *cost* <u>us</u> <u>$50</u> ⇒ **X** The lessons cost <u>$50</u> *to/for* <u>us.</u>
      IO DO   DO   PP

Larry *fined* <u>them</u> <u>ten dollars each.</u> ⇒
     IO   DO
X Larry fined <u>ten dollars each</u> *to/for* <u>them.</u>
        DO   PP

We *wished* <u>them</u> <u>a great trip.</u> ⇒
     IO   DO
X We wished <u>a great trip</u> *to/for* <u>them.</u>
       DO   PP

The verb *ask* is unusual in that it uses the preposition *of* in forming the indirect object + direct object paraphrase. For example:

I *asked* <u>Mary</u> <u>a favor.</u> ⇒ I asked <u>a favor</u> *of* <u>Mary.</u>
     IO   DO   DO PP

If both the indirect object and the direct objects are pronouns, then the *to/for* paraphrase is obligatory in American English (but not in all dialects of British English). For example:

X The company *gave* <u>them</u> <u>it</u>.   ⇒   The company gave <u>it</u> *to* <u>them</u>.
         IO DO   DO   PP

X My parents *got* <u>them</u> <u>it</u>.   ⇒   My parents got <u>it</u> *for* <u>them</u>.
         IO DO   DO   PP

The *to/for* paraphrase poses a special problem for nonnative speakers. Nonnative speakers sometimes mistakenly interpret a noun phrase followed by a prepositional phrase beginning with *to* or *for* as being a *to/for* paraphrase of an indirect object + direct object complement. Here are some examples:

Problems with *to*
X He *said* me the answer.

To see what caused this mistake, compare the following sentences:

He *told* the answer **to** me.
He *said* the answer **to** me.

These two sentences look alike, but they are constructed completely differently. The *to* in the first sentence is the result of the *to/for* paraphrase:

He told <u>me</u> <u>the answer</u>.   ⇒   He told <u>the answer</u> *to* <u>me</u>.
        DO   IO   IO   PP

However, the *to* in the second sentence is not the result of the *to/for* paraphrase. It comes from a completely different source: the verb *say* is a phrasal verb that takes a noun phrase + *to* prepositional phrase complement. That is, we say something to somebody. The prepositional phrase beginning with *to* is, of course, locked in place following the first noun phrase.

The mistake is a result of the nonnative speaker's interpreting a sentence such as the one in the following example as a *to* paraphrase and then incorrectly assuming that the unparaphrased indirect object + direct object version of the sentence would also be grammatical. Here is the sentence:

He *said* the answer to me.

If this sentence is a grammatical *to/for* paraphrase, the nonnative speaker mistakenly assumes, then the following sentence should also be grammatical:

X He *said* me the answer.

The reasoning is logical, but it is based on a false premise.

Here are examples of similar mistakes using phrasal verbs that take noun phrase + *to* prepositional phrase complements:

George *addressed* his remarks **to** the crowd.
X George *addressed* the crowd his remarks.

The president *announced* his decision **to** us.
X The president *announced* us his decision.

The teacher *explained* the lesson **to** them.
X The teacher *explained* them the lesson.

Problems with *for*
X Roberta *unwrapped* her mother a gift.

To see what probably caused this mistake, compare the following sentences:

Roberta *made* a gift **for** her mother.
Roberta *unwrapped* a gift **for** her mother.

Again, these two sentences look alike, but they are constructed completely differently.

The *for* in the first sentence is a result of the *to/for* paraphrase:

Roberta *made* <u>her mother</u> <u>a gift</u>. ⟹
            IO   DO

Roberta *made* <u>a gift</u> <u>***for*** her mother</u>.
            DO   PP

The *for* in the second sentence, however, has nothing to do with the *to/for* paraphrase. This particular use of *for* is in an optional adverb prepositional phrase that we can add to nearly any action-verb sentence to indicate for whose benefit the action of the verb was performed. We can even add this optional adverb prepositional phrase to an intransitive verb, for example:

She *smiled **for*** <u>you</u>.
        adverb phrase

The mistake is a result of the nonnative speaker's interpreting a sentence such as the one in the following example as a *for* paraphrase and then incorrectly assuming that the unparaphrased indirect object + direct object version of the sentence would also be grammatical. Here is the sentence:

Roberta *unwrapped* <u>a gift</u> <u>***for*** her mother</u>.

If this sentence is a grammatical *to/for* paraphrase, the nonnative speaker mistakenly assumes, then the following sentence should also be grammatical:

X Roberta *unwrapped* her mother a gift.

Again, the thought process is perfectly logical, but it is based on a false premise.

Verbs That Take the to Paraphrase

Most verbs that take the indirect object + direct object complement use *to* in forming the *to/for* paraphrase. In general, the verbs that use *to* describe something being transferred from one person to another, either physically or metaphorically.

Physically:	give, hand, lend, offer, pass, sell, send, throw
	I *gave* the books *to* them.
	We *loaned* our truck *to* the neighbors.
	Did you *send* the memo *to* everyone?
	Throw that pencil *to* me, will you?
Metaphorically:	grant, leave, owe, phone, promise, read, show, sing, teach, tell, write
	I *left* the decision *to* them.
	We *owe* our success *to* our loyal customers.
	They *promised* my office *to* the new manager.
	He *showed* his new car *to* his parents.

Verbs That Take the for *Paraphrase*

Most of the indirect object + direct object verbs that use *for* in forming the *to/for* paraphrase have the basic meaning of doing or making something for the benefit of someone else: *bake, call, build, cook, do, find, fix, make, order, pour, reserve, save.* Here are example sentences:

We *built* a birdhouse *for* our kids.
They *did* a favor *for* them.
My mother *made* some cookies *for* the reception.
We *saved* some of the cookies *for* you.

Object + Predicate Adjective Complement

Some verbs take an object + a predicate adjective (abbreviated PA) complement. For example:

He *drives* me crazy.
　　　　O　PA

The proposal *left* us cold.
　　　　　　O　PA

The jury *found* them innocent of all charges.

　　　　　　 O　　　 PA

I *like* my steak medium-rare.

　　　　 O　　　　 PA

Most uses of this complement type are phrases that allow relatively little substitution for the predicate adjective. For instance, in the four preceding examples of this complement type, each of the predicate adjectives will allow only a few other predicate adjectives to be used with that verb.

Consider the first example:

He *drives* me **crazy.**

We can substitute only a few close synonyms for *crazy*. For example:

He *drives* me **mad.**

He *drives* me **nuts.**

Now consider the second example:

The proposal *left* us **cold.**

About the only obvious substitute for *cold* is *lukewarm*:

The proposal *left* us **lukewarm.**

The same is true of the remaining two examples. We can substitute only *guilty* for *innocent* in the third example. In the fourth example, we can substitute only words for describing meat (such as *rare, well done, juicy,* and *pink*) for *medium-rare*.

A list of the most commonly used verbs that take an object + adjective phrase complement follows. Since this complement type is so idiomatic, an example is included with each verb.

Verb	Example
believe	She *believed* him **honest**.
color	We *colored* them **orange**.
consider	They *consider* him **reliable**.
drive	They *drove* their parents **crazy**.
find	We *found* their suggestions **helpful**.
get	The senator always *got* his critics **angry**.
keep	The insulated cover *will keep* the food **cold**.
like	Jazz fans *like* their music **hot**.
make	Their attitude *made* us **angry**.
need	I *need* them **ready** by noon.
paint	We *painted* the deck **a light brown**.
prefer	I *prefer* my eggs **well cooked**.
presume	The law *presumes* them **innocent**.
prove	The evidence *proved* their theory **correct**.
rate	I *would rate* their food **only average**.
think	We *think* the offer **adequate**.
turn	Too much smoking *turns* your teeth **yellow**.
want	I *want* the rooms **bright and cheery**.

Dummy It *with* That *Clauses as Objects*

The object position in this complement type can be filled by noun clauses and gerunds. For example:

Noun clause: I found what you said hard to accept.
Gerund: I found commuting to work easy.

However, *that* clauses are normally shifted to a position following the predicate adjective. A dummy *it* is then put in the place of the object. (A *dummy it* is an *it* that does not refer to anything. The dummy *it* acts as a kind of grammatical place marker.) This is a fairly common construction. Here are some examples:

I *found* it **odd** that they were in such a hurry to leave.
We *believe* it **certain** that they will accept our offer.

Don't you *think* it **strange** <u>that the meeting was canceled so suddenly?</u>
John *considers* it **unlikely** <u>that they will have to go to New York.</u>

Object + Object Complement

Strictly speaking, the heading for this section should be "Object + Object Complement Complement." The confusion involving the word *complement* results from the fact that *object complement* is a technical term in grammar. An **object complement** (OC) is a noun phrase that follows an object and renames that object. That is, the object complement and the object must refer to the same person or thing. Here is an example:

The committee *named* <u>Mary Smith</u> <u>the new chair of the committee.</u>
                O   OC

In this sentence, Mary Smith is the new chair. In other words:

Mary Smith = the new chair of the committee

Here are some more examples of this type of complement:

The Supreme Court *declared* <u>George Bush</u> <u>president.</u>
            O   =   OC

I *pronounce* <u>you</u> <u>man and wife.</u>
     O = OC

The critics *considered* <u>her latest book</u> <u>a great success.</u>
        O   =   OC

I have often *wished* <u>myself</u> <u>a better person.</u>
      O   = OC

Distinguishing Object Complements from Objects

One of the problems with object complements is that they look so much like the (more common) indirect objects in an indirect object + direct object complement construction. Both object complements and direct objects follow other noun phrases. How can we tell them apart? There are two easy ways to do so.

The first way, in an indirect object + direct object complement construction, we can use the *to/for* paraphrase. However, this paraphrase will never work with an object + object complement construction. To see the difference, compare the ability of the following sentences to undergo the *to/for* paraphrase:

Indirect object + direct object:	The kids made John a birthday present.
***to/for* paraphrase:**	The kids made a birthday present *for* John.
Object + object complement:	The outcome made John a happy man.
***to/for* paraphrase:**	X The outcome made a happy man *to/for* John.

The sentence with the object complement is completely ungrammatical, while the sentence with the indirect object and direct object is used quite naturally with the *to/for* paraphrase.

The second way, in an object complement sentence, the person or object in the object complement must be the same person or object as the preceding noun (the object). In an indirect object + direct object sentence, they are never the same person or object. Compare the following two sentences:

Object + object complement:	The outcome made <u>John</u> <u>a happy man</u>.
	John = a happy man
Indirect object +direct object:	The kids made <u>John</u> <u>a birthday present</u>.
	John ≠ a birthday present

Object Complements Used as Part of *Be Infinitive Verb Phrases*

Some verbs that take as their complement an object + object complement also allow the object complement to be in an infinitive verb phrase that uses the verb *be*. Consider the following example:

> I always *imagined* <u>him</u> <u>a wealthy man.</u>
>   o   oc

We can also say it this way:

> I always *imagined* him **to be** a wealthy man.

The two versions mean exactly the same thing. In fact, with the verb *imagine*, most native speakers would probably prefer the version with the *be* infinitive. Here are some more examples, with the *to be* in parentheses:

> I always *found* him (**to be**) a good listener.
> The board *chose* her (**to be**) the next CEO of the company.
> I *consider* myself (**to be**) a fair person.

This use of an infinitive *be* with an object complement is only one instance of a more general complement type that is discussed here in an upcoming section on the object + infinitive verb phrase complement.

Verbs That Take Object Complements and *Be Infinitive Object Complements*

Here is a list of the commonly used verbs that take as their complement object + object complements. The verbs that can also take the *be* infinitive are indicated by (B). For example, the verb *appoint* can be used either with or without the *to be*:

> They *appointed* him the new secretary.
> They *appointed* him **to be** the new secretary.

appoint (B)	consider (B)	keep	rate
baptize	crown	make	suppose (B)
believe (B)	declare (B)	name (B)	think
call	elect (B)	presume (B)	vote
certify (B)	find (B)	proclaim (B)	wish (B)
choose (B)	hold (B)	profess (B)	
christen	imagine (B)	pronounce (B)	
confess (B)	judge (B)	prove (B)	

Object + Adverb of Place Complement

A few verbs require an expression of place after the object. For example:

I *put* the box **on the table.**

The verb *put* requires an expression of place. When you *put* something, you have to put it somewhere. If we delete the expression of place, the sentence becomes ungrammatical:

X I *put* the box.

The expression of place can be an adverb prepositional phrase (as in the example) or merely a single-word adverb. For example:

I *put* the box **there.**

The adverb of place can also include adverbs that have a sense of motion or direction toward a place. For example:

I *pushed* a coin **into the slot of the vending machine.**

All of the verbs that take this complement type have a sense of causing someone or something to be placed somewhere or to be moved to some place. Here are some more examples:

Can you *take* me **to the airport**?
Carefully, I *laid* the eggs **in the carton**.
Show me **where to go**.
Send any mail **to my home address**.

One particular pair of verbs that take this complement type causes some nonnative speakers a problem: *bring* and *take*. In English, as in many other languages, *bring* and *take* are directional words. *Bring* implies "toward the speaker," and *take* implies "away from the speaker." For example:

Please *bring* the books **to me**. (toward the speaker)
Please *take* the books **to his office**. (away from the speaker)

Some languages do not have directional words like *bring* and *take*. For native speakers of these languages, the directional use of *bring* and *take* can be surprisingly difficult to master.

Object + *That* Clause Complement

Some verbs can take an object followed by a *that* clause. For example:

I *told* <u>him</u> **that** <u>his plan was very risky</u>.
　　　O　　　　　　that clause

We *reminded* <u>the kids</u> **that** <u>it was time to go to bed</u>.
　　　　　　O　　　　　　　that clause

As is true with *that* clauses used in nonsubject roles, the *that* is often omitted, especially in rapid speech. For example:

I *told* <u>him</u> Ø <u>his plan was very risky</u>.
　　　O　　　　　that clause

We reminded <u>the kids</u> Ø <u>it was time to go to bed</u>.
　　　　　O　　　　　　　that clause

The deletion of the word *that* from a *that* clause poses special problems for nonnative speakers by erasing one of the key signals on which people can rely to identify *that* clauses. Therefore, the examples that follow show the *that* in parentheses as a reminder that the word is often omitted.

The verbs that take this complement type have a restricted range of meaning. Most of the verbs express some form of communication, such as *convince, tell, warn,* and *write.* Here are some example sentences using these verbs:

We *convinced* them (**that**) it was a bad idea.
I *told* you (**that**) I needed to leave early.
The lifeguards *warned* the swimmers (**that**) the tide was dangerous.

Here are the most commonly used verbs that take an object + *that* clause complement:

advise	notify	show
assure	order	teach
beg	persuade	tell
bet	promise	wager
convince	remind	warn
inform	satisfy	write
instruct		

To *Phrase* + That *Clause*

A few verbs that express communication have an unusual feature: they use a prepositional phrase beginning with *to* (a **to** phrase) instead of the expected object. For example, with the verb *say,* we might expect the following construction:

X I said <u>him</u> <u>*that* we needed to leave soon.</u>
       O   *that* clause

We find instead a *to* phrase in place of the object:

I said **to him** *that* we needed to leave soon.

    to phrase   *that* clause

Using an object with verbs that take a *to* phrase is a common error for nonnative speakers.

Here are some more examples of sentences that correctly use the *to* phrase:

He *wrote* **to my sister** *that* they had finally moved.
The professor *explained* **to the students** *that* they had all failed the test.
Let me *prove* **to you** *that* my idea will work.
We *pointed out* **to them** *that* they were behind schedule.

Note that we can delete the "*to* + noun phrase" from any of the preceding examples, giving us an ordinary transitive verb with a *that* clause as an object. For example:

I said **to him** *that* we needed to leave soon.

Deleting *to him* gives us this sentence:

I said *that* we needed to leave soon.

                NP

Here is a list of the most common verbs that use the *to* phrase:

acknowledge	explain	remark
admit	mention	report
announce	point out	say
complain	propose	signal
confess	prove	state
declare	recommend	suggest

Object + Infinitive Complement

In this construction, the object is followed by an infinitive. For example:

Ralph *expected* the office *to be* empty on a Sunday morning.
           O   Infinitive phrase

Many verbs take this complement type. They can be arranged into four general groups based on meaning, as shown here; some of the more common verbs within the group are then listed alphabetically, followed by an example:

Verbs of permission:	allow, enable, elect, help, inspire, permit, require
	The company *authorized* the project team *to go* ahead.
Verbs of cognition:	assume, expect, feel, imagine, know, understand
	John *considered* his job *to be* vital to the company's success.
Verbs of causation:	cause, drive, force, get, intend, lead, mean, prompt
	I *got* a friend *to drive* me to the station.
Verbs of naming:	appoint, choose, elect, name, vote
	They *chose* Alice *to lead* the new task force.

Object + Base-Form Complement

Only a few verbs take this complement type, but they are commonly used. Here is an example:

He *made* me *do* it.
    O   base form

The **base form** is also called an **unmarked** or **bare infinitive**. All of these terms refer to the same thing: a verb phrase that contains a base-form verb followed by that verb's complement. We can see that this complement type is indeed a base form by using the verb *be*. For example:

They *let* <u>Mary</u> ***be*** <u>the leader in the new project.</u>
　　　　　DO　　　　　　　base form

If the verb *be* were not in its base form, it would agree with its subject, *Mary*:

X They *let* Mary ***is*** the leader in the new project.

Nonnative speakers commonly make mistakes with this complement type because it is easily confused with the much more frequent object + infinitive complement. That is, nonnative speakers sometimes overgeneralize the *to* of the object + infinitive complement to the less common object + base-form complement. For example, compare the following two sentences:

Object + infinitive:　　We *allowed* them *to* finish.
Object + base form:　X　We *let* them ***to*** finish.

In the second example, the *to* has been added to the base form in mistaken analogy to the more common infinitive complement.

Here are some more examples of the correct use of the base-form complement:

Please *let* me *help* you.
I once *saw* Pelé *play* soccer.
We *listened to* them *debate* the issue.

You may not be familiar with the use of *have* with this complement type. *Have* means something like to "cause somebody to do something." For example:

I *had* my secretary *take* notes during the meeting.

Here is a list of the verbs that take the base-form complement:

feel	let	observe
have	listen to	overhear
hear	make	see
help	notice	watch

Note: The causative use of *have* can also be extended to the passive. See Chapter 18.

Many verbs that take the base-form complement also take the present-participle complement (discussed in the next section). For example:

Base form: They *watched* the plumber ***fix*** the leak.
Present participle: They *watched* the plumber ***fixing*** the leak.

The difference between the two is completed act versus process. The base-form complement means that they observed a completed event. The present-participle complement emphasizes that they sat through the entire process of the plumber fixing the leak, step by step.

Object + Present Participle Complement

This final type uses a present-participle (PP) verb phrase (VP) as a complement. For example:

I *saw* him ***working on*** his report.
    O   PP   VP

One of the difficulties in recognizing this complement type is that present-participle verbs look just like present participles used as **gerund phrases** (see Chapter 6). Gerund phrases are *-ing* forms of the verb used as noun phrases. Here is an example:

Working on his report kept Rudolph up all night.
              NP

The gerund phrase *working on his report* is a noun phrase playing the role of subject. Fortunately, there is a simple and highly reliable way to identify gerund phrases: they can always be replaced by *it*. For example:

Working on his report kept Rudolph up all night.
              It

When we try to substitute *it* for a present-participle verb phrase, the result will always be ungrammatical. For example:

I *saw* him **working on** his report.
              X *it*

Here are some more examples of verbs with present-participle complements:

She *found* them *watering* the garden.
I couldn't help *hearing* them *discussing* the project.
We *left* the painters *finishing up* the trim in the dinning room.

The verb *catch* often has the negative implication of discovering somebody doing something improper. For example:

The teacher *caught* several students *cheating* on the exam.
The manager *caught* some employees *sleeping* on the job.
The audit *caught* several offices *overcharging* customers.

Get and *have* both mean to "cause somebody to do something." For example:

The police *got* volunteers *searching* the woods.
We *have* the interns *searching* the records.

Here is a list of the verbs that are commonly used with object + present participle complements. Note that most of these are verbs of sense perception:

catch	hear	see
discover	leave	smell
feel	notice	spot
find	observe	spy
get	overhear	watch
have	perceive	

13

Predicate Adjective Complements

This chapter is concerned with the complements that can follow **predicate adjectives**. Predicate adjectives are adjectives that can be used as the complements of **linking verbs**. For example:

Eva *is **tall***.
Eva *is **brilliant***.
Eva *seems **likable***.

Predicate adjectives have two features that are helpful in identifying them: they have **comparative** and **superlative forms**, *and* they can be preceded by the modifiers *very* or *quite*. (*Quite* works better than *very* with some predicate adjectives. For example, ***quite** horrified* sounds better than ***very** horrified*.)

There are two sets of comparative and superlative forms, dependent on the length of the adjective. One-syllable adjectives use the endings *-er* and *-est* to form the comparative and superlative. For example:

tall, taller, tallest

Multiple-syllable adjectives use *more* and *most* to form the comparative and superlative. For example:

brilliant, more brilliant, most brilliant
likable, more likable, most likable

(See Chapter 2 for a detailed discussion of comparative and superlative forms.)

At first glance, the use of the modifiers *very* and *quite* may not seem to be all that helpful because *very* and *quite* can be used with both adjectives and adverbs. However, the real advantage of *very* and *quite* is that they can never be used with verbs. Thus, we can use *very* and *quite* to reliably distinguish between predicate adjectives and verbs. This is significant because, as we will see, many predicate adjectives are derived from verbs and retain verb endings.

Many predicate adjectives are derived from the present and past participles of verbs (see Chapter 2). For example:

Derived from Present Participle	Derived from Past Participle
amusing	amused
disgusting	disgusted
frightening	frightened
tiring	tired
upsetting	upset

All of these derived predicate adjectives can be used with *very* and *quite*:

very amusing, *very* amused; *quite* amusing, *quite* amused
very disgusting, *very* disgusted; *quite* disgusting, *quite* disgusted
very frightening, *very* frightened; *quite* frightening, *quite* frightened
very tiring, *very* tired; *quite* tiring, *quite* tired
very upsetting, *very* upset; *quite* upsetting, *quite* upset

To see how useful *very* and *quite* can be, compare the two present participles in these examples:

The baby was *smiling*.
The baby was *amusing*.

The two present participles look the same, but they are not the same thing at all, as we can see when we use *very* and *quite* with them:

X The baby was **very** *smiling*.   X The baby was **quite** *smiling*.
   The baby was **very** *amusing*.   The baby was **quite** *amusing*.

The failure of *very* and *quite* with *smiling* shows us that *smiling* is not a predicate adjective. It is actually a verb; it is part of the progressive form of the verb *was smiling*. The success of *very* and *quite* with *amusing* tells us that *amusing* is a predicate adjective. It is the complement of the linking verb *was*.

Predicate adjectives are used as complements of two types of verbs. Most predicate adjectives, as we have seen, are the complements of **linking verbs**. The other source of predicate adjectives is a group of verbs that take **object + predicate adjective** complements (Chapter 12). Here are some examples of this latter type:

> We always *found* the staff very **helpful**.
> Please *keep* the hallways **clear**.
> The frost *had turned* the leaves bright **red**.
> We *found* the images quite **disturbing**.

Prepositional Phrase Complement

Many predicate adjectives (both complements of linking verbs and complements of verbs that take object + predicate adjective complements) are used with specific prepositions. The accepted pairing of a given predicate adjective with a preposition is largely unpredictable. As is true of verb + preposition combinations, these predicate adjective + preposition combinations are a considerable problem for nonnative speakers. The combinations have to be learned one-by-one, and often the meanings are unpredictable. Also as with verb + preposition combinations, the list of prepositions is limited. In fact, the list is nearly the same as the list of prepositions that are used with inseparable transitive phrasal verbs and with prepositions that follow noun phrase objects (see Chapter 10). The most common prepositions used with predicate adjectives are *about, at, from, of, on, to,* and *with.* Here are examples (using both types of predicate adjectives) of each preposition:

about
I am very *worried **about*** the election.
We believed him *knowledgeable **about*** the election.

at
He was always quite *alarmed **at*** having to speak in public.
Being nervous rendered him *hopeless **at*** public speaking.

from
He was quite *different **from*** what I thought he would be.
I always imagined the village *distant **from*** civilization.

of
He was quite *ashamed **of*** himself.
They supposed him *capable **of*** anything.

on
The team was very *dependent **on*** the captain.
They proclaimed themselves *set **on*** their course of action.

to
We are quite *accustomed **to*** it.
The lawyers considered their clients *responsible **to*** no one.

with
The teacher was quite *pleased **with*** their progress.
The teacher got *bored **with*** the students' poor responses.

Certain predicate adjectives even require a particular preposition or else we cannot use the predicate adjective at all. For example, if we use *intent* as a predicate adjective, it must be followed by *on:*

They are *intent **on*** finding a solution.

If we delete the *on* and its noun phrase object *finding a solution*, the result-ing sentence is ungrammatical:

X They are *intent.*

Some predicate adjective + preposition combinations are idiomatic. That is, the combination has a special, unpredictable meaning. For example:

I am *short of* time this afternoon.

Short of means to "be lacking." We can delete the *of* and its noun phrase object, but then we are left with a sentence that has a new meaning totally unrelated to the original meaning with *of:*

I am *short* this afternoon.

Here are examples of other obligatory predicate adjective + preposition units:

of
I am *conscious of* my obligations.
The kids are really *fond of* pizza.
We are *proud of* you.

on
The proposal is *based on* solid research.
He is completely *dependent on* his parents.
They are *set on* their plans.

to
I am *accustomed to* her face.
Their failure is totally *due to* their own mistakes.
We are completely *opposed to* the proposal.

with
His idea is not *compatible* **with** ours.
We were quite *taken* **with** their suggestions. (*taken with* = "impressed by")

Many adjectives that take prepositions will allow abstract nouns as objects in the prepositional phrases. (Abstract nouns are nouns such as *idea, answer, outcome,* and *plan.*) Any noun position that will allow abstract nouns will also allow gerunds, certain infinitives, and noun clauses. For example, *worry about* will allow an abstract noun:

We are very *worried about the idea.*

We can predict that *worry about* will allow gerund phrases (GP), *wh*-infinitives (infinitives that begin with words like *when, where, what*), and noun clauses (NC). For example:

We are very worried about *John's hacking cough.*
                          GP

We are very worried about *what to do.*
                          wh- infinitive

We are very worried about *what John told us.*
                          NC

That Clause Complement
Some predicate adjectives (PA) that are complements of linking verbs take *that* clause complements. For example:

I am *afraid that* you will have to come back later.
     PA   *that* clause

As is often the case with *that* clauses in post-verb positions, the word *that* may be (and often is) omitted from the beginning of the *that* clause.

Naturally, deleting the word *that* makes these clauses much more difficult for nonnative speakers to recognize. From this point on, related examples will show the word *that* in parentheses as a reminder that the word can be left out.

We were quite <u>*disappointed*</u> <u>*(that)* you were not able to come.</u>
              PA   *that* clause

Her parents were very <u>*pleased*</u> <u>*(that)* she did so well in her exams.</u>
                     PA   *that* clause

I'm <u>sorry</u> <u>*(that)* I'm late.</u>
      PA   *that* clause

Here are the most commonly used predicate adjectives that take *that* clause complements; as you can see, most of them express emotion:

afraid	astonished	happy	sad
alarmed	disappointed	hopeful	shocked
amazed	disturbed	horrified	sorry
amused	frightened	irritated	thankful
angry	glad	pleased	upset
annoyed	grateful	proud	

Dummy It *with* That *Clauses*

A large number of predicate adjectives can take *that* clauses as subjects. For example:

<u>*That* we did so badly</u> was <u>*unfortunate*.</u>
     that clause   PA

While this sentence is perfectly grammatical, few people would actually say it that way. Instead, we would move the *that* clause to a position after the predicate adjective and then use a "dummy" or "empty" *it* as a kind of placeholder for the subject. For example:

It was *unfortunate (that)* we did so badly.
   PA   *that* clause

A grammatical curiosity of sorts arises here. We can delete the word *that* from the *that* clause, but only after the *that* clause has been moved to a position after the verb. If we leave the *that* clause in the subject position, we cannot delete the word *that*:

X We did so badly was *unfortunate*.
   that clause   PA

Different predicate adjectives take different verb forms in the *that* clause. One group of verbs takes ordinary tenses; a second group takes the helping verb *would*; and a third group takes base-form subjunctives.

Dummy *It* with *That* Clauses That Use Regular Tense. A few predicate adjectives that refer to truth or knowledge take regular-tense *that* clauses. For example:

It is *clear (that)* we have a problem.
    PA   *that* clause

We can use any present, past, or future tense that is appropriate to the context:

It is *clear (that)* we **have** a problem.
It is *clear (that)* we **had** a problem.
It is *clear (that)* we **will have** a problem.

Here are some more examples with regular-tense *that* clauses:

It is *obvious (that)* there will be trouble.
It was *plain (that)* they had made a big mistake.
It is *possible (that)* we are totally wrong.

Here are the most commonly used predicate adjectives that take this type of *that* clause complement:

apparent	likely	unlikely
certain	obvious	untrue
clear	plain	well known
evident	possible	
implicit	true	

Dummy-*It That* Clauses That Use *Would*. A surprisingly large number of predicate adjectives that take dummy-*it that* clauses are used with the helping verb *would*. (Speakers of British English use *should* rather than *would*—a usage that is alien to most speakers of American English.) Here are some examples:

It is *unfortunate (that)* they **would** feel so unwelcome.
It was *strange (that)* he **would** take it that way.
It is *silly (that)* they **would** make such a big deal out of it.

The use of *would* is not absolutely obligatory with these verbs, but it is the normal usage.

Nearly all the predicate adjectives that take this complement type either express surprise or otherwise convey the speaker's (usually negative) emotional attitude about the information contained in the *that* clause.

Here are the most commonly used predicate adjectives that take this type of *that* clause complement:

awkward	fortunate	sad
curious	irrational	silly
disastrous	logical	strange
dreadful	odd	tragic
extraordinary	peculiar	unfortunate

In addition to the predicate adjectives just listed, this complement type uses two other groups of predicate adjectives derived from verbs. One group ends in *-able* or *-ible*. These endings are used to change abstract verbs into abstract predicate adjectives. For example:

Verb	Predicate Adjective
admire	admirable
commend	commendable
comprehend	comprehensible, incomprehensible
deplore	deplorable
justify	justifiable, unjustifiable
remark	remarkable
understand	understandable

Here are some examples that illustrate the use of these predicate adjectives derived from verbs:

It is *understandable (that)* her feelings **would** be hurt.
It is *deplorable (that)* they **would** get so upset over nothing.
It is *incomprehensible to me (that)* we **would** do nothing about it.

The second group is derived from the present-participle form of verbs. For example:

alarming	discouraging	perplexing
annoying	embarrassing	pleasing
depressing	frightening	shocking
disappointing	irritating	surprising

Here are some examples that illustrate the use of these predicate adjectives derived from present-participle verb forms:

It is *embarrassing (that)* we **would** be so badly misunderstood.
It is *shocking (that)* he **would** get himself into such a situation.
It was *discouraging (that)* the team **would** play so badly.

Dummy-*It That* Clauses That Use Subjunctive Base Forms. A few verbs that take a dummy-*it that* clause can use an uninflected base form in the *that* clause. This base form is a type of **subjunctive**. In this case, the subjunctive is used for commands or strongly stated desires. Here is an example:

It is *essential (that)* they **be** notified of the court's decision as soon as possible.

Because the verb *be* has a base form that is different from all of the present-tense forms, we know that this is a subjunctive (or else it would be *they* **are** *notified . . .*).

Here are some more examples:

It is *improper (that)* he **appoint** a close relative to such a high post.
It was *necessary (that)* you **be** personally involved.
It is *advisable (that)* she **stay** out of politics for a while.
It is *important (that)* the report **be** released as soon as possible.

Here are the most commonly used predicate adjectives that can take a subjunctive *that*-clause complement:

advisable	fitting	necessary
appropriate	imperative	obligatory
compulsory	important	preferable
crucial	impossible	proper
desirable	improper	vital
essential		

Infinitive Complement

Most predicate adjectives that express emotion can take infinitive complements (IP is the abbreviation for infinitive phrase). For example:

We are <u>happy</u> **to see** you.
      PA   IP

We are <u>ready</u> **to go**.
     PA   IP

Even predicate adjectives that follow objects can easily take infinitive-phrase complements. For example:

We *made* *them* *proud* **to be** members of the team.
        O   PA   IP

There are two different types of infinitive phrases, dependent on the relation of the subject of the sentence to the infinitive phrase. In the most common type of infinitive, the subject of the sentence carries over to also become the understood subject of the infinitive (as we would expect). For example:

Bob is *eager* **to start** as soon as possible.

We understand from this sentence that the person who is going to start as soon as possible is Bob.

In the less common type, the subject of the sentence is not the understood subject of the infinitive. For example:

Bob is *hard* **to reach** by telephone.

Bob is not trying to reach us by telephone; we are trying to reach him. Bob is not the understood subject of the infinitive *to reach*. In fact, Bob is the object of *to reach*.

Infinitives with Automatically Assigned Subjects

In this type of complement, the subject of the sentence is the understood subject of the infinitive unless something intervenes to tell us otherwise. For example:

Alice was *astonished* **to find** her ex-husband at the party.

We understand from this sentence that Alice is the person who found her ex-husband at the party, not some other person. Again, the subject of the sentence is automatically assigned to be the subject of the infinitive.

Here are some more examples of infinitive complements with understood subjects:

I am *willing **to answer*** all of your questions.
They are *likely **to be*** upset by what happened.
You are *welcome **to visit*** us anytime.

Here are examples of the same complement type, this time with the predicate adjective following an object:

The movie *made* me *eager **to take*** dancing lessons.
I would *like* the children *ready **to go*** to bed.
I *thought* myself *able **to start*** all over again.

Virtually all predicate adjectives that can take infinitive phrases belong to this type. The exceptions are listed in the next section.

Infinitives Without Automatically Assigned Subjects

In this much less common type of complement, the subject of the sentence is *not* the understood subject of the infinitive. For example:

Donald is very *unpleasant **to deal*** with.

Donald is not the subject of the infinitive verb *to deal with*. Donald is the object of the verb in the infinitive—the person everybody else has to deal with.
　　We can make the subject of the infinitive explicit by means of a *for* phrase (a prepositional phrase beginning with *for*). For example:

Donald is very unpleasant ***for his staff*** to deal with.

His staff is now the explicit subject of the infinitive *to deal with*.
　　When there is no expressed *for* phrase to serve as subject, the implied subject is an implied indefinite "everyone" or "everyone":

Donald is very unpleasant (***for everyone***) to deal with.

Here are some more examples in which the subject of the sentence is not the subject of the infinitive:

Linda is *easy **to be*** around.
(= It is easy ***for everyone*** to be around Linda.)
Rupert is *impossible **to get*** an appointment with.
(= It is impossible ***for anyone*** to get an appointment with Rupert.)
Juan is *hard **to get*** to know.
(= It is hard ***for anyone*** to get to know Juan.)
Alice is *pleasant **to talk*** to.
(= It is pleasant ***for everyone*** to talk to Alice.)

Here is a list of the more commonly used predicate adjectives that take infinitives without automatically assigned subjects:

awkward	hard	tough
convenient	impossible	tricky
difficult	nice	unpleasant
easy	pleasant	

Sometimes only context tells us whether an infinitive has an assigned subject. For example:

Assigned subject: We are ready to eat lunch.
    (= We are the ones eating the lunch.)
Unassigned subject: Lunch is ready to eat.
    (= Somebody is going to eat the lunch—*lunch* is not the subject of the verb *eat*; *lunch* is the object of *eat*.)

14

Adverbs

This chapter discusses how adverbs are formed at the word level, at the phrase level, and at the clause level. Chapter 15 describes how these different kinds of adverbs are used.

Word-Level Adverbs

There are three types of adverbs at the word level: simple adverbs, compound adverbs, and adverbs derived from other parts of speech. **Simple adverbs** are uncompounded words whose primary meaning is adverbial. **Compound adverbs** are made up of two or more freestanding words, and **derived adverbs** are other parts of speech that have been changed into adverbs by an ending (usually -*ly*—for example, *quick–quickly*). While most of the top fifty adverbs used are simple, uncompounded words (such as *then* and *now*) whose primary meaning is adverbial, more and more of the next most common adverbs are compounds and -*ly* adverbs derived from adjectives. In fact, if we were to look at a list of the one thousand most common adverbs, we would see that 95 percent of them are -*ly* adverbs.

Adverbs Derived from Adjectives by Adding an -ly *Suffix*

Adverbs as a part of speech are peculiar in that the vast majority actually come from another part of speech, as just noted. Most adverbs are formed from adjectives by adding an -*ly* suffix. Here are some examples:

Adjective	Adverb
abrupt	abruptly
firm	firmly
honest	honestly
quick	quickly
sad	sadly
slow	slowly
soft	softly

Even adjectives formed from the **present participle** and **past participle** of verbs can be changed to adverbs by adding -*ly*. For example:

PRESENT PARTICIPLE

Adjective	Adverb
amusing	amusingly
frightening	frighteningly
interesting	interestingly
laughing	laughingly
pleasing	pleasingly

PAST PARTICIPLE

Adjective	Adverb
assured	assuredly
disgusted	disgustedly
learned	learnedly
marked	markedly
reported	reportedly

Given that so many adjectives can be turned into adverbs by adding -*ly*, it is easy to conclude that *all* adjectives can be made into adverbs. Not quite. Here are some groups of adjectives that have no corresponding -*ly* adverb forms:

NATIONALITY

American	X	Americanly
Chinese	X	Chinesely
French	X	Frenchly

DIMENSION

big	X	bigly
fat	X	fatly
tall	X	tally

AGE

old	X	old<u>ly</u>
teenage	X	teenage<u>ly</u>
young	X	young<u>ly</u>

The spelling of -*ly* adverbs is largely what we would expect when we add a suffix beginning with a consonant to any word. For example, adjectives ending in a final silent *e* retain the *e*:

Adjective	Adverb
accurate	accurate<u>ly</u>
complete	complete<u>ly</u>
entire	entire<u>ly</u>
loose	loose<u>ly</u>
rare	rare<u>ly</u>
sparse	sparse<u>ly</u>

Also as we would expect, for adjectives that end in a consonant + *y*, we change the *y* to *i* before the -*ly* suffix:

Adjective	Adverb
hardy	hard<u>ily</u>
merry	merr<u>ily</u>
mighty	might<u>ily</u>
sleepy	sleep<u>ily</u>

There are only a few exceptional spellings for -*ly* adverbs. Here are familiar examples:

Adjective	Adverb
due	duly
gay	gaily
true	truly

(*Truly* is one of the most commonly misspelled words in English.)

Adverbs Derived from Adjectives Without an -ly Suffix

Historically, certain adverbs (nearly all of which are one syllable) have been derived from adjectives without using the -*ly* suffix. Here are examples of the more common ones along with how they are used in a typical sentence:

fast	We drove really *fast*.
fine	It works *fine*.
hard	He hit the ball *hard*.
high	We flew *high* over the desert.
late	We arrived *late*.
long	Did you have to wait *long*?
loud	Their voices sounded *loud*.
sharp	We turned *sharp*.
short	She had her hair cut *short*.
slow	Please drive *slow*.
soon	Dawn came all too *soon*.
tight	Their eyes were shut *tight*.

Over time, many of these adverbs have also developed forms with -*ly*. So, for example, we can say either of the following:

The day seemed to pass terribly *slow*.
The day seemed to pass terribly *slowly*.

In almost all cases in which there are competing adverb forms derived from adjectives—one form *with* the *-ly* and one *without* the *-ly*—the historically older form is steadily losing ground to the newer, *-ly* form. Every now and then, for example, there are letters to the editors of newspapers complaining about the poor grammar of highway signs that say "Drive Slow." The writers point out with great certainty (but with little historical knowledge) that *slow* is an adjective and that the sign should use the adverb *slowly*:

Drive **Slowly**

Comparative and Superlative Forms of Adverbs

As with adjectives, adverbs form their comparative and superlative constructions in one of two fundamentally different ways: by adding an *-er* and *-est* ending, *or* by using the helping words *more* and *most*. For example:

-er/-est
George finished *faster* than Frank.
George finished the *fastest* of all the runners in his age-group.

more/most
George moved *more* quickly than Frank.
George finished the *most* quickly of all the runners in his age-group.

However, as we will see, the rules that govern which adverbs use the *-er/-est* pattern and which use the *more/most* pattern are completely different from the rules that govern use of *-er/-est* and *more/most* in adjectives.

In addition to these two standard patterns, there is a small minority of adverbs that form the comparative and superlative forms in an irregular way. For example, the base-form adverb *well* has the comparative form *better* and the superlative form *best*:

Base form:	Sally did *well*.
Comparative:	Sally did *better* than I did.
Superlative:	Sally did the *best* of any of us.

Adverbs That Form Their Comparatives and Superlatives with -er and -est Suffixes. Only simple, uncompounded adverbs can use the -er/-est endings. For example:

high
The ball went *higher* and *higher*.
John's kite went the *highest* of anyone's.

loud
The bells rang *louder* as we came nearer.
The old church bell rang the *loudest* of all.

sharp
I answered *sharper* than I had intended.
His criticisms stung the *sharpest* of all.

tight
She smiled *tighter* and *tighter*.
She smiled the *tightest* at Bill's stupid comments.

Adverbs That Form Their Comparatives and Superlatives with *More* and *Most*. Adverbs that are formed from adjectives by adding the -ly suffix must use *more* and *most*. For example:

amusingly
She spoke *more* amusingly than ever.
She spoke the *most* amusingly of all the presenters.

brightly
The light shone *more* brightly as the room grew darker.
The stars shone the *brightest* that dark night.

charmingly
They laughed *more* charmingly than ever.
They laughed the *most* charmingly about their own mistakes.

eagerly

I spoke **more** *eagerly*.

I spoke the **most** *eagerly* on the topics I knew most about.

Adverbs with Irregular Comparative and Superlative Forms. A few adverbs have historically irregular forms. Here are examples:

Base Form	Comparative	Superlative
badly	worse	worst
far	farther	farthest
far	further	furthest
little	less	least
much	more	most
well	better	best

Farther and *farthest* refer to physical distance. For example:

His golf ball went *farther* than mine did.
His shot went the *farthest* from the tee.

Further and *furthest* are used in all other meanings. For example:

His comments on the incident went *further* than theirs.
His comments went the *furthest* of anybody's in explaining what happened.

Adverbial Phrases

There are two types of phrases that play the role of adverbs: **adverb prepositional phrases** and **adverbial infinitive phrases**.

Adverbial prepositional phrase:	Sally met her friends *after work*.
Adverbial infinitive phrase:	Sally met her friends *to plan the reception*.

Adverbial Prepositional Phrases

Prepositional phrases consist of prepositions followed by noun-phrase objects. The noun-phrase objects are nouns (with or without modifiers), pronouns, gerunds, or noun clauses. Here are examples of adverbial prepositional phrases with various types of objects; the entire prepositional phrase is in italics, and the object is in bold:

Noun phrase:	We had dinner *at **that new restaurant on Eighth Street**.*
Pronoun:	There is a drugstore *by **us**.*
Gerund:	We finished on time only *by **everyone's working overtime**.*
Noun clause:	They have an apartment *near **where we live**.*

Adverbial Infinitive Phrases

An infinitive phrase consists of the **infinitive** form of the verb together with that verb's complements and/or modifiers (if any). Here are some examples of infinitive phrases used as adverbs; the entire infinitive phrase is in italics, and the infinitive verb itself is in bold:

We went to the post office *to **get** some stamps.*
You need a prescription *to **get** your medicine at the drugstore.*
You must practice hard *to **win**.*
We turned off the water *to **fix** a leak in a pipe.*

We can assign a specific subject to the infinitive verb by using a prepositional phrase beginning with *for* (also called a ***for* phrase**). For example:

We turned off the water *for **the plumber** to fix a leak in the pipe.*

If we do not use a *for* prhase as the explicit subject, there is an automatically assigned subject. The subject of the main verb carries over as the understood subject of the infinitive. For example:

The children went to the zoo *to **see** the new panda.*

Here the understood subject of the infinitive *to see* is *children*, the subject of the main verb *went*. (Chapter 6 offers a detailed discussion of how subjects are assigned to infinitive phrases used as nouns. All of that discussion would also apply to infinitives used as adverbs.)

We can paraphrase all infinitives used as adverbs with the words *in order*. Here is the *in order* paraphrase applied to the preceding example sentences:

We went to the post office **in order** *to get some stamps.*
You need a prescription **in order** *to get your medicine at the drugstore.*
You must practice hard **in order** *to win.*
We turned off the water **in order** *to fix a leak in a pipe.*

We can even combine the *in order* paraphrase with the *for* phrase. For example:

We turned off the water **in order** *for the plumber to fix a leak in the pipe.*

Note: We cannot use the *in order* paraphrase with infinitives used as adjectives or nouns.

Adverb Clauses

Clauses are grammatical constructions that contain both a subject and a **finite verb**. A finite verb is a verb form (present or past tense) that can enter into a subject-verb relationship with the subject. Adverb clauses (like adjective clauses and noun clauses) are **dependent clauses**—clauses that cannot stand alone as independent sentences. Dependent clauses must always be attached to at least one **independent clause**.

Structure of Adverb Clauses

Compared with adjective and noun clauses, adverb clauses have a simple and uniform structure: an introductory subordinating conjunction followed by a complete sentence. (Adverb clauses, on the other hand, are more difficult in that there are numerous subordinating conjunctions, versus the handful of words that can begin adjective and noun clauses.) In the following examples, the subordinating conjunctions are in bold, and the complete adverb clauses are in italics:

> I'll give them a call **when** *I get a chance.*
> Go get a cup of coffee **while** *I am finishing up here.*
> I went home **because** *I wasn't feeling well.*
> We decided to go ahead, **although** *we certainly had our doubts about it.*
> We could go to a movie **unless** *you would rather stay home.*
> The children enjoyed themselves **everywhere** *we went.*
> He will do it **if** *he can.*

There is also a group of compound subordinating conjunctions, many ending in *that* or *as.* For example:

> We will meet our goals **assuming that** *our sales hold up.*
> We should make plans **in the event that** *all the flights are canceled.*
> I'll join you for dinner **provided that** *I can get done in time.*
> Let's finish up here **so that** *we will have some time to talk later.*
> She has worked here **as long as** *I have known her.*
> We will eat **as soon as** *I can set the table.*

Some compound subordinating conjunctions are long fixed phrases. For example:

> I watched an old movie **despite the fact that** *I had a lot of work to do.*
> The game was delayed **due to the fact that** *the team bus broke down.*
> We will have to wait **until such time as** *all of our calendars are free.*

Reduced Adverb Clauses

Reduced adverb clauses are so-called because they are not true clauses. They have neither subjects nor finite verbs. There are two types of reduced adverb clauses. One type uses **past-participle** verb forms, and the other type uses **present-participle** verb forms. In the examples that follow, the participles are in bold, and the entire reduced adverb clauses are in italics:

> *Although not yet formally **admitted** to college,* she has already taken many courses.

The preceding sentence contains the past-participle verb form. The following example is of a reduced adverb clause using the **present-participle** verb form:

> *Though **knowing** no Italian,* we still had a great time in Rome.

It is easy to see the complete clauses underlying the reduced adverb clauses:

> *Although she is not yet formally admitted to college,* she has already taken many courses.
> *Though we know no Italian,* we still had a great time in Rome.

As you can see from the examples, the subject of the main clause automatically becomes the understood subject of the reduced adverb clause.

Here is an example in which it is harder to see what the subject of the reduced adverb clause is:

> *When **playing** tennis,* be sure to check for blisters.

What makes this sentence hard to analyze is that the subject in the main clause is itself an understood *you* in an **imperative sentence** (a command). The understood *you* in the main clause then becomes the understood subject in the reduced adverb clause. For example:

> When **(you are)** playing *tennis,* **(you)** be sure to check for blisters.

In the examples so far, all the reduced adverb clauses have been moved from the (normal) sentence-final adverb position to a sentence-initial position—to a position in front of the main clause. Though most of the time, reduced adverb clauses are indeed sentence-initial, there is no grammatical requirement that they be moved. It is perfectly grammatical for them to remain in their original sentence-final position. For example:

*When **answering** the phone*, be sure to give your name and title.
Be sure to give your name and title *when **answering** the phone*.

15

Using Adverbs

This chapter addresses a variety of topics relating to how we use adverbs, paying particular attention to punctuation problems. Eight major topics are discussed: movement and punctuation of adverbs, adverb classification, the order of adverbs at the ends of sentences, the meaning of sentence-initial adverbs, conditional clauses, concession clauses, split infinitives, and misplaced and squinting adverb modifiers.

The term *adverb* can be used both narrowly to refer to single-word adverbs and broadly to refer to any grammatical unit (word, phrase, or clause) that functions as an adverb. We use the term in its broad sense here to include all types of adverbs, unless specified otherwise. For example, in some sections, you will see references to specific parts of speech such as "single-word adverb," "adverb phrase," and "adverb clause."

Adverbs are conventionally defined as grammatical elements (words, phrases, or clauses) that "modify verbs, adjectives, and other adverbs." The use of adverbs to modify adjectives and other adverbs is limited to a handful of words (*quite* and *very* being the most common) that serve to emphasize the meaning of an adjective or adverb. In the following examples, modifying adverbs are in bold, and the adjectives or adverbs being modified are in italics:

Adverbs Modifying Adjectives
a **completely** *false* idea
unusually *good* results
very *accurate* guess
quite *dangerous* weapons

Adverbs modifying other adverbs
They answer their mail **very** *promptly.*
Harvard fought **rather** *fiercely.*
The meeting ended **quite** *abruptly.*

Ninety-nine percent of the time, adverbs are used to modify verbs, so the remainder of this discussion focuses exclusively on adverbs that modify verbs. (We also exclude from discussion adverbs that are used as **complements** of verbs. See Chapters 11 and 12).

Movement and Punctuation of Adverbs That Modify Verbs

There are three different forms of adverbs: **single-word adverbs**, **adverb phrases**, and **adverb clauses**. All of these forms of adverbs are used to modify verbs. Adverbs that modify verbs all come from the same place in the sentence. They are the final component of the verb phrase, following the verb and its complement, as shown in the following diagram:

Sentence

| Subject Noun Phrase | Verb Phrase | Verb Complement | (Optional Adverbs) |

Optional adverbs can be single, word-level adverbs; adverb prepositional phrases or adverb infinitive phrases; or adverb clauses. For example:

	Subject Noun Phrase	Verb	Complement	Adverb
Word-level adverb:	John	met	Mary	*recently.*
Adverb prepositional phrase:	John	met	Mary	*on the weekend.*
Adverb infinitive phrase:	John	met	Mary	*to borrow her computer.*
Adverb clause:	John	met	Mary	*when he was on campus.*

Single-word adverbs and adverb phrases in their normal position at ends of sentences are never set off with commas. In American English, the only type of sentence-final adverb clause that is ever set off with commas is a somewhat different kind of adverb clause that begins with *although*, *even though*, or *though* (see "Concession Clauses" later in this chapter). In British English, however, it is not unusual to find final adverb clauses set off with commas for emphasis. For example:

We ended up rejecting the offer, *because it was too low.*

In American English, the punctuation of the preceding sentence would be considered marginal, and incorrect by many grammarians.

One of the defining characteristics of adverbs that modify the verb is that they are movable. All of the other grammatical components (including the other uses of adverbs) are fixed in place. Only adverbs that modify verbs can be shifted forward to other positions in the sentence. For example:

Single-word adverb
Original: John met Mary *recently.*
Shifted: *Recently* John met Mary.
Shifted: John *recently* met Mary.

Adverb prepositional phrase
Original: John met Mary *on the weekend.*
Shifted: *On the weekend* John met Mary.

Adverb infinitive phrase
Original: John met Mary *to find out what was going on at school.*
Shifted: *To find out what was going on at school,* John met Mary.

Adverb clause
Original: John saw Mary *when he was on campus.*
Shifted: *When he was on campus,* John saw Mary.

When we shift adverbs from their original position to the beginning of a sentence, we do have some limited choice about comma punctuation. The general rule is that individual adverbs and short adverb phrases are not set off with commas. How long does an introductory adverb prepositional phrase have to be before we use a comma? Many composition books suggest that any introductory prepositional phrase that is longer than five words or that itself contains a prepositional phrase should be set off with commas. For example:

No comma: *After the ball* Cinderella's coach turned into a pumpkin.

Comma: *Just after the clock had struck midnight,* Cinderella's coach turned into a pumpkin.

Comma: *After the ball at the palace,* Cinderella's coach turned into a pumpkin.

The one clear-cut rule is that adverb clauses shifted to the front of the sentence *must* be set off with commas. For example:

No comma: Cinderella's coach turned into a pumpkin *when the clock struck midnight.*

Comma: *When the clock struck midnight,* Cinderella's coach turned into a pumpkin.

Many editors consider the failure to set off sentence-initial adverb clauses with commas a hanging offense!

Adverbs Classified by Meaning

Adverbs fall into four broad categories of meaning, as determined by the kind of adverb question they answer. The four adverb questions are *when, where, why,* and *how:*

Adverb Question	Adverb Category
When:	Adverbs of time
Where:	Adverbs of place
Why:	Adverbs of reason
How:	Adverbs of manner

The following discussion of each of the four adverb categories features examples of the three different types of adverbs (word-level, phrase, and clause) that answer each question word (though not all types of adverbs are used in all categories).

The word-level type of adverb includes both single-word adverbs and short adverb expressions. Note that these expressions are not adverb phrases because they do not contain either prepositions or verbs.

Most of the adverb phrases are prepositional phrases. However, in the category of adverbs of reason, we can also use infinitive phrases.

There can be severe restrictions on the subordinating conjunctions that are used with particular categories of adverbs. For example, the only subordinating conjunctions that can be used as adverbs of frequency are *when* and *whenever*. Accordingly, there is only one example of each given for that category.

After the examples of words, phrases, and clauses, you'll find a list of the most common subordinating conjunctions that are used with each category of adverb.

Adverbs of Time

Adverbs of time fall into three groups: **point in time**, **frequency**, and **duration**. There are three time-word questions. *When* is used (ambiguously) for either point-in-time or frequency adverbs. *How often* is used for frequency adverbs. *How long* is used for duration adverbs. For example:

Point in time: *When* were you there?

Word/ Expression	Prepositional Phrase	Clause
Tuesday.	On the third of April.	When John gave his talk.
Yesterday.	At Christmastime.	Before we went on vacation.
Just last week.	In August.	Just after the strike was settled.

Conjunctive adverbs commonly used with point in time are *after, before, just after, just before, since, until,* and *while.*

Frequency: *When* do you go there?

How often do you go there?

Word/Expression	Prepositional Phrase	Clause
Tuesdays.	On the weekends.	When we are in the neighborhood.
Frequently.	Throughout July.	
Every now and then.	About once a week.	Whenever we get a chance.

Conjunctive adverbs commonly used with frequency are *when* and *whenever.*

Duration: *How long* are you staying there?

Word/Expression	Prepositional Phrase	Clause
All day Tuesday.	During the week.	While I am working in New York.
A week.	For the whole month.	
Several months.	Until next Thursday.	Until I get the job finished.
		As long as I am needed.

Conjunctive adverbs commonly used with duration are *as long as, until,* and *while.*

Adverbs of Place

Adverbs of place have two different meanings. One meaning is **position**. The other meaning is **direction**—that is, to some place. The question word *where* is (ambiguously) used for both meanings. For example:

Position: *Where* were you?

Word/ Expression	Prepositional Phrase	Clause
Here.	At the office.	Where I could use my cell phone.
Next door.	On the road.	
Outside.	In the kitchen.	Everywhere you could imagine.
		Somewhere where it was quiet.

Conjunctive adverbs commonly used with position are *everyplace, everywhere, someplace, somewhere, where,* and *wherever.*

Direction: *Where* did you go (to)?

Word/ Expression	Prepositional Phrase	Clause
There.	To the office.	Someplace where I could rest.
Back home.	Onto the road.	Where I could use my cell phone.
Out.	Into the kitchen.	Wherever I could find some quiet.

Conjunctive adverbs commonly used with direction are *everyplace, everywhere, someplace, somewhere, where,* and *wherever.*

Adverbs of Reason

Adverbs of reason also have two different meanings. One meaning is **cause**; the other meaning is **goal**. To see the difference between the two meanings, compare the following sentences:

Cause: We did it *because we had to.*
Goal: We did it *in order to make some extra money.*

The question word *why* is used (ambiguously) for both cause and goal. For example:

Cause: *Why* did they do it?

Word/Expression	Prepositional Phrase	Clause
(None commonly used)	For appropriate reasons. From necessity. Out of a sense of duty.	Because they had to. As it was part of their job. Since their boss asked them to do it.

Conjunctive adverbs commonly used with cause are *as, because, inasmuch as,* and *since.*

Goal: *Why* did they do it?

Prepositional Phrase	Infinitive Phrase	Clause
For the money.	To get promoted. To achieve success. To please their families.	So that they could finish early. Because it would be profitable. As it was in their interest to do so.

Conjunctive adverbs commonly used with goal are *as, because, inasmuch as,* and *so that.*

Adverbs of Manner

Adverbs of manner also have two different meanings. One meaning is **instrument**; the other meaning is **style**. To see the difference between the two meanings, compare the adverb prepositional phrases in the following sentences:

Instrument:	He opened the door *with a key.*
Style:	He opened the door *with a big smile.*

The question word *how* is used (ambiguously) for both instrument and style meanings. For example:

Instrument:	*How* did they do it?
Prepositional phrase:	With reinforcing rods.
	By a new technique.
	Through computer simulation.
Style:	*How* did they do it?

Word/ expression	Prepositional phrase	Clause
Gracefully.	With time to spare.	As well as anyone could do it.
Clumsily.	Without complaint.	As if their lives depended on it.
Alone.	By good teamwork.	As though it were the most important project in the world.

Conjunctive adverbs commonly used with style are *as, as if, as though,* and *as well as.*

Order of Adverbs at the Ends of Sentences

In general, the four categories of adverbs just described are used in the following left-to-right order when there is more than one modifying adverb at the end of a sentence: manner, place, time, reason.

For example:

Ralph worked <u>hard</u> <u>at his desk</u> <u>all afternoon</u> <u>so he could finish by five.</u>
    manner place   time   reason

As you can see from this example, it is immaterial what form the adverbs actually take: individual word, phrase, or clause. Here are several more examples:

	Manner	Place	Time	Reason
I bought some sandwiches		at the grocery	this morning	for lunch
You need to practice	seriously		every day	to get any any better
The plane circled the field	with its engine roaring		all afternoon	
It rained	heavily	in the mountains	during the night	due to a warm front
I found an apartment for Anne	by advertising	in the paper	Sunday	
The pipe started leaking	badly	under the sink	this morning	

The very fact that there is a largely predictable left-to-right order for adverbs means that none of them is singled out for special emphasis. However, we often want to single out one particular adverb. The most common way to give special emphasis is to move the adverb out of the normal position, usually by shifting it to the front of the sentence. For example, here is a sentence with the adverbs in the normal order:

The kids worked <u>quietly</u> <u>at home</u> <u>all evening</u> <u>to finish their paper.</u>
                manner   place   time   reason

Manner emphasis:	*Quietly,* the kinds worked at home all evening to finish their paper.
Place emphasis:	*At home,* the kids worked quietly all evening to finish their paper.
Time emphasis:	*All evening,* the kids worked quietly at home to finish their paper.
Reason emphasis:	*To finish their paper,* the kids worked quietly at home.

Sentence-Initial Adverbs

Some adverbs that are commonly used at the beginning of sentences do not seem to originate from a sentence-final position because none of them can answer **manner, place, time,** or **reason** questions. These sentence-initial adverbs fall into three groups, based on meaning: **possibility, presumption,** and **desirability.** Here is an example from each group:

Possibility:	*Usually,* we go to the beach over the Fourth of July.
Presumption:	*Obviously,* they were not ready to go.
Desirability:	*Hopefully,* they will do better next time.

One of the distinctive features of these sentence-initial adverbs is that most of them convey the feeling that the speaker is somehow stepping outside the sentence to comment on the likelihood of the action's taking place or to pass judgment on what the sentence is saying. Many of the adverbs can even be paraphrased as self-contained clauses. Here is an example:

	Usually, we go to the beach over the Fourth of July.
Clause:	*It is usually the case that* we go to the beach over the Fourth of July.
	Obviously, they were not ready to go.
Clause:	*It is obvious that* they were not ready to go.
	Hopefully, they will do better next time.
Clause:	*We hope that* they will do better next time.

Possibility

Adverbs in the possibility group are by far the most commonly used type of initial adverb. One study found that more than 50 percent of initial adverbs belonged to this group. The most commonly used possibility adverbs are the following: *certainly, generally, maybe, perhaps, surely, typically, usually.*

As you can see, the adverbs range in meaning from high possibility (*certainly*) to low possibility (*occasionally*). Here are example sentences:

Generally, I am able to reboot my computer without any problem.
Maybe this is not such a good idea.
Surely you know what I mean.
Typically, we have very hot summers here.

Presumption

Adverbs of presumption are used to assert the speaker's confidence that the information contained in the rest of the sentence is valid. The most commonly used presumption adverbs are *clearly, evidently, obviously,* and *of course.* Here are some examples:

Clearly, the salesman did not know what he was talking about.
Obviously that is not what we wanted to happen.
Of course, it may not work out that way at all.
Evidently he had something else in mind.

Desirability

Adverbs in the desirability group are used to express the speaker's attitude (both positive and negative) toward the events mentioned in the sentence. The most commonly used adverbs are *(un)fortunately, hopefully, luckily,* and *regrettably.* Here are some examples:

Fortunately, I had a change of clothing in my car.
Hopefully, they will reconsider their hasty decision.
Luckily, we knew just what to do in such an emergency.
Regrettably, the board turned down your proposal.

Notice that adverbs that belong to this class are usually set off with commas.

Conditional Clauses

Conditional clauses are a group of adverb clauses that do not fit into the time, place, reason, and manner classification because they do not answer any adverb question. Also in contrast to time, place, reason, and manner adverbs, there are no word-level or phrase-level conditional adverbs that correspond to the clause-level conditional adverbs (subordinating conjunctions).

The commonly used subordinating conjunctions for conditional clauses are *as long as, assuming that, if, in case, in the event that, on condition that, provided that, so long as,* and *unless.* In the following examples, subordinating conjunctions are in bold and the entire conditional clause is in italics.

> We will order out **as long as** *it is OK with everybody.*
> We are going to the play tonight **assuming that** *we can get tickets.*
> We will take our jackets **in case** *it rains.*
> The game will be rescheduled for Saturday **in the event that** *the field is unavailable.*
> We agree **on condition that** *everybody else does too.*
> The company is interested in the deal **provided that** *the terms are financially viable.*
> We will go there **so long as** *our friends can come too.*

As is possible with all other adverb clauses, we can shift the conditional clause to the beginning of the sentence:

> **As long as** *it is OK with everybody,* we will order out.
> **Assuming that** *we can get tickets,* we are going to the play tonight.
> **In case** *it rains,* we will take our jackets.
> **In the event that** *the field is unavailable,* the game will be rescheduled for Saturday.
> **On condition that** *everybody else does too,* we agree.
> **Provided that** *the terms are financially viable,* the company is interested in the deal.
> **So long as** *our friends can come too,* we will go there.

Notice that when the conditional adverb clause follows the main clause, no comma is used; that's because the clause is in its normal position. However, when the conditional clause has been shifted to the front of the sentence, it is set off from the main clause by a comma. This use of the comma is obligatory.

In all of these examples, the conditional clause states a requirement that must be met as a condition for performing the action stated in the main clause. That, of course, is why this type of clause is called a **conditional** clause.

Two subordinating conjunctions—*unless* and *if*—function somewhat differently from the other subordinating conjunctions in conditional clauses.

Unless *Clauses*

The subordinating conjunction *unless* signals essentially a negative condition. For example:

Unless you eat your spinach, you can't have dessert.

This sentence is essentially saying the same thing as a negative *if* clause. For example:

*If you **don't** eat your spinach*, you can't have dessert.

Here are some more examples of *unless* clauses:

Unless we get some decent weather, we can't have a picnic.
Unless I lose some weight, I won't fit into my bathing suit.
Unless the tide is in, we can't sail across to the island.

While an *unless* clause is often associated with a negative main clause, it is not necessary that the main clause be negative. For example:

Unless I miss my guess, our plane will take off on time.
Unless the package weighs less than a pound, it will have to go by
surface mail.
Unless we are out of flour, we will make a cake.

If *Clauses*

Among all the conditional clauses, clauses beginning with *if* have by far the most complexity for users. *If* clauses are used in making three different kinds of statements: **factual**, **conditional**, and **hypothetical**.

Factual *If* Clauses. *If* clauses can be used for factual statements and generalizations. Here are some examples:

Factual statement:	*If you mix red and white*, you will get pink.
	Water freezes *if the temperature drops below 32 degrees.*
Generalization:	*If I catch a cold*, I always get a sore throat.
	If it rains, the roof leaks.

The key to recognizing this use of *if* clauses is to see whether you can replace *if* with *when* or *whenever.* In each of these examples, this substitution is perfectly natural:

Factual statement:	*If you mix red and white*, you will get pink.
	When *you mix red and white*, you will get pink.
	Water freezes *if the temperature drops below 32 degrees.*
	Water freezes **whenever** *the temperature drops below 32 degrees.*
Generalization:	*If I catch a cold*, I always get a sore throat.
	Whenever *I catch a cold*, I always get a sore throat.
	If it rains, the roof leaks.
	Whenever *it rains*, the roof leaks.

As you may have noticed from the examples, we rarely use *then* with factual *if* clauses. That's because *then* implies a specific point in time, a meaning that is incompatible with the basic time-less meaning of the factual *if* clause.

Conditional *If* Clauses. The conditional *if* clause represents the classic conditional statement expressed as follows:

> *If* A, *(then)* B.

Here is an example:

> *If I have some time, **(then)** I will stop by.*

This conditional *if* statement is not a generalization about what will happen whenever the speaker may have some time. It is a statement about the speaker's present intention to carry out a specific action within a limited time frame. Unlike the situation with factual *if* clauses, there is absolutely no presumption in conditional *if* clauses that the conditions are going to be met. Here are some more examples:

> *If we have enough money, **(then)** we will take a trip to Greece.*
> *If I can, **(then)** I will get tickets on the earlier flight.*
> *If you eat your vegetables, **(then)** you can have some dessert.*

We often use conditional *if* statements for giving advice:

> *If you're cold, **(then)** turn up the heat.*
> *If you can't get tuna, **(then)** get halibut instead.*
> *If you are getting tired, **(then)** take a break.*

When the main clause comes first, we usually do not use *then*. Compare the two versions of the following sentence:

> *If you are going to be late, **(then)** give us a call.*
> Give us a call **if you are going to be late.**

We can also use the past tense in the *if* clause along with various possible tenses in the main clause. For example:

If Jack got an A, *(then)* he passes the course.
                 (then) he passed the course.
                 (then) he will pass the course.
                 (then) he will have passed the course.
                 (then) he would pass the course.

Even though these sentences contain a past tense in the *if* clause, they are not hypothetical statements. They are actually statements of fact, only the speaker doesn't know whether the "fact" is true. The sentence is saying that if it is a fact that Jack got an A, then it is also a fact that he will pass the course. (The hypothetical *if* clauses outlined in the section that follows reflect statements that we know are not true.)

Another use of the past tense in conditional *if* clauses is for polite distancing. For example, compare the following two sentences:

Present tense: *If you do that*, they will be offended.
Past tense: *If you did that*, they would be offended.

These two sentences mean the same thing. The difference is that the use of the past tense softens the tone of what the speaker is saying. In conversational settings, this use of the past tense is common in conditional *if* clauses. Here are some more examples of past-tense *if* clauses:

If you really cared, you would not make these unnecessary mistakes.
If we simplified the procedure, we could make it much easier to use.
If you took I-5, you could avoid a lot of traffic.
If we didn't spend so much on advertising, we would be able to improve quality control.
If you didn't stay up so late, you would get more done in the morning.

Hypothetical *If* Clauses. Hypothetical *if* statements are past-tense or past-perfect statements that refer to hypothetical alternatives to present or past realities.

Past *tense*. A common use of the past-tense hypothetical *if* clause is to talk about unrealized possibilities. For example:

If I had the manual, I could fix the problem.

We know from the use of the past tense, *had*, in the *if* clause that the speaker does not actually have the manual. This use of the past tense does not signal past time because historically it comes from a present-tense **subjunctive**. Typically, the verb in the main clause will also be a subjunctive modal, usually *could* or *would*. Here are some more examples:

If I had the time, I would visit Aunt Jane.
If we were at the office now, we would easily get that information.
If you didn't eat so much, you could lose some weight.

Another common use of the past tense with hypothetical *if* clauses is to offer advice. For example:

If I were Susan, I wouldn't try to drive on those icy roads.

This construction is hypothetical in the sense that the speaker knows that he is not Susan. Here are some more examples of this common construction:

If I were you, I would stay at home.
If I were you, I would assume the worst.
If I were you, I would not order the raw tuna at that restaurant.

Past perfect. We use past-perfect hypothetical *if* clauses to talk about things in the past that could have been different. For example:

If I had had my passport with me, I would have gone to London.

The clear implication of this sentence is that the speaker did not have the passport and thus could not go to London. Here are some more examples of hypothetical *if* clauses in the past perfect:

If the movie had ended earlier, we would not have missed dinner.
If we had been smarter, we would have taken their offer.
If I had known then what I know now, I would have done things very
    differently.

Concession Clauses

Concession clauses are another group of adverb clauses that, like conditional clauses, do not fit into the time, place, reason, and manner classification because they do not answer any adverb question. Also in contrast to time, place, reason, and manner adverbs, there are no concession word-level or phrase-level adverbs that correspond to the clause-level adverbs of concession (subordinating conjunctions).

There are only three subordinating conjunctions that introduce concession clauses: *although, even though,* and *though.* Here is an example of each:

I went along with his plan, **although** *it was against my better judgment.*
We decided to go for a walk, **even though** *it was getting late.*
He was still gaining weight, **though** *he said he ate only carrot sticks.*

Notice that concession clauses in their normal adverb position at the end of the sentence are still set off from the rest of the sentence with a comma. This use of the comma is unique among adverb clauses. The convention for using a comma with *although, even though,* and *though* probably came about because these three subordinating conjunctions are used to introduce a clause that is contrary to the expectations set up in the main clause. Using a comma with any other type of sentence-final adverb clause would be ungrammatical. However, in the cases of *although, even though,* and *though,* the comma is obligatory. In fact, leaving off this comma is one of the more prevalent punctuation errors in English.

As we would expect, we can easily shift concession clauses in front of the main clause:

Although *it was against my better judgment,* I went along with his plan.
Even though *it was getting late,* we decided to go far a walk.
Though *he said he ate only carrot sticks,* he was still gaining weight.

Split Infinitives

A **split infinitive** occurs when an adverb appears between the *to* and the base form in an infinitive. For example:

We need *to **seriously** consider* what they said.

Grammarians in the latter part of the nineteenth century condemned the split infinitive on the grounds that the infinitive in Greek and Latin is never split (which is not surprising given that the infinitive in those languages is only a single word). In more modern times, most grammar and usage books adopt an equivocal approach that amounts to saying, "There is nothing wrong with splitting infinitives, but don't do it in writing because it bothers some people." *The Macmillan Handbook of English* offers a typical view:

> *It is not true that the parts of an infinitive are inseparable. But since a split infinitive still causes many persons (especially composition instructors) discomfort, it is better not to split infinitives too rashly or promiscuously. A good rule to follow is this: place the adverbial modifier between* to *and the verb of an infinitive only when such an arrangement is necessary to avoid an awkward phrase.*

It is clear from research that even carefully spoken, educated people split infinitives in conversation all the time. Nevertheless, since some people are truly bothered by split infinitives in writing, the foregoing advice from the *Macmillan Handbook* is probably a reasonable guide.

Misplaced and Squinting Adverb Modifiers

The placement of adverbs can make a big difference in meaning. For example, changing the placement of *only* in the following sentence totally changes the message:

Only I love you. (You have no other admirers but me.)
I love *only* you. (You alone are the one I love.)

Misplaced modifiers do not make sentences ungrammatical. Rather, misplaced modifiers are mistakes because they say something the person did not intend to say. There are two main causes of misplaced modifiers: either a small group of ambiguous adverbs that can modify either verbs or noun phrases of quantity or the placement of adverbs at clause boundaries so that the reader or listener cannot tell which clause the adverb goes with.

Misplaced Adverbs

A few adverbs have the unusual property of being able to modify noun phrases that are expressions of quantity in addition to adverbs. For example, consider the following sentence:

John *almost* ate a dozen doughnuts.

This sentence is grammatical, but it does not mean what the writer or speaker intends. How many doughnuts did John eat? According to this sentence, John didn't eat any at all (though he nearly ate a lot). The intended meaning is this:

John ate *almost* a dozen doughnuts.

In the first example, the adverb *almost* is modifying the verb, which, after all, is what adverbs are for. The problem is that *almost* actually modifies the noun phrase of quantity *a dozen doughnuts*.

The most commonly used adverbs that can also modify noun phrases of quantity are *almost, barely,* and *nearly.* Here are some more examples:

Original: We *barely* packed enough clothes for the trip.
Corrected: We packed *barely* enough clothes for the trip.

You can't barely pack. Either you actually do pack something or you don't pack anything at all.

Original: Strokes *almost* account for half of the reported deaths.
Corrected: Strokes account for *almost* half of the reported deaths.

Accounting for something is either-or. Either we account for it or we don't account for it. To almost account for something is meaningless.

Original: Our cat has been *nearly* pregnant for three weeks now.
Correction: Our cat has been pregnant for *nearly* three weeks now.

A cat is either pregnant or not pregnant. It can't be nearly pregnant.

Squinting Adverbs

The delightful label **squinting adverb** applies to an adverb placed at the boundary between two clauses so that the adverb appears to look in two directions at once. For example:

A friend whom I e-mail *frequently* has virus problems with his
computer.

Frequently is a squinting adverb here because it can modify either the verb in front of it (*e-mail*) or the verb that follows it (*has*). To illustrate where the confusion lies, let's break the sentence apart with parentheses to show how the word *frequently* can be paired with either the modifying adjective clause or the main clause:

Adjective clause: A friend (whom I e-mail *frequently*) has virus
problems with his computer.
Main clause: A friend (whom I e-mail) *frequently* has virus
problems with his computer.

Once we identify the problem, squinting adverbs can be fixed in several ways. If we want the adverb in our example to modify the verb *e-mail*, then we need to move it to an unambiguous position in front of that verb:

A friend whom I *frequently* e-mail has virus problems with his
computer.

If we want the adverb to modify the verb in the main sentence, we have the option of moving the adverb to the end of the sentence:

> A friend whom I e-mail has virus problems with his computer *frequently.*

Or we can change the adverb *frequently* to the adjective *frequent*:

> A friend whom I e-mail has *frequent* virus problems with his computer.

It it not difficult to find a solution to the problem of a squinting adverb; the difficulty is in recognizing the mistake to begin with. The key to avoiding squinting modifiers is to keep adverb modifiers away from places in the sentences where two clauses join. Adverb modifiers at these junction points always run the risk of being ambiguous as to which clause they go with.

PART III

Sentences

16

Conjunctions

A **conjunction** is the joining of grammatical units together as equals to form a larger unit. In this context, the opposite of conjunction is **subordination**, in which units are joined unequally. This chapter is designed to help you navigate through some of the problems we encounter when joining grammatical units together as equals. The first part is a guide to joining words and phrases, and the second part moves on to the joining of independent clauses.

Joining Words and Phrases

Writers as compared to speakers encounter three main problems related to joining words and phrases. The first is faulty parallelism. The second is a grammatical error with the use of colons in introducing a series. The third is a question of how to use commas with coordinating conjunctions in a series.

Faulty Parallelism

When we use a coordinating conjunction to join two or more elements of the same type, those elements are said to be **parallel** with each other. When we mistakenly join two or more elements together with a coordinating conjunction but the elements are **not** of the same grammatical category, then we have made an error called **faulty parallelism**. By far the most common type of faulty parallelism involves nonparallel verb forms. For example:

X A standard formula for a speech is beginning with a joke and to end
      with a summary.

The problem with this sentence is that the writer has made a **gerund** (an
-*ing* verb form) parallel with an infinitive, as we can see when we arrange
them separately:

X A standard formula for a speech is   *beginning* with a joke (gerund)
                                 and   *to end* with a summary.
                                        (infinitive)

To correct the faulty parallelism, we must make both verb forms the same:
either both gerunds or both infinitives:

A standard formula for a speech is   *beginning* with a joke (gerund)
                               and   *ending* with a summary. (gerund)
A standard formula for a speech is   *to begin* with a joke (infinitive)
                               and   *to end* with a summary.
                                      (infinitive)

Stacking the parallel elements one on top of the other is a simple technique
for making it visually obvious whether the elements that are supposed
to be parallel are actually parallel. Another advantage of what we might
call "parallelism stack" is that it makes it clear what exactly the parallel
elements are. For example, there is another way to make the verbs in the
example parallel:

A standard formula for a speech is to   *begin* with a joke (base form)
                               and   *end* with a summary. (base
                                      form)

Now the parallel elements are the **base-form** verbs that follow the *to* of the
infinitive. This somewhat more sophisticated form of parallelism is hard
to see at first without the parallelism stack.
      Probably the most common situation in which faulty parallelism is
likely to occur is with a series of three (or more) infinitives. For example:

X I need to take the garbage out, check the mail, and to bring in the
       paper.

When we arrange the supposedly parallel infinitives in a parallelism stack,
we can see the problem more easily:

X I need to   *take* the garbage out,
                check the mail, and
                to bring in the paper.

The writer has been inconsistent about what the parallel elements are. The
first two elements are parallel base-form verbs that share a common *to*:

I need to   *take* the garbage out,
             check the mail,

The problem is with the third element, ***to bring*** *in the paper*. The writer
has forgotten that the parallel elements are base-form verbs, not infinitives. One solution, of course, is either to make all of the parallel elements
infinitives:

I need   *to take* the garbage out,
             to check the mail, and
             to bring in the paper,

The other obvious solution is to make all of the parallel elements base-
form verbs with a shared *to*:

I need to   *take* the garbage out,
             check the mail, and
             bring in the paper.

Some more examples of faulty parallelism follow, but the errors here
are more subtle and can not be easily explained without using the parallelism stack.

It is easy to make parallelism errors with clauses that are joined by **correlative conjunctions**. (Correlative conjunctions are two-part conjunctions such as *either . . . or* and *not only . . . but also.*) Here is an example:

X Jayne would *either* campaign for the governor *or* the senator.

The parallelism stack shows that the elements made parallel by the conjunctions are not really the same thing:

X Jayne would *either*   campaign for the governor
                   or   the senator.

The problem is that the first element, *campaign for the governor,* is a verb phrase, while the second element, *the senator,* is a noun phrase.

Once we see what the problem is, we can find several ways to fix it. For example, we can make parallel verb phrases:

Jayne would *either* campaign for the governor
                     or campaign for the senator.

We can also make parallel noun phrases:

Jayne would campaign for *either*   the governor
                          or   the senator.

We can make parallel prepositional phrases:

Jayne would campaign *either*   for the governor
                      or   for the senator.

Any of these solutions is fine; the real challenge is seeing the faulty parallelism to begin with.

If we begin a sentence with a correlative conjunction, then we are committed to making two complete clauses parallel. Here is an example of what can go wrong when we do not:

X *Not only* did John reject their offer, *but* criticized their CEO as well.

The parallelism stack shows us the problem:

X *Not only*   did John reject their offer,
     but   criticized their CEO as well.

The first element is a complete clause with a subject and verb, while the second element is only a verb phrase (no subject). To correct the error, we need to make the second element a complete sentence:

   Not only   did John reject their offer,
      but   **he** criticized their CEO as well.

You can see how the complexity of the grammar required by the correlative conjunction makes it difficult to monitor for correct parallelism.

Sometimes what counts as faulty parallelism is surprising. For instance, when we use a string of three or more noun phrases, the first two noun phrases establish a pattern of modification; if that pattern is then broken by subsequent noun phrases, the result is faulty parallelism. For example:

X Sue always takes   her briefcase,
              her cell phone, and
              Blackberry to the office.

The first two noun phrases set the pattern of *her* + noun, which the third noun phrase breaks. One repair option is to repeat the *her* in the third noun phrase:

  Sue always takes   her briefcase,
             her cell phone, and
             her Blackberry to the office,

Or we can make the parallel elements nouns with the *her* shared:

  Sue always takes her   briefcase,
                cell phone, and
                Blackberry to the office.

Faulty parallelism is a problem of sophistication. If we use only short, simple sentences, we can avoid trouble. When we attempt to express more complex relationships, we need to exploit complex grammatical relationships such as parallelism.

Using Colons to Introduce Items in a Series

A series is a list of three or more parallel grammatical elements. For example:

Nouns:	apples, oranges, and bananas
Verbs:	singing, laughing, and dancing
Adverbs:	quickly, silently, and menacingly

We often use colons to introduce lists. For example:

Four states have active volcanoes: Alaska, California, Hawaii, and
   Washington.

One restriction on using colons with lists is that the portion of the sentence before the colon must be a complete independent clause. Violating this restriction is a common error. For example:

X Our requirements are: adequate space, reliable water, and highway
   access.

The problem is that the portion of the sentence to the left of the colon, *our requirements are*, is not a complete independent clause. Here is one way to correct the error:

Our requirements are *the following*: adequate space, reliable water, and
   highway access.

Now the portion to the left of the colon is a complete independent clause.
   Often we use the expression *such as* with lists. If we're not careful when we do, we may change a valid sentence into an ungrammatical one. There

is nothing wrong with *such as* in itself; the problem is knowing where to put it. For example, the following sentence is correct as it stands:

My kids are into a lot of sports: football, basketball, and swimming.

However, if we add *such as* to the left of the colon, we make the sentence ungrammatical:

X My kids are into a lot of sports, *such as*: football, basketball, and swimming.

The problem is that the portion of the sentence to the left side of the colon is no longer a complete independent clause:

X My kids are into all kinds of sports, *such as*:

We can easily solve this problem by moving *such as* to the right side of the colon:

My kids are into all kinds of sports: *such as* football, basketball, and swimming.

Now the portion of the sentence to the left side of the colon is a valid independent clause.

Using Commas with Coordinating Conjunctions in a Series

There are two different schools of thought on punctuating a series of three or more elements. One way of punctuating a series is to think of the comma as a substitute for the coordinating conjunction (usually either *and* or *or*). For example:

The restaurant had a fixed price for a salad, an entree *and* a dessert.

The comma is required between *a salad* and *an entree* because they are not joined by a coordinating conjunction. Since *an entree* and *a dessert* are joined by a coordinating conjunction, no comma is necessary. The other school of thought is to always use a comma and a coordinating conjunction between the last two elements in a series. For example:

The restaurant had a fixed price for a salad, an entree, *and* a dessert.

One advantage of this second approach is that the comma + the coordinating conjunction clearly signals the end of the series.

A more significant advantage is that adding the comma solves what might be called the *bacon and eggs* problem. The phrase *bacon and eggs* is a single, fixed unit. When it is used as a subject, the verb that agrees with it is singular. For example:

Bacon and eggs **is** my favorite breakfast.

If we use *bacon and eggs* as part of a series, we run into a problem if we follow the first approach and do not use a comma with the final coordinating conjunction. To see the problem, compare the following sentences:

My favorite breakfast is toast, orange juice, bacon and cereal.
My favorite breakfast is toast, orange juice, bacon and eggs.

The two series in these examples are punctuated exactly alike, but they are not the same at all. The lack of a comma following *bacon* in the first example is parallel to the lack of a comma following *bacon* in the second example, but we know that *bacon and cereal* is not a single unit and that *bacon and eggs* is. So, we have the problem of the same punctuation for two completely different relationships.

The *bacon and eggs* problem is avoided if we always use a comma with the coordinating conjunction when it is part of a series:

My favorite breakfast is toast, orange juice, bacon, *and* cereal.
My favorite breakfast is toast, orange juice, *and* bacon and eggs.

The absence of any comma between *bacon* and *eggs* tells the reader that *bacon and eggs* is a single unit.

A third reason for always using commas with coordinating conjunctions that end series is consistency. It is obligatory to use commas with coordinating conjunctions when we have a series of parallel clauses. For example:

> The lawn was raked, the shrubs were trimmed, *and* the driveway had been recently swept.

Adding the comma when we are joining words or phrases makes all series (parallel words, parallel phrases, and parallel clauses) have exactly the same punctuation.

Joining Independent Clauses (Compound Sentences)

There are two fundamentally different ways of joining clauses together to form larger sentences. One way is by joining clauses unequally to create a **complex sentence**. In a complex sentence, we make one clause the independent (or main) clause and reduce the other clause(s) to the role of dependent (or subordinate) clause.

In the remainder of this chapter, however, we are concerned with the second way of joining clauses together to form larger sentences, which is by combining clauses equally to create a **compound sentence**. In a compound sentence, no clause is subordinated to another; all of the clauses retain their status as independent clauses. This process is call **conjunction**. There are two main ways of conjoining independent clauses: by using a comma and a coordinating conjunction, or by using a semicolon or colon.

Joining Independent Clauses with Commas and Coordinating Conjunctions

The most common way of joining two independent clauses together to form a single compounded sentence is by using a comma and a coordinating conjunction. For example:

> It was getting late, *so* we decided to quit.

There are seven single-word coordinating conjunctions. A helpful acronym for remembering them is FANBOYS:

F	for
A	and
N	nor
B	but
O	or
Y	yet
S	so

Each of the seven single-word conjunctions has its own range of meanings.

For. *For* typically means "because" or "since." For example:

They knew all the answers, *for* they had already taken the exam.

For is not as commonly used in this sense as *because*. Although *for* and *because* mean the same thing, they have different grammatical characteristics and are punctuated differently. Compare the following:

Conjunction: We celebrated, *for* it was her birthday.
Adverb: We celebrated *because* it was her birthday.

For is a conjunction that stands between the two independent clauses it joins. *Because* is a subordinating conjunction that begins an adverb clause. *For,* being a coordinating conjunction joining two independent clauses, is always used with a comma. An adverb clause following an independent clause would never be set off with a comma.

And. *And* in logic joins two propositions that are claimed to be true independently. For example:

John is British, *and* Sue is Chinese.
Sue is Chinese, *and* John is British.

Since the two clauses are totally independent of each other, we can give them in either order without affecting their meaning.

However, most of the time, *and* implies some kind of a link between the two independent clauses. Often the link is an implied cause-and-effect. For example:

John caught a terrible cold, *and* he had to miss work for a week.

Lacking any other information, we would naturally assume that the reason John missed work was that he caught a bad cold. If we reverse the order of the two clauses, we get a completely different meaning because the cause-and-effect relationship is destroyed:

John had to miss work for a week, *and* he caught a terrible cold.

This sentence says that John had two things happen to him: he missed work (for unknown reasons), and on top of that the poor guy caught a cold.

We often encounter this cause-and-effect use of *and* in conversation when a speaker makes a statement that does not seem to lead anywhere. The listener will often prompt the speaker by pointedly saying, "And . . . "

Sometimes the link between the two sentences is merely chronological. For example:

John stood up, *and* he went to the door.

The sentence describes two events that took place in this order: first John stood up, and then he went to the door.

Nor. *Nor* is used to join two negative sentences. For example:

Loren can't eat nuts, *nor* can her children.

Nor is not as widely used as *and neither.* For example:

Loren can't eat nuts, *and neither* can her children.

In terms of meaning, *nor* and *and neither* are completely interchangeable. The use of *nor/and neither* and the complex grammar of the second independent clause is discussed later, in the section "*So, Nor/Neither,* and Elliptical Clauses."

But. *But* has two slightly different meanings. One meaning is called "denial of expectations," which we encounter when the second independent clause negates the expectations that would follow from the first independent clause. Here are some examples that illustrate this meaning:

We were worried about the weather, *but* it turned out fine after all.
John started out in economics, *but* then he switched to art history.
I really like the movie, *but* I thought it went on too long.

The second meaning of *but* merely states the difference between two things, without any denial of expectations. For example:

Louise likes curry, *but* Anne does not.

The fact that Louise likes curry does not lead us to expect that Anne would like curry too. Since no expectation is set up, there can be no denial of that expectation. The following example, on the other hand, is a denial of expectations:

Louise likes curry, *but* she doesn't eat in Indian restaurants very often.

Or. *Or* is used to join independent clauses in two different ways. The more common way is to state mutually exclusive alternatives. For example:

I can pay you in cash, *or* I can use my credit card.

The other use of *or* has an ominous tone. We can call this the *or else* meaning. For example:

Move your car, *or (else)* I will call the police.
Stop that, *or (else)* I will leave.
Turn down your music, *or (else)* we will file a complaint.

In all of these examples, the clause beginning with *or (else)* is a threat—or at the least, a hostile statement. This use of *or else* is so well established that we often do not need to complete the second independent clause. For example:

I told my kids to clean up their room, *or else.*

Yet. *Yet* is generally similar to *but* in that the second clause is different from what we might expect from the first clause. For example:

I slept for eight hours, *yet* I didn't feel rested when I woke up.

But can be used for situations in which the second clause is a complete violation of the expectations set up in the first clause. *Yet* tends to be used for situations in which the second clause, while unexpected, is not a flat contradiction of the first clause. For example, compare the following sentences:

> **but:** Louise likes curry, *but* Anne does not.
> **yet:** X? Louise likes curry, *yet* Ann does not.

The sentence with *yet* seems odd, because the use of *yet* implies that Louise's dislike of curry would somehow lead to Ann's dislike of curry. Here is a more natural use of *yet*:

Louise likes curry, *yet* she seldom eats in Indian restaurants.

The second clause is unexpected, but it is not necessarily contradictory. Maybe Louise does not like eating out, or maybe the Indian restaurants are not very good where she lives.

So. *So* means "therefore" or "as a result." The second clause follows from the information given in the first clause. The second clause can be a direct, necessary cause-and-effect result from the first clause. For example:

>   It started raining, *so* I turned on my windshield wipers.

Or the second clause can be only indirectly connected to the first clause by prior information. For example:

>   I really love curry, *so* I jumped at the chance to eat at Louise's house.

Here the second clause makes sense only if we already know that Louise likes to cook curry.

There is a second use of *so* with *and (and so)* in sentences like the following:

>   Louise loves curry, *and so* do I.

In this example, there is a subject and verb reversal in the second clause. This use of *so* is discussed later, in the section "*So, Nor/Neither,* and Elliptical Clauses."

Run-On Sentences, Comma Splices, and Fused Sentences. When we join two independent clauses together to form a compound sentence, the rule is that we must use both a comma and a coordinating conjunction. This section capsules a well-developed set of terms for describing the three principal types of error that are possible when we form compound sentences incorrectly.

   Run-on sentence: the writer has used the coordinating conjunction correctly but has failed to use the comma. For example:

X Ron answered the phone *but* he failed to take down the message.
X He heard what you said *and* he will address the problem.
X We can't go to there *so* they will have to come to us.

   Comma splice: the writer has used the comma correctly but has failed to use a coordinating conjunction. For example:

X Ron answered the phone, he failed to take down the message.
X He heard what you said, he will address the problem.
X We can't go there, they will have to come to us.

Fused sentence: the writer has used neither a coordinating conjunction nor a comma. For example:

X Ron answered the phone he failed to take down the message.
X He heard what you said he will address the problem.
X We can't go there they will have to come to us.

To form these compound sentences correctly, we must use both a comma and a coordinating conjunction:

Ron answered the phone, *but* he failed to take down the message.
He heard what you said, *and* he will address the problem.
We can't go there, *so* they will have to come to us.

So, Nor/Neither, **and Elliptical Clauses.** The coordinating conjunctions *so* (actually, *and so*) and *nor* (together with *and neither*, which is a commonly used paraphrase of *nor*) have an unusual property. When they are used to join together two independent clauses, the duplicate information in the second clause is deleted. This deletion process is called **ellipsis**.

To see how the *and so* ellipsis works, let us begin with two simple independent clauses:

Betty moved to Los Angeles.
Lois moved to Los Angeles.

We can combine these two clauses with the coordinating conjunction *and*:

Betty moved to Los Angeles, *and* Lois moved to Los Angles.

While this sentence is perfectly grammatical, it seems somewhat childlike. Most of us would consolidate the information in the sentence by combining the subjects and eliminating the repetition. (This is in itself a form of ellipsis.) For example:

Betty *and* Lois moved to Los Angeles.

We can also combine the two original simple independent clauses by using the coordinating conjunction *and so*:

Betty moved to Los Angeles, *and so* did Lois.

Notice that two things have happened to the second clause:

- The verb *did* has been inserted in front of the subject *Lois*.
- The entire original verb phrase *moved to Los Angeles* has been deleted by ellipsis.

The basic rule that governs ellipsis is that grammatical components cannot be deleted unless there is sufficient redundancy in the rest of the sentence to reconstruct what has been deleted. In other words, no real information can be lost. Looking again at the preceding example, every speaker of English knows what underlies the following elliptical sentence:

Betty moved to Los Angeles, *and so* did Lois.

It is clearly the following complete sentence:

Betty moved to Los Angeles, and so did Lois *(move to Los Angeles)*.

What is the difference in meaning between the two ways of combining the original independent clauses? Here are the combined sentences again:

and: Betty *and* Lois moved to Los Angeles.
and so: Betty moved to Los Angeles, *and so* did Lois.

The first way, with *and*, implies that Betty and Lois moved to Los Angeles together.

The second way, with *and so*, does not have the implication of joint action. Betty and Lois may not even know each other. The sentence is saying only that Betty and Lois both moved to Los Angeles. Whether they did it together or totally independently we have no way of knowing.

Note that if the two independent clauses already contained a modal verb, then we would not use *do*. For example:

Betty *can* go to Los Angeles, *and so can* Lois.
Betty *should* go to Los Angeles, *and so should* Lois.
Betty *will* go to Los Angeles, *and so will* Lois.

(The modal verbs are *can, may, must, shall*, and *will*. See Chapter 8.)

Nor and its paraphrase *and neither* are the counterpart of *and so* in negative sentences. For example:

Betty didn't move to Los Angeles, *nor* did Lois.
Betty didn't move to Los Angeles, *and neither* did Lois.

We find the same use of modals with *nor/and neither*:

Betty *can't* go to Los Angeles, *nor/and neither can* Lois.
Betty *shouldn't* go to Los Angeles, *nor/and neither should* Lois.
Betty *won't* go to Los Angeles, *nor/and neither will* Lois.

Joining Two Independent Clauses with Semicolons and Colons

Both semicolons and colons are effective ways to join two independent clauses to form a single sentence. Both semicolons and colons stand somewhat in between the full separation of a period and the close connection of a comma. Writers use semicolons and colons to show that two independent clauses are closely related—so close, in fact, that the writer did not want to put them into separate sentences. Nevertheless, both semicolons and colons are like periods in that they require grammatically independent clauses. Semicolons and colons cannot be used to join an independent clause with a dependent clause. For example:

X I need to find their office; which is somewhere in the next block.
X I finally found it: right in front of me.

In both examples, the material to the right of the semicolon and colon is not an independent clause; therefore, the use of the semicolon and colon is incorrect.

Semicolons. Semicolons are used to show that the second of two independent clauses follows from or is related to the first independent clause. This section summarizes the three most common relations between the two clauses.

• **Cause-and-effect.** The second independent clause results from or is a consequence of the first clause. For example:

> The car had not been washed in months; there was dirt clear up to the windows.
> I have been on the phone all day; my ear actually hurts.
> It rained all day; by evening, the streets were flooded.

• **Generalization-and-example.** The second independent clause illustrates the point made in the first clause. For example:

> Baby giraffes are amazingly tall; their average height is six feet.
> I am really busy; I can't even find time for lunch.
> The weather is getting more unstable; rainfall patterns are becoming more and more irregular every year.

• **Statement-and-response.** The second independent clause is a response to what is said in the first clause. For example:

> Americans think British television is very cultivated; clearly, they have never sat through an evening of British sitcoms.
> Getting a new car is out of the question; we will have to get along with our old one for a while longer.
> We had dinner with some old friends last night; it was good to catch up on the news.

Colons. Colons are not used to join independent clauses nearly as often as semicolons. The main function of colons is to introduce second clauses that explain or illustrate the material in the first clause. For example:

Martha told George what he wanted to hear: his plans stood a good chance of succeeding.

The French had good reasons for intervening in the American Revolutionary War: they would gain a foothold in the New World while poking a finger in England's eye.

I am worried about their proposal: they have absolutely no way of reducing their losses if things go bad.

Using Conjunctive Adverbs

Conjunctive adverbs are words such as *moreover, however,* and *thus.* They are "signpost" words that allow readers to see the connection between the ideas contained in two independent clauses that are joined by semicolons or periods. For example:

The peace negotiations had run into problems; *moreover,* public support for the treaty was beginning to slip.

The beach was gradually eroding; *however,* the winter storms have added a fair amount of sand lately.

My husband has become a vegetarian. *Thus,* we all have been eating a lot less meat lately.

The term *conjunctive adverb* is not very helpful because it implies that these words are conjunctions like coordinating conjunctions. This is incorrect. Conjunctive adverbs are adverbs, not conjunctions. As such, they have no power to join grammatical units together. Since the term *conjunctive adverb* is so misleading, some texts refer to these words as **transitional terms.** However, because *conjunctive adverb* is in much wider use, we retain that term in this book.

The most frequent punctuation error involving conjunctive adverbs is a direct result of the name: people sometimes join two independent clauses with a comma + conjunctive adverb in the assumption that it is just like joining two independent clauses with a comma + a coordinating conjunction. For example:

X John is working full-time, *however*, he is still trying to take a full load at the university.

This sentence is technically a **comma splice**: two independent clauses have been (inadequately) joined by just a comma without a coordinating conjunction. One reason why it is so easy to make this mistake is that conjunctive adverbs convey so much information that it seems as if they should count as at least the equivalent of a coordinating conjunction. Notwithstanding, since conjunctive adverbs are only adverbs, they do not count for anything at all.

Here is a list of the more commonly used conjunctive adverbs sorted into four groups according to their meaning:

In Addition	Example	Contrast	Result
again	for example	however	accordingly
also	for instance	instead	as a result
besides	in fact	subsequently	consequently
likewise	otherwise	thus	
moreover	still		
similarly			

Here are some examples of each group:

In addition
We arranged the meeting time; *in addition*, we reserved the conference room.
I stopped for gas; *besides*, I needed to stretch my legs for a minute.
Rain is forecast for tomorrow; *furthermore*, it may rain all weekend.

Example
The movies this summer are not very original; *for example*, most of the big studio releases are sequels.
Jason was pretty upset; *in fact*, he went home right after the meeting.

The high cost of gas is affecting carmakers; *namely,* it is forcing them
to produce smaller, more fuel-efficient models.

Contrast

We were going to fly; *instead,* we ended up taking the train.

Remodeling our house turned out to be more expensive than we
expected; *nonetheless,* it was worth every penny.

I made money on the investment; *still,* I am not sure the return was
worth taking such a big risk.

Result

Our old supplier has gone out of business; *as a result,* we need to get
bids from some other companies.

There is a big storm in the Midwest; *consequently,* all flights to Chicago
have been canceled.

Our business has increased 200 percent this quarter; *thus,* we need to
hire several new employees.

One of the distinctive features of conjunctive adverbs is that we can
move them around inside their independent clause. After all, conjunctive
adverbs are adverbs, and adverbs are movable. Here is an example:

The team has had a bad year; *consequently,* attendance has been poor.

The team has had a bad year; attendance, *consequently,* has been poor.

The team has had a bad year; attendance has, *consequently,* been poor.

The team has had a bad year; attendance has been poor, *consequently.*

Notice that the punctuation stays exactly the same no matter where
we place the conjunctive adverb. We must separate the two independent
clauses with either a period or a semicolon, and the conjunctive adverb is
itself set off with commas from the rest of its clause—one comma if it is
at the beginning or end of the clause; two commas if it is in the middle of
the clause.

17

Questions

Questions are a central part of all human languages. There is a universal division of type into *yes-no* questions and information questions. *Yes-no* questions ask for "yes" or "no" answers, whereas information questions ask for specific details and cannot be answered with a simple affirmative or negative reply. In English, nearly all information questions are introduced by a word beginning with the letters *wh-*, such as *who, what, when, where,* and *why.* For this reason, information questions in English are usually called *wh-* questions.

Yes-No Questions

A **yes-no question** asks for a "yes" or "no" response. For example:

Should we call them?
Can I come, too?
Will they be home late?

This first section describes the three main forms of *yes-no* questions in English: inverted *yes-no* questions, informal *yes-no* questions, and tag questions.

Inverted Yes-No *Questions*

In most languages in the world, spoken *yes-no* questions are formed by merely raising the intonation at the end of the sentence, rather than letting it fall as it does in statements. We can certainly do that in English too, but the predominant way of forming *yes-no* questions is by inverting the normal subject-verb word order of statements. For example:

Are you OK?
Can we stop now?
Did you see that?

The specific details of how the subject-verb inversion works are actually pretty complicated.

How Inverted *Yes-No* Questions Are Formed. As a first approximation of how the inversion process works, the following examples compare the word order of statements with the word order of *yes-no* questions (subjects are in italics; verbs are in bold):

Statement	Inverted Yes-No Question
I **can** come, too.	**Can** *I* come, too?
They **will** be home late.	**Will** *they* be home late?
You **are** leaving tonight.	**Are** *you* leaving tonight?
John **has** returned.	**Has** *John* returned?

Again, the *yes-no* inversion is more complicated than these examples would imply. All of the verbs in the examples are **helping verbs** (verbs that precede the **main verb**). We can see that when the first verb is a helping verb, we form the *yes-no* question by inverting the subject and that helping verb.

What happens, though, when there is no helping verb? The answer seems improbable: we use *do* as a kind of substitute or "dummy" helping verb and invert *do* and the subject. For example:

Statement	Inverted *Yes-No* Question
John smiled.	**Did** *John* smile?
Mary and Susan laughed.	**Did** *Mary and Susan* laugh?
They work in New York.	**Do** *they* work in New York?

Using *do* is trickier than using the other helping verbs, in that *do* carries with it the tense marker that was attached to the main verb in the original statement. For example, compare the verbs in the following statement and corresponding *yes-no* question:

Statement: *The children* **walked** to the park this afternoon.
Question: **Did** *the children* **walk** to the park this afternoon?

The dummy helping verb *do* is inverted with the subject noun phrase *the children*, taking with it the past-tense marker that was originally part of the past-tense verb *walked*. In effect, *do* strips away the past-tense marker from *walked*, leaving behind the **bare-stem** form *walk*. Note: *walk* is not a present tense. There can be only one tense-carrying (**finite**) verb in a clause. That tense-carrying verb is *always* the first verb in the clause.

Here are some more examples of the construction; both the dummy helping verb *do* and the bare-stem main verb are in bold:

Statement	Inverted *Yes-No* Question
The TV works.	**Does** *the TV* **work**?
Roberta **found** the missing book.	**Did** *Roberta* **find** the missing book?
The brothers **look** alike.	**Do** *the brothers* **look** alike?
He **returned** your call.	**Did** *he* **return** your call?

There are two **main verbs** that are exceptional: *be* and *have*.
Be. *Be*, when used as a main verb, behaves just like the helping verb *be*. That is, it is inverted with the subject. For example:

Statement	Inverted *Yes-No* Question
They **were** classmates of mine.	**Were** *they* classmates of yours?
He **is** busy this afternoon.	**Is** *he* busy this afternoon?
The train **was** on time.	**Was** *the train* on time?

Have. There are not many differences in grammar between British and American English, but the use of *have* as a main verb is one of them. In American English, *have* as a main verb is just like any other main verb (except *be*, of course). To form a *yes-no* question, we must use the dummy helping verb *do*. For example:

Statement	Inverted *Yes-No* Question
She **has** a cold.	**Does** *she* **have** a cold?
They **had** a good time.	**Did** *they* **have** a good time?
I **have** a question.	**Do** I **have** a question?

In British English, however, *have* can also be treated like the main verb *be*. That is, it is inverted with the subject without the use of *do*. For example:

Statement	Inverted *Yes-No* Question
She **has** a cold.	**Has** *she* a cold?
They **had** a good time.	**Had** *they* a good time?
I **have** a question.	**Have** *you* a question?

According to some studies, in British English the use of *do* with *have* as a main verb is becoming more common in informal situations. So, for example, you would hear both of these usages in conversation:

Has *she* a cold?
Does *she* **have** a cold?

Negative Inverted *Yes-No* Questions. Negative markers are attached to the first helping verb and are moved along with that verb when the verb and subject noun phrase are inverted. For example:

Negative Statement	Negative Inverted *Yes-No* Question
I **can't** come.	**Can't** I come?
They **won't** be home late.	**Won't** *they* be home late?
You **aren't** leaving tonight.	**Aren't** *you* leaving tonight?
John **hasn't** returned.	**Hasn't** *John* returned?

When there is no helping verb, the negative marker is attached to the dummy helping verb *do*. When we turn the negative statement into an inverted *yes-no* question, the negative marker is moved along with *do*. For example:

Negative Statement	Negative Inverted *Yes-No* Question
The TV **doesn't** work.	**Doesn't** *the TV* work?
Roberta **didn't** find the book.	**Didn't** *Roberta* find the book?
The brothers **don't** look alike.	**Don't** *the brothers* look alike?
He **didn't** return your call.	**Didn't** *he* return your call?

Be used as a main verb behaves just like the helping verb *be*: we attach the negative marker directly to it. When we invert *be*, the negative marker automatically goes along with it. For example:

Negative Statement	Negative Inverted *Yes-No* Question
They **weren't** classmates.	**Weren't** *they* classmates?
He **isn't** busy this afternoon.	**Isn't** *he* busy this afternoon?
The train **wasn't** on time.	**Wasn't** *the train* on time?

Have used as a main verb is treated differently in British and American English. In American English, *have* is like any other main verb (except *be*, of course). That is, we need to attach the negative marker to the dummy helping verb *do*. For example:

Negative Statement	Negative Inverted *Yes-No* Question
She **doesn't** have a cold.	**Doesn't** *she* have a cold?
They **didn't** have a good time.	**Didn't** *they* have a good time?
We **don't** have any questions.	**Don't** *we* have any questions?

In British English, on the other hand, *have* used as a main verb is typically treated just like *have* as a helping verb. That is, speakers of British English usually do not add the dummy helping verb *do*. For example:

Negative Statement	Negative Inverted *Yes-No* Question
She **hasn't** a cold.	**Hasn't** *she* a cold?
They **hadn't** a good time.	**Hadn't** *they* a good time?
I **haven't** any questions.	**Haven't** *you* any questions?

Negative questions differ from positive questions in terms of their assumptions. For example, compare the following sentences:

Positive question: Is Francine taking Spanish this year?
Negative question: Isn't Francine taking Spanish this year?

The positive question is neutral in the sense that the speaker genuinely does not know whether Francine is taking Spanish. The negative question, however, is far from neutral. The negative question sends several messages. One message is that the speaker is expressing surprise. The speaker fully expected Francine to take Spanish, but now he or she has heard that Francine may not be taking Spanish after all.

Another message that a negative question can send is disappointment. For example:

Didn't you say we were going to the movies tonight?

Here the speaker uses the negative question to signal disappointment or even a sense of betrayal. The meaning is something like, "Hey, I thought we had an agreement that we were going to the movies, and now you tell me we're not. I'm kind of upset by this."

Responses to Inverted *Yes-No* Questions. We can respond to inverted *yes-no* questions with a grammatically complete answer. For example:

Question	Full Answer
Is Anne in her office?	Yes, I saw her there a minute ago.
	No, I haven't seen her all day.

Most of the time, however, we respond to inverted *yes-no* questions with a shortened answer that omits redundant information already supplied in the question. For example:

Question	Short Answer
Is Anne in her office?	Yes, she is.
	No, she isn't.

The short answer presumes that the listener can fill in the redundant information. For example:

Question	Short Answer
Is Anne in her office?	Yes, she is (in her office).
	No, she isn't (in her office).

The form the short answer takes depends on the form of the question. If the question contains only a single helping verb, then that helping verb (and only that helping verb) is used in the short answer. For example:

Question	Short Answer
Can I help you?	Yes, you can. No, you can't.
Will you be there?	Yes, I **will**. No, I **won't**.
Are you working?	Yes, I **am**. No, I'm **not**.
Have you seen Anne?	Yes, I **have**. No, I **haven't**.
Did you finish?	Yes, I **did**. No, I **didn't**.

Notice that it makes no difference what the nature of the helping verb is. It can be a modal (*can* and *will*), the helping verb *be* from the progressive, the helping verb *have* from the perfect, or the dummy auxiliary *do*. The result is always the same: we must use the same helping verb in the short answer.

Notice also that in the affirmative short answer, the helping verb is not contracted. That is, we do not say, "Yes, I'm"; we say, "Yes, I am." The helping verbs in the negative short answers are contracted in the expected way.

As we would expect, the main verb *be* has the same short answer as the helping verb *be*. For example:

Question	Short Answer
Are you on the phone?	Yes, I **am**. No, I'm not.

If the question contains two helping verbs, both are used in the short answer. For example:

Question	Short Answer
Could you **have** finished sooner? (modal + perfect)	Yes, I **could have**. No, I **couldn't have**.
	Yes, I **could've**. No, I **couldn't have**.
Could they **be** working late? (modal + progressive)	Yes, they **could be**. No, they **couldn't be**.
Have they **been** studying? (perfect + progressive)	Yes, they **have been**. No, they **haven't been**.

Note: When *have* is the second helping verb in the short answer, *have* can be either fully stressed or contracted.

When a question contains three helping verbs (a modal + the perfect + the progressive), we have an option: we can use just the first two helping verbs (modal + *have*), or we can use all three. For example:

Question	Short Answer
Will they **have been** worrying?	Yes, they **will have (been)**.
	No, they **won't have (been)**.

Again, *have* can be either contracted or uncontracted.

Informal Yes-No *Questions*

One problem nonnative speakers face with *yes-no* questions is that in informal conversational English, nobody seems to follow the rules. In listening to casual conversation among Americans, you will be surprised at how prevalent informal *yes-no* questions are. In one study of conversational English, informal questions were found to make up an astonishing 41 percent of the total number of questions.

Using an informal *yes-no* question is a signal to the other party that we feel comfortable enough in our relationship with the person to presume a certain level of intimacy. Obviously, nonnative speakers need to be confident in themselves and in the nature of their relationships to risk using these informal questions.

There are two commonly used informal variants of *yes-no* questions: uninverted and elliptical.

Uninverted *Yes-No* Questions. An uninverted *yes-no* question, as its name suggests, is a *yes-no* question in which the subject and finite verb are not inverted. Here is an example of a statement (by party A) followed by an uninverted *yes-no* question (by party B):

> A: I just got some good news.
> B: You got your promotion? (said with a rising intonation)

Uninverted *yes-no* questions are highly contextual. We would use them only with people we know well and in situations in which we can reasonably anticipate the answer to the question we are asking. (In this sense, uninverted *yes-no* questions are more like exclamations than real questions.) In more formal situations or if we really do not know the answer to the question, we would use the standard *yes-no* inverted question:

> Did you get your promotion?

Elliptical *Yes-No* Questions. Elliptical *yes-no* questions are questions in which the inverted helping verb is omitted. For example:

Standard *Yes-No* Question	Elliptical *Yes-No* Question
Are you going to the meeting?	You going to the meeting?
Do you know where the sugar is?	You know where the sugar is?
Have you had lunch yet?	You had lunch yet?

In contrast to the uninverted *yes-no* questions, elliptical *yes-no* questions are genuine questions; that is, the speaker does not know the answer. Elliptical *yes-no* questions are used only in informal situations in which the questioner can assume at least a casual familiarity with the other person.

Tag Questions

A tag is a word or phrase added on to an otherwise already completed sentence. A common type of tag (called a **question tag**) is used to turn a statement into a kind of *yes-no* question that does not invert the subject and verb. The question created by adding the question tag is not usually a genuine request for information. It is typically a request for confirmation that the information in the main body of the sentence is correct. For example:

> You can come tonight, **can't you**?
> You are not feeling very well, **are you**?

While question tags are common in languages around the world, the question tag in English is unusually complicated. One reason is that it has two different forms. (In many languages, the tag is a single fixed phrase, such as *nicht wahr* "Isn't that right?" in German.) If the main sentence is positive, then the question tag must be negative. If the main sentence is negative, then the question tag must be positive.

Further, the verb in the question tag is dependent on the verb in the main sentence. The tense of the tag must be the same as the tense of the **finite verb** in the main sentence. (The finite verb always precedes any other verb in the clause. It is the verb that the subject must agree with. A finite verb must be in either the present tense or past tense. See Chapter 9.) For example, the following sentence is ungrammatical:

X You **were** taking notes, **aren't** you?

The tense in the main sentence is past, while the tense in the tag is present. Both verbs must be the same: either both in the present tense, or both in the past tense. For example:

Present:	You **are** taking notes, **aren't** you?
Past:	You **were** taking notes, **weren't** you?

The correct verb to use in the tag is totally dictated by the finite verb in the main sentence. So, if the finite verb is a helping verb, then the tag must be that same helping verb. For example:

Modal:	They **should** go, **shouldn't** they?
be:	We **are** going soon, **aren't** we?
have:	Joan **has** finished the job, **hasn't** she?

Likewise, if the finite verb is *be* used as a main verb, then the tag must also use *be*. For example:

You **are** ready, **aren't** you?

If the finite verb is any other main verb except *be*, then we must use *do* in either its present-tense or past-tense form, as determined by the tense of the finite verb in the main part of the sentence. For example:

James **paid** the taxi, **didn't** he?
We **saw** that movie already, **didn't** we?
He **seems** upset, **doesn't** he?

Have in American English is like any other main verb; it obliges us to use *do* in the question tag. For example:

They **have** a problem with that, **don't** they?

In British English, main verb *have* is just like helping verb *have*. For example:

They **have** a problem with that, **haven't** they?

The addition of a negative tag to a positive main sentence does not really affect the positive assumption of the main sentence. For example:

We **are** seeing the Smiths tonight, **aren't** we?

The person being addressed here would readily interpret the tag as asking for confirmation that their original plan to see the Smiths is unchanged.

Likewise, the addition of a positive tag to a negative main sentence does not really affect the negative assumption of the main sentence. For example:

We **aren't** seeing the Smiths tonight, **are** we?

The other party would interpret this tag as asking for confirmation that their original plans, which did *not* include seeing the Smiths, are unchanged.

How we say the tag makes a difference in how the listener will interpret it. If we use a rising intonation, the tag comes close to being a real question. For example:

You **have** enough cash with you, **don't** you?

Said with a rising intonation, this means something like, "I really don't know if you have enough cash." The same sentence said with a falling intonation is asking only for confirmation of the fact that the person indeed has enough cash.

Wh- Questions

A ***wh*- question**, as the term is applied in Modern English grammar, is an information question. Information questions ask for specific kinds of information, as opposed to *yes-no* questions, as previously discussed. *Wh*-questions are so-called because most information questions in English happen to begin with the letters *wh-*, such as *who, what, where, when,* and *why.* Here are some examples:

Who(m) did you call?
What did he say about the meeting?
Where is the meeting?
Why did they call this meeting?
When will it be over?

The most obvious feature of *wh-* questions is that they all begin with *wh-* words. Note, however, that a few *wh-* words don't actually begin with *wh-*: *how, how long, how many, how much,* and *how often.* Each *wh-* word is a request for a certain kind of information. *Who* and *whom* ask about people; *what* asks about things or ideas; *where* asks about place; *why* asks for reasons; *when* asks about time, and so on.

Technically, *who* is used for subject noun phrases, and *whom* is used for object noun phrases. For example, compare the following:

Subject noun phrase:	**Who** answered the phone? (*Who* is the subject of *answered*.)
Object noun phrase:	**Whom** did they want to talk to? (*Whom* is the object of *talk to*.)

In spoken English, however, most speakers actually prefer to use *who* rather than *whom* for the object *wh-* word. The use of *who* versus *whom* illustrates the sometimes great difference between written English and spoken English. In written English, *whom* must be used where it is called for. In spoken English, people blithely ignore the rule and use *who* for the object *wh-* word (even if English teachers squirm in anger!).

It is possible in English to leave the *wh-* word in its original position in an information question. We do this when we want to express surprise or irritation. For example, here are some responses a mother might make to her teenager, with emphasis on the *wh-* word:

You had **what** for breakfast?
You are going **where**?
You are coming back **when**?

These are rhetorical questions. The mother heard perfectly well what her son or daughter had said. She is using the *wh-* word in this position (unfronted, as explained in the following section) as a way of expressing her unhappiness with the child's statement.

How *wh-* *Questions Are Formed*

The process of forming *wh-* questions in English is unusual and complicated. Its convolutions lead to many errors by nonnative speakers.

In virtually every language in the world, information questions are formed by moving an appropriate question word (the equivalent of the *wh-* word in English) forward to the first position. This process of moving the *wh-* word is called **fronting**. What makes English information questions unique is that a second movement also must take place: an inversion of the subject noun phrase and the first helping verb (or *be* used as a main verb).

The fact that information questions in English have two inversions, not just one, makes them remarkably difficult to process. Even fluent nonnative speakers are inclined to make certain mistakes in the construction when they are under any kind of time or social pressure. In the following examples of typical cases, the subject noun phrase is in italics, and the helping verb is in bold:

	Error	Standard
X	Where *you* **are** going?	Where **are** *you* going?
X	When *they* **will** be back?	When **will** *they* be back?
X	What *they* **have** done?	What **have** *they* done?
X	Why *he* **can't** come, too?	Why **can't** *he* come, too?

The problem in all the erroneous examples is that the speaker was not able to handle two inversions at the same time. In order to form these *wh-* questions correctly, the speaker has to do two things. First, move the *wh-* word to the front of the sentence, and then invert the helping verb and the subject noun phrase. The speaker was able to perform the first task—moving the *wh-* word to the front of the sentence—but was not able to simultaneously perform the second task of inverting the subject and the helping verb. Clearly, it was one task too many for the speaker to manage at the same time.

Here is a second group of errors of a similar nature:

	Error	Standard
X	What *he* **means** by that?	What **does** *he* mean by that?
X	Why *they* **want** to do that?	Why **do** *they* want to do that?
X	Who *he* **wants** to talk to?	Who **does** *he* want to talk to?
X	Where *they* **live**?	Where **do** *they* live?

In these examples as well, failing to invert the subject and verb results in an error, but this time the problem is compounded by the need to also insert the dummy helping verb *do*. This mistake is pretty understandable given how much manipulation these sentences require. First, move the *wh-*

word to the front of the sentence. Second, invert the tense marker (present or past tense) and the subject noun phrase. And finally, insert the dummy helping verb *do* to carry the tense marker. This is a lot of language to process on the spur of the moment, and in a foreign tongue, too.

There are three other types of *wh-* questions we have not discussed. One type uses *have* as a main verb. Remember that in American English, *have* is just like any other main verb in that it requires *do*. For example:

Why **did** *they* **have** a meeting?

In British English, the main verb *have* can also be treated the same way as the helping verb *have* and form questions without *do*. Thus, both of the following versions can be used in British English:

What kind of computer **have** *they*?
What kind of computer **do** *they* **have**?

A second type of *wh-* question is one in which the main verb is *be*. As explained in the discussion of *yes-no* questions, we do not use *do* with the main verb *be*. Instead, we invert the subject noun phrase and *be*. Here are some examples of *wh-* questions that use *be* as a main verb:

Where **is** *my cell phone?*
Who **is** *that girl?*
Why **are** *the kids* so upset?
When **was** *my appointment?*

Third and finally, there is the mysterious case of *wh-* questions in which the *wh-* word plays the role of subject. Here are some examples using *who* playing the role of subject with all the different types of verbs:

Helping verb:	**Who** *is* working on the Smith papers?
	Who *will* take care of the children?
	Who *has* had lunch already?
***be* as main verb:**	**Who** *is* the visitor?
No helping verb:	**Who** *reported* the accident?

As you can see, these *wh-* questions seem to break all the rules: there is no inversion of subject and helping verb, *and* we do not use *do* when there is no helping verb. Obviously, there is something special that happens when the *wh-* word plays the role of subject.

What is going on is that the two inversions (moving the *wh-* word to the beginning of the sentence, and inverting the first verb and subject) cancel each other out. Let us take as an example the following information question with *who* again playing the role of subject:

Who *should* go next?

Underlying this question is the following statement:

<u>Subject noun phrase</u> should go next.
      Who

The *wh-* word *who*, playing the role of the subject noun phrase, starts out at the beginning of the sentence, so we go to the next step in the process and invert the subject and the verb, producing the following:

Should **who** go next?

But to form an information question properly, we have to move the *wh-* word *who* back to the beginning of the sentence:

Who *should* go next?

As a result of the two changes, we end up right where we started, with no apparent change at all. The two inversions have canceled each other out.

The most peculiar consequence of this general canceling out is that we do not need to use the dummy helping verb *do* when the *wh-* word plays the role of subject. For example, consider the following construction:

Who *said* that we were ready to go?

Underlying the question is the following statement:

<u>Subject noun phrase</u> said that we were ready to go.
      Who

We would begin by inverting the past-tense marker from *said* with the subject noun phrase, producing the following:

Past-tense **who** *say* that we were ready to go?

But now we must move the *wh-* word *who* back in front of the past-tense marker, producing the following:

Who <u>past-tense *say*</u> that we were ready to go?
        said

Moving *who* back to the beginning of the sentence puts the past-tense marker right back where it started—attached to the verb *said*. So, there is no need for the dummy helping verb *do* to carry a stranded tense marker. Only English could have something this strange.

Negative wh- Questions

Negative *wh-* questions are formed like negative *yes-no* questions: negative markers are attached to the first helping verb (or the dummy helping verb *do* if there is no real helping verb), and then the negative markers and the verbs they are attached to are inverted with the subject noun phrase.

Here are some examples with a helping verb:

Who **hasn't** had *a turn*?
Where **haven't** *they* been?
When **won't** *you* be available?
Where **can't** *they* clean?
Why **aren't** *you* coming?

Here are some examples with the dummy helping verb *do*:

Who(m) **didn't** *I* introduce?
Why **don't** *you* send them an e-mail?

Where **didn't** *we* look?
What **don't** *they* want to do?

Here are some examples with *be* used as a main verb:

Why **isn't** *he* at the meeting?
When **aren't** *the trains* late?
Who **isn't** here?
What **aren't** *you* ready to do yet?

Why don't is used frequently to make polite suggestions. For example:

Why **don't** *we* take a break?
Why **don't** *you* start without us?
Why **don't** *we* give them a chance?
Why **don't** *you* let them finish the job?

Why don't can also have a critical or irritable tone. For example:

Why **don't** *you* give it a rest?
Why **don't** *you* listen?
If you're in so much pain, why **don't** *you* see a doctor?

In American English, *why don't I* and *why don't we* are used for offers. For example:

Why **don't** *I* give you a hand with that?
Why **don't** *we* help you get moved in?

Why don't can be shortened to *why not*. For example:

Why not take the subway?
Why not just do what we had already planned?
Why not stay home tonight?

Informal wh- *Questions*

As with *yes-no* questions, there are several nonstandard variations of *wh-* questions. All of them are used exclusively in informal situations, and all presume some degree of social intimacy. These are definitely not structures that nonnative speakers should try out on their bosses. Nevertheless, nonnative speakers need to be aware of them because they are common in conversational settings.

Truncated *wh-* Questions. Truncated *wh-* questions are verbless fragments that begin with *wh-* words. Truncated questions play an important role in casual conversational English. This section highlights some of the more common constructions.

How about *How about* is used to introduce a new topic. For example, at a meeting a member of the group might use *how about* as a way to propose a new alternative for the group to consider. For example:

> *How about* changing the meeting time?

Making the proposal in this form shows that it is being suggested tentatively and that the person making the proposal would not be offended by its rejection.

How about is often used for informal invitations that do not demand immediate formal answers. For example:

> *How about* going to a movie sometime?

The person being asked is free to make a polite, noncommittal, face-saving response, such as the following:

> Sure, let's do it sometime.

Now consider the standard equivalent to the same *how about* example:

> Would you like to go to a movie sometime?

This phraseology forces the other party to make a formal "yes" or "no" response—a response that could be embarrassing for both people.

How about you? is used to get a person's opinion. For example:

I love kung fu movies; *how about you?*

This can be a neutral question, but it can also express a sense of demanding (rather than just asking) someone's opinion.

What about. *What about* is often used to raise a question or to call for clarification. For example, in a discussion about hiring a person, a member of the committee might say this:

Well, *what about* his college record?

This is a way of reminding the committee not to overlook the importance of the candidate's college career.

Be very careful with the following expression:

What about it?

This particular question has a strongly confrontational tone. It is often a direct challenge to what someone else has said. Don't use it unless you plan to pick a fight.

How come. *How come* asks (often with more than a hint of demanding) that someone explain or justify an action. For example, a parent might ask a teenager this question:

How come you didn't call when you said you would?

How come often replaces *why* in informal conversation.

What for. *What for?* can be a neutral request for information, but it can also be used to challenge the validity of another person's request. For example, you might use *what for* in response to a request from a colleague for a time-consuming and seemingly unnecessary report.

Why not. *Why not?* is an affirmative response to a request. It is more or less the equivalent of saying, "Sure, let's do it."

Since when. *Since when* is a dismissive (and somewhat confrontational) response to a statement or request. *Since when* is an implied contraction of "*Since when* is that a rule/requirement/law?" For example, we might use *since when* in response to a request to provide what we consider to be unnecessary paperwork:

Since when do we need to do that?

What now *and* now what. These phrases are often used to express irritation or exasperation. Depending on the tone of voice used, the effect can range from mild ironic amusement to real frustration.

Elliptical *wh-* Questions. Elliptical *wh-* questions are much like elliptical *yes-no* questions. They are *wh-* questions that omit the first helping verb. Here are examples:

Standard *wh-* Question	Elliptical *wh-* Question
Where **have** you been staying?	Where you been staying?
What **are** you doing?	What you (watcha) doing?
How **are** we going to fix that?	How we going to (gonna) fix that?

Elliptical *wh-* questions are used only in informal situations in which the speaker can assume casual familiarity with the other person. They are genuine questions to which the speaker does not already know the answer.

The Passive

In traditional terminology, verbs are said to have **voice**. Voice refers to whether the subject performs the action of the verb. If the subject does perform the action of the verb, the verb is said to be in the **active voice**. If the subject is instead the recipient of the action of the verb, the verb is said to be in the **passive voice**. For example:

Active voice: The dog *bit* the man
Passive voice: The man *was bitten* by the dog.

In the active-voice sentence, the subject (*dog*) is the performer of the action of the verb; that is, the dog is the one engaging in the act of biting. In the passive-voice sentence, the subject (*man*) is not the performer of the action of the verb; that is, the man is not engaged in the action of biting. Instead, the subject (*man*) is the recipient of the action of the verb; the man is the one getting bitten, not the one doing the biting.

In practice, we rarely use the term *active* (except in discussions of the passive), and we use the term *passive* in a much narrower way than the traditional term would suggest. We reserve the term *passive* for sentences that contain a **passive auxiliary**. In the introductory example, the passive auxiliary is the helping verb *be* (in the past tense) followed by the main verb in the **past-participle** form (*bitten*). The details of how the passive auxiliary works are discussed later in the chapter. The critical point for now is that a sentence is passive if and only if the sentence contains a passive auxiliary.

Note also that our definition of the passive auxiliary requires the use of the helping verb *be*. In the final section of this chapter, we broaden the definition of the passive auxiliary to include two other helping verbs that can also be used to form passives: *get* and *have*.

Two Ways of Forming the Passive

There are two distinct ways to think about how the passive is formed:

1. Passive sentences are derived from preexisting active sentences. In other words, a set of rules converts appropriately formed active sentences into their passive-sentence counterparts.

2. Passive sentences are derived independently of active sentences. Passive sentences, along with all other types of sentences, must follow certain rules in order to be grammatically well-formed English sentences.

Passives Derived from Active Sentences

The most common way of teaching the passive is to derive passive sentences from corresponding active-voice sentences. For example, we might show how the following active sentence can be transformed into a passive by a three-step process:

Active: John saw Mary.

1. The subject of the active sentence (*John*) is turned into the object of the preposition *by* (sometimes *with*) and moved to the end of the sentence:

    John saw Mary ⇒ saw Mary by John

    Note: When a passive sentence retains the original subject in a *by* phrase, that retained subject is called the **agent**. The term *agent* is helpful because it allows us to distinguish between the semantic subject of the sentence (the doer of the action) and the grammatical subject (the subject that the verb agrees with). In active-voice sentences, the grammatical subject and the agent are, of course, the same thing. In passive-voice sentences, however, they are two quite different things.

2. The original object (*Mary*) is moved into the now empty subject position:

saw Mary by John ⇒ Mary saw by John

3. The active verb (*saw*) is changed into the corresponding passive verb *was seen*:

Mary *saw* by John ⇒ Mary *was seen* by John.

The mechanism of how *saw* changes into *was seen* is complicated. Two things must happen. First, we need to insert the passive helping verb *be* into the sentence immediately before the main verb. The verb *be* inherits whatever tense the main verb in the active sentence was carrying. In the current example, *be* inherits the past tense of *saw* and becomes *was*. We also need to change the main verb into its past-participle form. The result is the unmistakable signature of the passive: some form of the helping verb *be* followed by a main verb in the past-participle form. Nothing but a sentence in the passive voice can have this sequence.

Here are some more examples of active sentences with their corresponding passives. The distinctive passive auxiliary is in bold and italics:

Active: Mary has seen John.
Passive: John has ***been seen*** by Mary.

Active: Mary might see John.
Passive: John might ***be seen*** by Mary.

Active: Mary is seeing John.
Passive: John is ***being seen*** by Mary.

The great advantage of deriving passive sentences from preexisting active sentences is that it helps us think of the passive as a kind of stylistic alternative to the active. When we consider using a passive sentence in our own writing, we do need to consciously weigh the pros and cons of using that passive instead of the corresponding active sentence that underlies the passive alternative.

The disadvantage of deriving the passive directly from the active is that it makes the agent *by* phrase a major component of the new passive sentence. Certainly, the agent *by* phrase can be important, but most of the time it actually is not. In fact, about 85 percent of the time, the *by* phrase does not even appear in the new passive sentence.

When you think about the function of the passive, the deletion of the agent *by* phrase is not surprising. After all, most of the time, we use the passive to emphasize what happened to the object and to de-emphasize what the subject did. To see the difference, compare the following sentences:

Active: John saw Mary.
Passive: Mary **was seen** by John.

The whole point of shifting the sentence into the passive is to talk about what happened to Mary, not to talk about what John did. In that case, why would we want to keep the original subject in the passive *by* phrase?

Here are some of the many possible reasons why we would not keep the agent *by* phrase in a passive sentence:

The agent is unknown to the speaker: His car **was broken** into last night.

The agent is unknowable: My computer **was assembled** in Korea.

The agent is implicit or obvious: John **was promoted** last week.

The agent is an impersonal entity or institution: Our flight **has been canceled**.

The agent is vague or highly generalized: World War I **has been** largely **forgotten**.

Sometimes, we know the agent but choose to deliberately withhold or suppress it. For example, we might want to be tactful and avoid direct criticism of an individual:

Robin **was given** some bad advice about getting his car repaired.

We might even want to deflect criticism or blame for our own behavior. For example:

Mistakes **were made.**

This last example illustrates what gives the passive its bad reputation: it can be a way to avoid taking personal responsibility for our own actions.

Passives Formed Directly from the Passive Auxiliary (Be + Past Participle)

Most modern grammar books do not derive the passive from the active. Instead, they look at passive sentences solely in their own terms without any reference to the active-sentence counterparts.

The unique feature that makes a passive a passive is the presence of the **passive auxiliary**. The passive auxiliary consists of two obligatory components: the helping verb *be* (in some form as determined by the rest of the sentence) + the present-participle marker that is attached to the following verb.

The passive auxiliary (*be* + past participle) must immediately precede the main verb in the sentence (automatically ensuring that the passive auxiliary will always follow any other helping verbs, such as the perfect or the progressive). For example, here is how the passive sentence *John was promoted last week* would be derived:

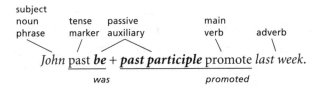

The tense marker (past, in this example) is automatically attached to the following verb (*be*, in this example) and the past-participle marker is automatically attached to the verb following it (*promote*, in this example).

Here is the derivation for the present-tense sentence *John is promoted now*:

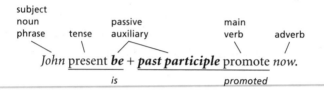

Here is the derivation for the future-modal sentence *John will be promoted soon*:

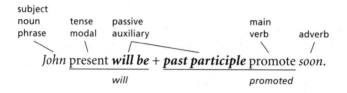

Obligatory Interpretation of the Subject Noun Phrase. When a sentence contains the passive auxiliary, then there is a forced interpretation of the meaning of the subject noun phrase. The "subject" noun phrase in a passive sentence *must* be interpreted as playing the role of the object of the passive verb. For example, consider the following passive sentence:

Dorothy **was invited** to the party.

We would interpret the sentence in this manner: The "subject" noun phrase *Dorothy* is actually playing the role of the object of the passive verb *was invited*. In other words, Dorothy did not issue the invitations to the party; she received an invitation.

We have to look at the noun phrase *Dorothy* in two different ways at the same time:

1. *Dorothy* functions as the **subject** of the finite verb *was*. We can verify that the finite verb agrees with *Dorothy* by changing the subject to the plural pronoun *they*:

   > They **were** invited to the party.

   Now the finite verb is plural (*were*) to agree with the new plural subject.

2. *Dorothy* plays the role of the **object** (the recipient of the action) of the passive verb *was invited*.

   So, is *Dorothy* a subject or an object? The answer is both: *Dorothy* is a subject as far as subject-verb agreement is concerned. *Dorothy* is an object as far as meaning is concerned. This peculiar double nature makes the passive very hard to master.

Here are some more examples:

The cars ***are parked*** in the garage.

The cars is the **subject** of the finite verb *are*. *The cars* is the **object** of the passive verb *are parked*.

The children ***were put*** to bed early.

The children is the **subject** of the finite verb *were*. *The children* is the **object** of the passive phrasal verb *were put to bed*.

The plan ***had*** been *proposed* before.

The plan is the **subject** of the finite verb *had*. *The plan* is the **object** of the passive verb *had been proposed*.

These problems should have ***been anticipated***.

These problems is the **subject** of the finite verb *should* (a past-tense modal). *These problems* is the **object** of the passive verb *should have been anticipated*.

Optional Use of the Agent *by* Phrase. The agent *by* phrase is a prepositional phrase beginning with *by* (sometimes *with*) that contains a noun phrase that will be interpreted as the doer of the action of the verb. For example, consider this passive sentence:

Mary **was seen** by John.

We interpret John as the person who saw Mary.

It is important to understand that the agent *by* phrase is optional. It is there if we want it; it need not be there if we do not. There is no obligation that a passive sentence contain an agent *by* phrase. In fact, as we have seen, most passive sentences do not contain an agent *by* phrase.

We are most likely to use the agent *by* phrase when the agent contains new information, specific information, or information that will be used in a sentence that follows the passive sentence. For example:

We stopped at the address given in the ad. I knocked on the door,
    which was opened *by a short dark woman wearing an apron*. I asked
    her if **she** had placed an ad for a piano.

The *by* phrase provides specific new information about the person who opened the door. This information is used in the subsequent sentence as the antecedents of the pronouns *her* and *she*.

The advantage of deriving the passive independently of the active is that it gives a simpler and more accurate description of how the passive actually works. It also avoids the overemphasis on the agent *by* phrase that deriving the passive from the active necessarily entails. The disadvantage is that it totally isolates the passive from the active. In our own writing, however, we often treat the active and passive as stylistic alternatives that we must evaluate against each other to see which is the more effective.

Verbs Incompatible with the Passive

As we would expect, **linking verbs** that take **noun-phrase complements** (Chapter 11) cannot be used in the passive. For example:

X An investment banker *was been* by Susan.
X A well-adjusted man *was seemed* by John.
X A political leader *was become* by John.

The verb *have* can be used in the passive, but only in the sense of "experience." For example:

A good time *was had* by all.

In its more usual sense of "possession," *have* is ungrammatical in the passive. For example:

X Some serious problems *were had* by the proposal.

Some other classes of verbs that are incompatible with the passive are the following:

Verbs of measure: *comprise, contain, cost, hold, last, weigh*
X Fifty-five gallons *is comprised* of a barrel.
X $5 *is cost* by the license.
X Twenty-five pounds *is weighed* by the box.

Reciprocal verbs: *equal, look like, resemble*
X Four *is equaled* by two plus two.
X His sister *is looked like* Fred.
X A mushroom *is resembled* by the bush.

Other Passive Verbs

While *be* is the most common and important passive auxiliary verb, there are two other verbs that are also used to form passives: *get* and *have*. *Get* can be used to form a passive auxiliary parallel to the normal passive auxiliary with *be*. For example:

be **passive:**   The thieves *were caught* by the police.
get **passive:**   The thieves *got caught* by the police.

Both *get* and *have* can be used to create passive forms in a **causative verb** construction. For example:

get: I **got** my hair **cut** by the new barber.
have: I **had** my hair **cut** by the new barber.

Get *Passive Auxiliary* (Get + *Past Participle*)

Get can be used in place of *be* to make another form of the passive auxiliary. For example:

Alex **got replaced** by Steve.

In many cases, passives formed with *be* and passives formed with *get* seem interchangeable. For example:

be **passive:**   The files **were destroyed** in the fire.
get **passive:** The files **got destroyed** in the fire.

be **passive:**   The cats **were fed** this morning.
get **passive:** The cats **got fed** this morning.

be **passive:**   The job **was finished** just in time.
get **passive:** The job **got finished** just in time.

Despite a certain amount of overlap, *get* and *be* passives are different in a number of ways. The most important difference is in degree of formality. *Get* passives are much more informal than *be* passives. Consequently, it is relatively rare to find the *get* passive in formal writing. For example, it would be unimaginable that we would find this in a book or article:

X?   The Civil War **got caused** by irreconcilable differences over slavery.

The standard form of that sentence is as follows:

The Civil War **was caused** by irreconcilable differences over slavery.

The fact that *get* passives are primarily used in casual, spoken language means that nonnative speakers who mostly come into contact with formal, written English have virtually no exposure to the *get* passive.

A second difference is that the *get* passive is largely restricted to actions and activities. Verbs that don't express action are often ungrammatical when used with a *get* passive. For example, compare the following sentences with both *get* and *be* passives:

get **passive:** X He has not ***gotten pain*** in weeks.
be **passive:** He has not ***been paid*** in weeks.

get **passive:** X The noise ***got heard*** everywhere in the building.
be **passive:** The noise ***was heard*** everywhere in the building.

get **passive:** X The party ***got enjoyed*** by everyone.
be **passive:** The party ***was enjoyed*** by everyone.

A third difference is that *get* passives are almost always used with animate subjects—90 percent of the time, according to one study. Inanimate subject are often ungrammatical. For example, compare the following *get* passives:

Animate subject: Fred ***got photographed*** right after it happened.
Inanimate subject: X? The accident ***got photographed*** right after it happened.

The first sentence, with an animate subject, is fully grammatical, but the sentence with an inanimate subject is marginally grammatical at best. However, both of these sentences are fully grammatical with a *be* passive:

Animate subject: Fred ***was photographed*** right after it happened.
Inanimate subject: The accident ***was photographed*** right after it happened.

For nonnative speakers, the biggest problem with *get* passives is that they are so highly idiomatic. This is not a very surprising fact given that *get* passives are almost exclusively used in informal, oral language. For example, *get* passives can be used in the *let's* construction. *Let's* + a base-form verb is used to make a suggestion or a polite command. For example:

> Let's go home.
> Let's get back to work.
> Let's eat! I'm starved.
> Let's quit.

Here are examples of *get* passives used as the base-form verb in the *let's* construction:

> Let's **get married.**
> Let's **get dressed.**
> Let's **get washed up.**

As we would expect, it is impossible to use a *be* passive in the *let's* construction:

X Let's **be married.**
X Let's **be dressed.**
X Let's **be washed up.**

Get *and* Have *Passives Used in Causative Verb Constructions*

Chapter 12 discusses both *get* and *have* used as causative verbs. The term *causative* refers to verbs whose meaning is to "cause something to happen" or "cause somebody to do something." The classic causative verb is *make.* For example:

> John **made** the kids turn down the TV.

In other words, John caused the kids to turn down the TV.

Here are examples of *get* and *have* used as causatives:

    get*:**   I ***got my secretary ***to take*** notes during the meeting.
           We ***got*** them ***to revise*** their plans.
           He ***got*** the judge ***to reduce*** the charges.

As you can see, when *get* is used as a causative, *get* is followed by a noun-phrase object and an infinitive verb phrase. The noun-phrase object of *get* also serves as the subject of the following infinitive verb. For example:

James ***got*** his boss to kill the proposal.

The noun phrase *his boss* is both the object of *get* and the subject of the infinitive verb *to kill*. In other words, the boss is the person killing the proposal, not James.

    have*:**   I ***had my secretary ***take*** notes during the meeting.
            We ***had*** them ***revise*** their plans.
            He ***had*** the judge ***reduce*** the charges.

When *have* is used as a causative, *have* is followed by a noun-phrase object and a base-stem infinitive verb phrase. The noun-phrase object of *have* also serves as the subject of the following bare-stem verb. For example:

James ***had*** his boss kill the proposal.

Here the noun phrase *his boss* is both the object of *had* and the subject of the bare-stem verb *kill*. In other words, the boss is the person killing the proposal, not James.

    When *get* and *have* are used as causative verbs, they differ in the exact form of the verb in their complements (infinitives with *get*; bare-stems with *have*), but in other aspects they seem interchangeable—with the predictable exception that *get* passives are more informal than *have* passives.

    They are also alike in that the verbs in their complements can be passives. Here are the active *get* and *have* sentences, together with their passive counterparts:

get

Active: James ***got*** his boss to kill the proposal.

Passive: James ***got*** the proposal ***killed*** by his boss.

have

Active: James ***had*** his boss kill the proposal.

Passive: James ***had*** the proposal ***killed*** by his boss.

These complicated structures are easier to understand if we treat the complements of *get* and *have* as freestanding sentences with an ordinary subject-verb-object structure (though we do have to ignore the tense for the moment):

get*:**   James ***got (his boss to kill the proposal)

    subject   subject   verb   object
               noun   noun phrase
               phrase

Turning subject-verb-object into the corresponding passive is straightforward:

Active: his boss to kill the proposal ⇒

Passive: the proposal ***killed*** by his boss

Final form of passive: James ***got*** (the proposal ***killed*** by his boss).

have*:**   James ***had (his boss kill the proposal)

    subject   subject   verb   object
               noun   noun phrase
               phrase

Active: his boss kill the proposal ⇒

Passive: the proposal ***killed*** by his boss

Final form of passive: James ***had*** (the proposal ***killed*** by his boss).

Here are the *get* and *have* sentences presented earlier along with their passive counterparts:

get
Active: I *got* my secretary *to take* notes during the meeting.
Passive: I *got* notes *taken* by my secretary during the meeting.

Active: We *got* them *to revise* their plans.
Passive: We *got* their plans *revised* (by them).

Active: He *got* the judge *to reduce* the charges.
Passive: He *got* the charges *reduced* by the judge.

have
Active: I *had* my secretary *take* notes during the meeting.
Passive: I *had* notes *taken* by my secretary during the meeting.

Active: We *had* them *revise* their plans.
Passive: We *had* their plans *revised* (by them).

Active: He *had* the judge *reduce* the charges.
Passive: He *had* the charges *reduced* by the judge.

Index

A lot of, agreement with, 46
A/an, 35–39
Abstract nouns, 115, 197
Action verbs, 196–98
Active voice, 319
Adjectival possessive pronouns,
    41–42
Adjectival prepositional phrases,
    49–50
Adjective clauses, 49, 51–62
    functions of, 58
    internal structure of, 51–57
    nonrestrictive, 52, 58–62
    relative pronoun forms and,
        52–57
    restrictive, 51–52, 58–62
    that clauses and, 105–6
Adjectives. *See also* Predicate
    adjectives
    comparative/superlative forms
        of, 23–24
    derived from present/past
        participles, 25–26
    overview, 21–22
    sequence/punctuation of
        multiple, 26–28

Adverb clauses, 250
    concession, 267
    conditional, 260–62
    present tense and, 140
    reduced, 246–48
    structure of, 245–46
Adverbial phrases, 250, 251
    infinitive, 243–45
    prepositional, 243–44
Adverbs
    from adjectives by adding an
        -ly suffix, 237–40
    from adjectives without an *-ly*
        suffix, 240–41
    classified by meaning, 252–53
    comparative/superlative forms
        of, 241–43
    compound, 237
    conjunctive, 293–95
    derived, 237
    desirability, 259, 260
    forms of, 249
    of manner, 256–57
    misplaced, 268–70
    movement/punctuation of,
        250–52

order of, at ends of sentences,
  257–58
of place, 254–55
possibility, 259–60
presumption, 259, 260
of reason, 255–56
relative pronouns as, 56–57
sentence initial, 259–60
simple, 237
squinting, 270–71
of time, 253–54
All/all (of) the, 47
And, 284–85
Antecedents, 80
Appositive phrases, 62–65
Articles, 29–41
  definite, 29–34
  indefinite, 34–40
  zero, 37–39

Base form, of verbs, 121–24
But, 286

Can/could, 150–52
Capitalization
  of persons, 3–4
  of places, 4–5
  of proper nouns, 3–5
  of things, 5
Causative verbs, 187–91
  get/have passives in
    constructing, 330–33
Clauses
  adjective, 49, 51–62
  adverb, 140, 245–48, 250,
    260–62, 267
  concession, 267

conditional, 260–62
conditional *if*, 264–65
if, 263–66
independent, 245, 283–93
nonrestrictive adjective, 52,
  58–62
noun, 103–4
that, 104–11, 229–33
unless, 262
wh-, 112–18
Collective nouns, 13–14
Colons, 280–81
  joining two independent
    clauses with, 293
Comma splices, 288–89, 294
Commands. *See* Imperatives
Commas
  with coordinating
    conjunctions in series,
    281–83
  joining independent clauses
    with, 283–91
Common nouns, 30–33
  count, 6, 8–13
  noncount, 6–7
  using definite article with,
    30–33
Complements, 193–94. *See
  also* Object complements;
  Predicate adjectives
  infinitive, 223–36
  prepositional phrase, 225–28
  that clause, 228–33
Complex sentences, 283
Compound adverbs, 237
Compound inseparable phrasal
  verbs, 178

Compound sentences, 283
Concession clauses, 267
Conditional clauses, 260–62
Conditional *if* clauses, 264–65
Conjunctions, 275
    correlative, 278
Conjunctive adverbs, 293–95
    commonly used, 294
Coordinating conjunctions
    commas with, in series, 281–83
    joining independent clauses
        with, 283–91
Correlative conjunctions, 278
Could/can, 150–52
Count nouns
    plural forms of, 8–13
        irregular, 10–13
        regular, 9–10
    using *a/an* with, 35–36
    using *some* with, 35–36

Dangling participles, 69–72
Data, 13
Definite articles, 29–34
    with common nouns, 30–33
    with proper nouns, 33–34
Demonstrative pronouns,
    85–86
Demonstratives, 42–43
Dependent clauses, 103, 245
Derived adverbs, 237
Determiners
    articles, 29–40
    demonstratives, 42–43
    overview, 29
    possessives, 40–42
    quantifiers, 43–48

Double possessive, 19–20
Dummy *it*, 101
    with clauses as objects, 210–11
    with *that* clause, 229–33
    for *that* clauses used as
        subjects, 106–7
    for *wh-* clauses used as
        subjects, 116–17

Ellipsis, 289–91
Elliptical *wh-* questions, 317
Elliptical *yes-no* questions, 305
"Empty" *it*. *See* Dummy *it*
English origin words, plural
    forms of, 8–9
-Er/-est, 23–24
External consideration, 62

Factual *if* clauses, 263
FANBOYS, 284–88
Faulty parallelism, 275–80
Few, comparative/superlative
    forms of, 47–48
Few/(a) little/any, 44–45
Fewer/less, 45
Finite verb, 245
For, 284
Fronting, 309–10
Fused sentences, 289
Future perfect, 157–58
    modals and, 158–63
Future progressive, 166
Future tenses
    forming, 122–23
    modals for, 147–52
    present progressive for, 153–54
    present tense for, 152–53

Generalizations, using zero
     article for, 37–39
Gerund phrases, 88
Gerunds, 88–89
     defined, 87
     subjects of, 89–93
     verbs that do not allow
          gerunds as objects,
          93–94
Get, 327–33

Habitual actions, describing,
     present tense and, 139
Have got to, 149–50
Have to, 149–50
How about, 315–16
How come, 316
Hypothetical *if* clauses, 265–66
Hypothetical statements, past
     tense for, 143–44

If clauses, 263–66
     conditional, 264–65
     factual, 263
     hypothetical, 265–66
Imperatives, 123
Indefinite articles, 34–40
     with proper nouns, 40
Indefinite pronouns, 82–85
Independent clauses, 245
     joining, with commas
          and coordinating
          conjunctions, 283–91
     joining, with semicolons and
          colons, 291–93
Infinitive complements, 233–36

Infinitive phrases, 72–74, 95
     uses for, 95
Infinitives, 87, 121
     defined, 94
     dummy *it* for, used as subjects,
          101
     forming, 122
     split, 268
     subjects of, 96–98
     verbs that do not allow
          infinitives as objects,
          98–99
     wh-, 99–100
Inflectional possessives, 14–17
Internal consideration, 62
Intransitive phrasal verbs, 170,
     174–75, 195
Intransitive verbs, 194
     transitive verbs as, 195
Inverted *yes-no* questions,
     297–302
     responses to, 302–4
Irregular comparatives,
     24–25
Irregular plurals
     of English origin, 10–12
     of Latin origin, 12–13
Irregular superlatives, 24–25
Its/it's, 79

Latin origin words, irregular
     plural forms of, 8–9, 12–13
Lay-lie, 190–91
Linking verbs, 198–201, 223
Little, comparative/superlative
     forms of, 48

Longman Dictionary of Phrasal Verbs, 169–70, 173
Lost opportunities, regret for lost, perfect tense and, 159, 162–63

Manner, adverbs of, 256–57
Many, comparative/superlative forms of, 48
Many/much, 44
May/shall, 150–51
Misplaced adverbs, 268–70
Modals, 133–34, 147–52
  defined, 136–37
  for future, 147–52
  perfect tense and, 158–63
  progressive tense and, 166–67
More/most, 24
Much, comparative/superlative forms of, 48
Must, 149–50

Near-time future actions/events, describing, present tense and, 141
Negative *wh-* questions, 313–14
Noncount nouns, 6–7
  using *some* with, 36–37
Nonfinite tenses, 135–36
Nonrestrictive adjective clauses, 52, 58–62
Nonrestrictive participial phrases, 66
Nonstative verbs, 185–86
Nor, 285–86

Noun clauses, 103–4
Noun phrases, 76, 87, 103
Nouns
  abstract, 115, 197
  collective, 13–14
  common, 6–13, 30–33
  count, 3–13, 35–36
  possessive forms of, 14–20
  proper, 3–6, 33–34
Now what, 317

Object complements, 211–14. *See also* Complements.
  distinguishing, from objects, 212
  used as part of *be*, 213
  verbs that take, 213–14
Objects, 197
  adverb of place complement and, 214–15
  base-form complement, 218–20
  direct, 203–6
  dummy *it* with *that* clauses as, 210–11
  indirect, 203–6
  infinitive complement and, 218
  object complement and, 211–14
  present participle complement and, 220–21
  that clause complement and, 215–16
Of possessive, 17–19
Or, 286–87

Organizational titles, definite
    articles and, 33
Ought to, 149–50

Parallelism, faulty, 275–80
Paraphrasing, 203–8
Participial phrases, 65–72
    movable, 69–70
    nonrestrictive, 66
    past, 68–69
    present, 67–68
    restrictive, 66
Passive auxiliaries, 319
    forming passive voice directly
        from, 323–26
Passive voice, 132, 319
    derived from active sentences,
        320–23
    formed directly from passive
        auxiliary, 323–26
    forming, 320–26
    get and, 327–33
    verbs incompatible with,
        326–27
Past participles, 121, 132–33
    adjectives derived from,
        25–26
    irregular, 132–33
    regular, 132
Past perfect, 156–57
Past progressive, 165
Past tense, 142–45
    for hypothetical statements,
        143–44
    irregular, 128–30

for polite requests, 144–45
    regular, 127–28
    shifting between present and,
        145–47
Past-participial phrases, 65–66,
    68–69
People, definite articles and, 33
Perfect tenses, 154–63
    future, 157–58
    past, 156–57
    present, 154–56
Personal pronouns, 75–79
    chart of, 77
    sexist use of, 78–79
Persons, capitalization of, 3–4
Phrasal verbs, 169–85. *See also*
    Verbs
    compound inseparable, 178
    distinguishing inseparable/
        separable, 182–83
    inseparable transitive, 172,
        175–78
    intransitive, 170, 174–75, 195
    noun phrase and
        prepositional, 184–85
    separable transitive, 172,
        179–82
    transitive, 170–71, 175–77
Places
    adverbs of, 254–55
    capitalization of, 4–5
    definite articles and, 34
Plural-only nouns, 13
Plurals
    of count nouns, 8–13

irregular, 10–13
regular, 9–10
of words ending in a
      consonant + *y*, 16
of words ending in *f*, 16
of words ending in *o*, 16
Possessive(s)
nouns, 40–41
of nouns, 14–20
double, 19–20
inflectional, 14–17
of possessive, 17–19
pronouns, 41–42
relative pronoun as, 56
Post-noun modifiers
adjectival prepositional
      phrases, 49–50
adjective (relative) clauses, 49,
      51–62
appositive phrases, 49, 62–65
infinitive phrases, 49, 72–74
participial phrases, 65–72
Predicate adjectives, 223–25
infinitive complement with,
      233–36
prepositional phrase
      complement with,
      225–28
that clause complement with,
      228–33
Predicate nominative, 88
Prepositional phrase
      complement, 225–28
Present participles, 121,
      130–31

Present perfect, 154–56
Present progressive, for future
      events, 153–54
Present tense, 124–26, 137–41
describing habitual actions,
      139
describing present plans for
      near-time future actions/
      events, 141
forming adverb clauses, 140
for future time, 152–53
for reports/reviews, 139–40
shifting between past and,
      145–47
for time-less statements,
      138–39
Present-participal phrases,
      65–68
Present-participles, adjectives
      derived from, 25–26
Progressive tenses, 163–67
future, 166
modals and, 166–67
past, 165
present, 163–64
Pronominal possessive
      pronouns, 41–42
Pronouns. *See also* Relative
      pronouns
demonstrative, 85–86
indefinite, 82–85
personal, 75–79
possessive, 41–42
reflexive, 79–82
sexist use of, 78–79

Proper nouns, 33–34
  capitalization of, 3–5
  plural forms of, 6
  using definite article with,
    30–33
  using indefinite article with, 40

Quantifiers, 43–48
  affected by count/noncount
    distinction, 44–46
  agreement with *a lot of*, 46–47
  comparative/superlative forms
    of *few, little, much*, and
    many, 47–48
Quasi-modal verbs, 148
Questions
  tag, 305–8
  wh-
    elliptical, 317
    forming, 309–13
    informal, 315–17
    negative, 313–14
    overview, 308–9
    truncated, 315–17
    word in *wh-* clauses and,
      117–18
  yes-no, 297–305
    elliptical, 305
    informal, 304–5
    inverted, 297–304
    responses to inverted,
      302–4
    uninverted, 305

Raise-rise, 187–88
Reason, adverbs of, 255–56

Reduced adverb clauses, 246–48
Reflexive pronouns, 79–82
  for emphasis, 80–81
  misuse of, 81–82
Regular plurals, of count nouns,
  9–12
Relative clauses. *See* Adjective
  clauses
Relative pronouns. *See also*
  Pronouns
  as adverb, 56–57
  forms, 52–53
  as object, 54
  as object of preposition, 54–56
  as possessive, 56
  as subjects, 53
  of time, 57
Reports, writing, present tense
  and, 139–40
Requests, past tense for, 144–45
Restrictive adjective clauses,
  51–52, 58–62
Restrictive participial phrases,
  66
Reviews, writing, present tense
  and, 139–40
Rise-raise, 187–88
Royal titles, definite articles and,
  33
Run-on sentences, 288

Semicolons, joining two
  independent clauses with,
  291–92
Sentence-initial adverbs, 259–60
Set-sit, 188–89

Shall/may, 150–51
Should, 149–50
Simple adverbs, 237
Since when, 316–17
Single-complement verbs, 196–201, 251
Single-word adverbs, 250
Sit-set, 188–89
So, 288
Some, 39
   with countable nouns, 35–36
   with noncount nouns, 36–37
Some/any, 46
Speculation, perfect tense and, 159–62
Split infinitives, 268
Squinting adverbs, 270–71
Stative verbs, 185–86
Subordination, 275

Tag questions, 305–8. *See also* Questions
Tense(s), 135–36
   future, 147–54
   past, 142–45
   perfect, 154–63
   present, 137–41
   progressive, 163–67
   shifting, between past/present, 145–47
That clause complements, 228–29
That clauses, 104–5
   adjective clauses and, 105–6
   deleting *that* from, used as objects of verbs, 107–8

dummy *it* with, 229–33
as objects with verbs of speech and cognition, 108–9
subjunctive, as objects, 110–11
That/those, 42–43
That/which, 60–62
These/this, 42–43
Things, capitalization of, 5
This/these, 42–43
Time, adverbs of, 253–54
Time-less statements, present tense and, 138–39
Titles, articles and, 33
To phrases, 216–17
To/for paraphrase, 203–8
Transitional terms, 293
Transitive phrasal verbs, 170–71, 175–77
Transitive verbs, as intransitives, 195
Truncated *wh-* questions, 315–17
Two-word verbs. *See* Phrasal verbs

Uninverted *yes-no* questions, 305
Unless clauses, 262

Verbs. *See also* Phrasal verbs
   action, 196–98
   base forms of, 121–24
   causative, 187–91
   infinitive, 121
   intransitive, 194
   linking, 198–201
   modal auxiliary, 133–34
   past participle, 121, 132–33

past tense, 121, 126–30
present participle, 121, 130–31
present tense, 121, 124–26
single-complement, 196–201
that do not allow infinitives as
    objects, 98–99
transitive, 195
voice and, 319
Voice, 319

Wh- clauses, 111–12
external role of, 115–16
internal structure of, 113–15
using *wh*- question word order
    in, 117–18
Wh- infinitives, 99–100
Wh- questions
elliptical, 317
forming, 309–13
informal, 315–17
negative, 313–14

overview, 308–9
truncated, 315–17
word order in *wh*- clauses and,
    117–18
Wh- words, 99–100
What about, 316
What for, 316
What now, 317
Which/that, 60–62
Why not, 316

Yes-no questions, 305–8. *See also*
    Questions
elliptical, 305
informal, 304–5
inverted, 297–302
responses to inverted, 302–4
uninverted, 305
Yet, 287

Zero article, 37–39